Table Saw Techniques

Roger W. Cliffe

 Sterling Publishing Co., Inc.   New York
Blandford Press   Dorset, England

Dedication

To Cathy and Austin

Edited and designed by Michael Cea

Library of Congress Cataloging in Publication Data

Cliffe, Roger W.
  Table saw techniques.

  Includes index.
  1. Circular saws. 2. Woodwork. I. Title.
TS850.C45 1984   684'.083   84-8676
ISBN 0-8069-5540-6
ISBN 0-8069-7912-7 (pbk.)

Copyright © 1984 by Roger W. Cliffe
Published by Sterling Publishing Co., Inc.
Two Park Avenue, New York, N.Y. 10016
Distributed in Australia by Oak Tree Press Co., Ltd.
P.O. Box K514 Haymarket, Sydney 2000, N.S.W.
Distributed in the United Kingdom by Blandford Press
Link House, West Street, Poole, Dorset BH15 ILL, England
Distributed in Canada by Oak Tree Press Ltd.
% Canadian Manda Group, P.O. Box 920, Station U
Toronto, Ontario, Canada M8Z 5P9
Manufactured in the United States of America

Photo Credits

The illustrations in this book display the products, creations and photography of many people and business organizations. Represented among them are: Biesemeyer Manufacturing Corporation, 27; Boice Crane Industries, 12, 13, 15; The Clemson Group (Sanblade™), 94–96; Delta International Corporation 4, 5 8–11, 15, 16, 18, 22, 24, 26, 28, 30, 42, 155, 197, 273, 452–457; Garrett Wade, 6, 17, 29, 40, 43, 181; Foley-Belsaw Company, 80–88, 90, 91, 103, 108, 109; The Foredom Electric Company (Brett Guard™), 52, 64, 438–441; Forrest Manufacturing, 104, 111, 112; Marvco Tool and Manufacturing, 71, 72; Oliver Machinery Company, 3, 25; Power Tool Institute, 133; Fisher Hill Products (Ripstrate™), 152, 153; Sears, Roebuck and Company, 2, 36, 37, 75, 105, 124, 209, 210, 428, 429,, 460, 461; Sprunger Tool Corporation, 1, 34.

Acknowledgments

Table Saw Techniques represents the work and cooperation of many people. No project of this magnitude could be done by the author alone.

The photos for this book were shot by Jim Schmitz and Bill Peters. The custom darkroom work was done by Bill Peters. Special thanks to the photo models, Dave Miles and Chris Sullens.

The drawings for projects and jigs were done by Don Simon and Steve Piatak. Their work has made project construction much easier for the reader.

The manuscript critique by Dr. John Beck has also been very helpful. His work and advice have made the written portion of the book easier to read and understand.

Manuscript typing by Bea Paulus and Ruth Odynocki transformed the writer's longhand into a workable product. Many thanks to these patient women.

Commercial photographs were generously furnished by the following people and organizations:

Roger Thompson
Marilyn Brock
The Foredom Electric Co.
Clayt Williams
John Greguric
Fred Slavic
John Baenisch
Jim Forrest and Wally Kunkel (Mr. Sawdust)

Garretson W. Chinn
Jay Dykstra
James Bates
Mike Mangan
Dale Fahlbeck

Biesemeyer Manufacturing Corporation
Boice Crane Industries
Brett Guard™
The Clemson Group (Sanblade™)
Delta International Corporation
Fisher Hill Products (Ripstrate™)
Foley-Belsaw Company
Forrest Manufacturing
Marvco Tool and Manufacturing
Garrett Wade
Oliver Machinery
Power Tool Institute
Sears, Roebuck and Company
Sprunger Tool Corporation

ROGER CLIFFE
CLIFFE CABINETS

Table of Contents

Preface

With over 10 million table saws in the United States, one can only wonder how many table saw operators there are worldwide. It is certain that these operators have varied interests and purposes for their table saw.

Regardless of interests and purposes, there is a certain core of operations and knowledge that applies to all table saw owners and operators. This book addresses that core of operations and knowledge.

Included in the knowledge core are topics such as:

1. Selection of blades for your table saw
2. Maintenance of blades and accessories
3. Maintenance of your table saw
4. Buying a new or used table saw
5. Design and construction of table saw jigs
6. Safety habits and procedures for operating the table saw
7. Tips for operating the table saw efficiently and correctly

Included in the operations core are topics such as:

1. Ripping and crosscutting procedures
2. Simple and compound mitring
3. Cutting feathers and splines
4. Cutting and shaping edge joints
5. Using the table saw to make drawer joints such as the dado, rabbet, dovetail and lock corner
6. Using the table saw to make door joints such as the lap, mortise-and-tenon, haunched mortise-and-tenon and mitre joint
7. Cutting coves and partial coves on the table saw with the aid of an inclined fence
8. Cutting finger joints and constructing related jigs
9. Constructing jigs for cutting circles, tapers, irregular parts, splines, mitres and many other joints or parts

Table Saw Techniques was written for both the novice and the experienced table saw operator. The collection of special set-ups and techniques represents the knowledge of many experienced cabinetmakers with whom I have had the pleasure of working. While many experienced table saw operators will be familiar with some of the operations, it is certain that they will not be familiar with all of them.

This book provides a ready reference for special set-ups. Many operations that are performed occasionally are easy to forget. This book will serve as a guide to those operations with photographs, simple, concise instructions and safe procedures.

Part I:
Table Saw Fundamentals

1
Introduction to the Table Saw

Types of Table Saws

There are many different types of table saws sold today. Each type of table saw has its own unique features, but all table saws can be classified according to the following categories or groups.

Motorized or Motor Driven   A table saw is classified as motorized or motor driven. A motor-driven table saw uses a motor and 1 or more belts to drive the blade (Fig. 1). The blade is mounted on 1 end of an arbor, and the driven pulley is mounted on the other end. The motor is usually mounted under the table.

The blade on a motorized table saw attaches directly to the motor (Fig. 2). The motor is mounted to the underside of the table. Some motorized table saws operate at a higher noise level than motor-driven saws. This is due to increased vibration and motor echo. Some motorized table saws are classified as universal table saws. These saws have 2 arbors and 2 blades (Fig. 3). The blade in the upper position is the only one that moves when the saw is turned on.

Universal saws are large industrial saws. Raising the blade causes it to move on a large arc. As 1 blade disappears beneath the table, the other blade appears. This minimizes the amount of blade changing, as 1 blade may be a rip blade and the other a crosscut blade.

Fig. 1. A motor-driven table saw uses a motor and 1 or more belts to drive the blade. The blade is mounted on 1 end of an arbor.

8

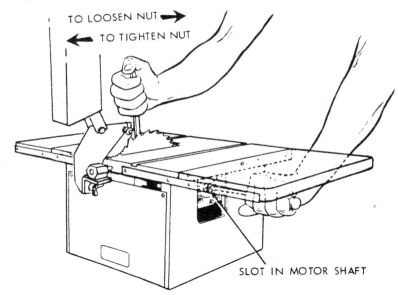

Fig. 2. This is a motorized table saw. The blade attaches directly to the motor.

TO LOOSEN NUT →

← TO TIGHTEN NUT

SLOT IN MOTOR SHAFT

Fig. 3. This motorized table saw is called a universal saw. It has 2 arbors. Only the arbor in the up position turns when the saw is turned on.

Variety Saw or Bench Saw Variety saws are large table saws. Saws with a 10-inch (25.4-cm) diameter blade are usually classified as variety saws. Table saws with a blade under 10 inches (25.4 cm) in diameter or a small table surface are classified as bench saws. Classification of a saw in the bench or the variety group is subjective in most cases.

Tilting Table or Tilting Arbor Cutting stock at an angle is done by tilting the blade or tilting the table. Most newer saws use a tilting blade (Fig. 4). This allows the stock to remain horizontal while it is being cut. The blade is attached to an arbor. The arbor moves on a gearlike mechanism that is controlled by a handwheel or crank on the side of the saw (Fig. 5). On a tilting table saw, the stock is at an angle when it is fed across the table. Stock is not as easy to handle when the table is tilted. The operator must contend with the forces of gravity.

Most table saws with a tilting table have a power take-off on the end of the motor opposite the blade (Fig. 6). The power take-off allows the attachment of other accessories such as a mortiser or drill bit.

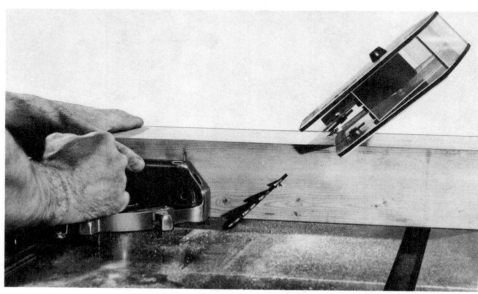

Fig. 4. Most newer table saws cut stock at an angle by tilting the blade. This large timber would be difficult to handle if the table tilted instead of the blade.

Fig. 5. A view from the bottom of the table saw allows you to see the worm gears that tilt the arbor and control its height.

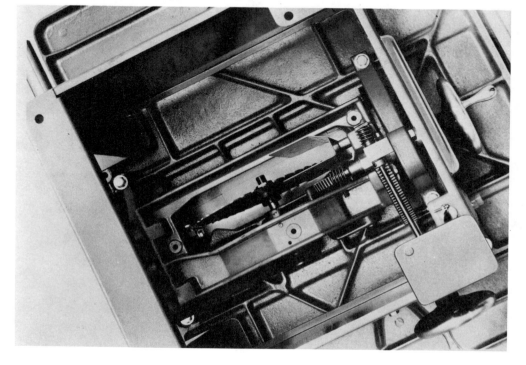

Fig. 6. The power take-off on this table saw allows the saw to be used for mortising and horizontal boring. The auxiliary table makes complex set-ups possible.

Sliding Table A sliding or rolling table (Fig. 7) is an option on larger industrial saws. The table on the left of the blade rolls when unlocked. This allows wider, heavier pieces of stock to be controlled more easily. The entire table rolls and moves the stock into the blade with little effort. Sliding tables have stops or travel limits at both ends. This keeps the table from sliding out of its track. Most of these tables also have provisions for adjustment.

Some companies offer a sliding table as an add-on accessory for their table saw (Fig. 8). These sliding tables do the same thing as the included sliding table, but take up more floor space. Add-on sliding tables can be purchased to fit almost any table saw. They allow a single operator to handle larger stock (Figs. 9–11). Be sure that the add-on table is compatible with the saw before you buy it.

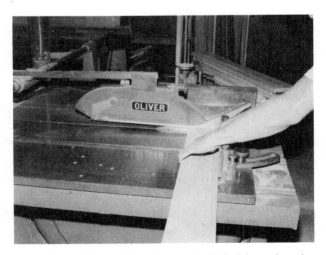

Fig. 7. This rolling table makes control of wider or heavier pieces much easier. This feature is common on large production saws.

Fig. 8. This add-on sliding table takes up slightly more floor space due to the rod extending beyond the table. The table rolls on this rod. Ball bearings reduce friction and make it roll easily.

Fig. 9. The operator saws a sheet of plywood easily without help.

Fig. 10. The operator cuts a mitre on a large timber with no problem of balancing stock. The clamping device holds the stock firmly in place.

Fig. 11. The operator cuts a compound mitre on a large timber. The clamp holds stock securely and eliminates blade binding.

13

Determining Table Saw Size

The size of a table saw is misleading. You can consider overall size, table size, blade diameter and many other measures of size. The following discussion of table saw size will help you determine what measures of size are important to your work.

Blade Diameter Blade diameter is the most common method of determining table saw size. The largest diameter blade that the table saw will take is its size. For example, a table saw that will take a blade with a 10-inch (25.4-cm) diameter is a 10-inch (25.4-cm) table saw. The diameter of the blade affects the maximum stock thickness that the table saw will cut.

Most table saws have lugs near the blade's periphery. They limit blade size and eliminate the chance of installing an oversized blade. Some people use an undersized blade on the table saw, but the largest blade that the saw will accommodate actually determines size.

Table Size The size of the table on a table saw is also important when considering table saw size. It is much easier to balance and control large sheets of stock on a large surface. Not all 10-inch (25.4-cm) table saws have the same size table or work surface (Fig. 12).

It is possible to build a large wooden table around a bench saw or small table saw. This increases the working area and makes the table saw more versatile. Extensions may also be attached to the fence or the sides or ends of the table saw. This allows greater support and control when cutting long, wide or thin pieces of stock.

Maximum Ripping Width The widest piece of stock that can be ripped (cut with the grain) is another size determi-

Fig. 12. Not all 10-inch (25.4-cm) table saws have the same size table. Some are larger (or smaller) than ordinary.

nant on the table saw. The length of the rails on which the rip fence travels determines the maximum ripping width (Fig. 13).

Most 10-inch (25.4-cm) saws have rails 28–30 inches (71.1–76.2 cm) long. These rails allow a 12-inch (30.5-cm) rip on the left and right of the blade. They can also be adjusted for a 24-inch (61.0-cm) rip on the right or left side of the blade. Some 10-inch (25.4-cm) saws allow for a 12-inch (30.5-cm) rip on the left side and a 24-inch (61.0-cm) rip on the right side of the blade. This is a desirable set-up. It allows rip cuts to the center (width) of panel stock on the right side of the blade and provides for occasional cuts on the left side of the blade.

Other rails are offered for certain table saws. They allow for a 50-inch (127.0-cm) rip on the right side of the blade. They allow the saw to crosscut to the center (length) of 4-foot × 8-foot (1.2-m × 2.4-m) panel stock. Many manufacturers of table saws offer more than 1 length of rails. Usually the saw is sold with the shortest rails available. This is because the longer rails require a

Fig. 13. The length of the rails on which the rip fence travels determines the maximum ripping width. This saw will rip 2 feet (61.0 cm) on the left of the blade and 4 feet (122 cm) on the right.

much larger working space. Consult the manufacturer's catalogue to determine what rails are available for your saw.

Distance from Table Front to Blade   The distance from the front of the table to the front of the blade (at full height) is also an important measurement (Fig. 14). The greater this distance, the greater the control over the work. This is important for cutting both with or across the grain.

It is much safer to balance a large piece of stock on the table before the cut begins. If the distance from the table front to the blade is minimal, cutting begins almost as soon as the stock touches the table. Greater strength and skill are needed to obtain a good cut under these circumstances. Larger tables usually have a greater distance between the front of the table and the blade (Fig. 15).

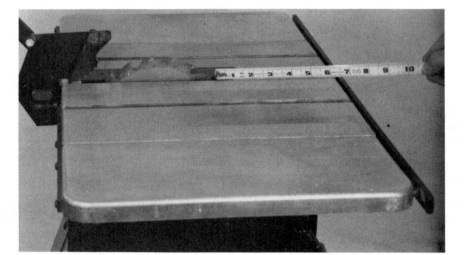

Fig. 14. The distance from the front of the table to the front of the blade (at full height) determines the size of the stock that can be cut. The greater this distance, the better control you have over the stock.

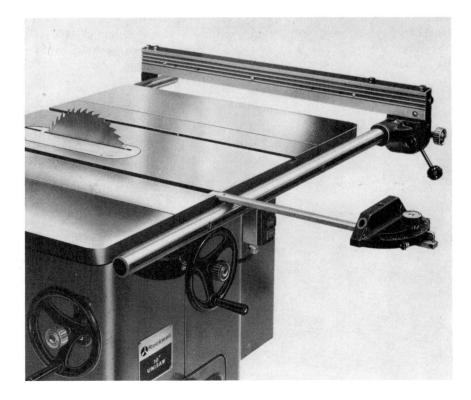

Fig. 15. This 10-inch (25.4-cm) table saw has great distance between the blade and the front of the table. It is easier to control stock on a table like this.

Horsepower

Horsepower is an important table saw size consideration. Several motors of varying horsepower ratings can be used on the same saw. The motors may all have the same outside dimensions, which makes motor selection even more difficult. The following discussion will help you determine which size motor your saw needs. It will also help eliminate confusion between the terms rated horsepower and peak horsepower.

Rated Horsepower vs. Peak Horsepower Horsepower is a function of torque and rpms (revolutions per minute). The peak or developed horsepower is the horsepower of the motor when it has no load. Rated horsepower is the horsepower under load, and is lower than the peak horsepower. The 2 horsepower evaluations are different. They cannot be used for comparison purposes.

Generally, the best comparison between motors is the amperage rating. A 10-ampere, 110-volt motor has an actual horsepower of 1.

How Much Horsepower is Needed Most table saws come equipped with a motor from ½ horsepower (rated) to 10 horsepower (rated). This is a considerable horsepower difference. The ½-horsepower motor would be found on a 7½-inch (19.1-cm) table saw. This is because the saw turns a smaller blade and is not designed to cut thick stock.

A 16-inch (40.6-cm) table saw would have a 5-horsepower to 7-horsepower (rated) motor on it. The 10-inch (25.4-cm) table saw would have a 1-horsepower, 1½-horsepower, 2-horsepower or 3-horsepower motor. The large variety is due to the different jobs these saws might perform. If a 10-inch (25.4-cm) saw is used to cut framing lumber, a 2-horsepower or 3-horsepower (rated) motor would be selected. This is because the stock is not as dry or true as furniture lumber. The twisted or warped condition may put extra strain on a smaller motor. The extra moisture in framing lumber means that more horsepower is needed to throw or eject the heavier sawdust.

Table saws that are purchased for heavy ripping or dadoing operations should have the largest available horsepower motor installed. Ripping requires about 5 times as much energy as crosscutting. Turning a large dado head and making dado cuts also requires more energy than general sawing.

In most cases, a 10-inch (25.4-cm) table saw is underpowered if it has a 1-horsepower (rated) or smaller motor. A 1½-horsepower (rated) motor should be the smallest motor installed on a 10-inch (25.4-cm) table saw for general duty. A 10-inch (25.4-cm) table saw with an 8-inch (20.3-cm) blade mounted on the arbor will have more power. More power is available to cut since less power is used to turn the smaller blade. When using a smaller blade, be sure that its rpm rating is correct for your saw.

Larger horsepower motors also have more energy to kick back (eject or kick stock towards you). I have taught many students table saw basics on a ½-horsepower, 7½-inch (19.1-cm) table saw. Stock that binds on this saw usually freezes the blade and does not kick back.

Remember, an over-powered saw in the hands of a beginner is similar to a sports car with a beginning driver at the wheel, Select the saw size according to the work you do. A 10-inch (25.4-cm) saw may be too large for miniature work and too small for panel work.

2
Table Saw Controls and Accessories

Controls

There are 3 common controls on all tilting-arbor table saws: the power switch, the blade-elevating wheel and the blade-tilting handwheel (Fig. 16). On tilting table saws (Fig. 17), there is a table-tilting mechanism and table-raising mechanism instead of a blade-tilting or blade-elevating mechanism. In addition, some table saws are equipped with a brake. The brake stops the blade as soon as the saw is shut off.

Power Switch   There are many types of power switches in use on table saws. Some use a conventional light switch, while others are more specialized. Specialized switches are easier to turn off than on (Fig. 18). This makes accidental starting of the saw more difficult. Usually these switches are color coded for increased safety. Green is on and red is off. The power switch should be positioned so that the operator can turn the saw on and off easily without reaching. The operator should be able to shut the saw off quickly in an emergency.

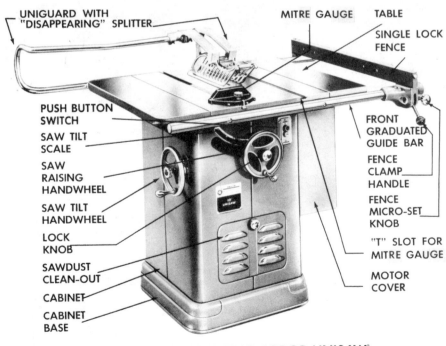

UNIGUARD WITH "DISAPPEARING" SPLITTER

MITRE GAUGE   TABLE

SINGLE LOCK FENCE

PUSH BUTTON SWITCH

SAW TILT SCALE

SAW RAISING HANDWHEEL

SAW TILT HANDWHEEL

LOCK KNOB

SAWDUST CLEAN-OUT

CABINET

CABINET BASE

FRONT GRADUATED GUIDE BAR

FENCE CLAMP HANDLE

FENCE MICRO-SET KNOB

"T" SLOT FOR MITRE GAUGE

MOTOR COVER

Fig. 16. Common table saw controls and parts are shown here. Refer back to this as new terms and operations are presented.

ROCKWELL DELTA 10″ TILTING ARBOR UNISAW

Fig. 17. This table saw has a table-tilting mechanism and a table-elevating mechanism. The blade does not tilt or move up and down. The table tilts in both directions, which allows easy cutting of dovetails.

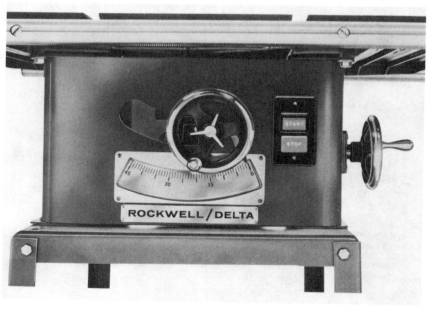

Fig. 18. This power switch is easier to turn off than on. The start switch is surrounded by a hood. This permits contact only from the front. The stop button can be contacted from the front or side.

Some power switches require that a key be inserted before the table saw can be used (Fig. 19). This type of switch keeps inexperienced operators and curious children from operating the saw. Any table saw (or other power tool) in a home where children are present should either have key-actuated switches or tools that are kept behind a locked door to prevent a mishap.

On high-voltage table saw motors, a low-voltage switching system is used. The system uses a 24-volt circuit to the motor. This system activates a solenoid on the motor to the on or off position. The 24-volt circuit minimizes the chance of high-voltage electric shock to the operator.

Blade-Elevating Handwheel The blade-elevating handwheel controls blade height through a worm-gear and rack-gear mechanism (Fig. 20). Most (but not all) handwheels are turned clockwise to elevate the blade. Most table saws have positive stops at full blade height and depth. Avoid overcranking the handwheel, as the elevating mechanism can become jammed.

When adjusting blade height, make the final setting as the blade is being raised. This increases the accuracy of the setting. When the blade is raised, there is positive contact between the worm and rack gears. This eliminates slippage due to gear lash.

Fig. 20. The blade-elevating handwheel controls blade height. On most saws, the wheel is turned clockwise to elevate the blade.

Fig. 21. The small knob in the center of the handwheel locks the blade height at the desired setting.

There is usually a locking device (Fig. 21) to lock the blade at the desired height. Be sure to loosen this device before changing blade height. Raising or lowering the blade while the locking device is on may damage the saw. Always check the locking device before making any adjustment.

Blade-Tilting Handwheel The blade-tilting handwheel (Fig. 22) controls the angle of the blade. Table saws have a protractorlike scale on the front of the saw (Fig. 23) to help you determine the blade angle. This scale is helpful, but it is not very accurate. It is more accurate to measure the angle between the table and the blade. Use a sliding T-bevel (Fig. 23) or other device to measure the angle.

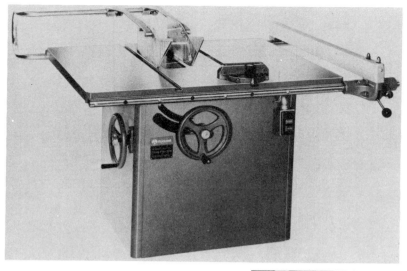

Fig. 22. The blade-tilting handwheel is located on the side of the saw. It controls blade tilt. It usually has a locking device to hold the blade setting.

Fig. 23. A sliding T-bevel is a more accurate measure of blade angle than the scale on the front of the saw.

Brakes Some table saws made today are equipped with brakes that stop the blade instantly after the power is shut off. The brakes may be mechanical or electronic. Mechanical brakes consist of a pad and a drum similar to those on a car. Some are activated by a solenoid and others are operated manually. These brakes must be adjusted periodically, and the pads must be changed when they become worn. Electronic brakes stop the blade by sending current through the motor. The current counteracts the motion of the motor, causing it to stop. Electronic brakes can easily be installed on most table saws.

Brakes make the table saw safer to operate, and minimize set-up time. The operator does not have to wait for the motor to coast to a stop before changing the set-up. The electronic brake causes no appreciable wear on the electric motor.

Accessories

There are many accessories available for the table saw. Some come with the saw and others are shop-made or sold as optional equipment. These accessories make the saw safer and easier to use.

Power-Feed Unit A power-feed unit (Fig. 24) is a motor-operated device that feeds stock into the blade. Used primarily for ripping stock, it reduces operator fatigue and eliminates the monotony that is often the cause of accidents. Operator contact with the blade is also eliminated since all the operator must do is supply stock to the feed unit.

Power-feed units are set so that they feed stock against the fence and into the blade. Some units have an adjustable feed speed, which compensates for wood of varying hardness or thickness. Gear motors are used for positive feed and have less chance of a kickback. Power-feed units are usually sold as optional equipment.

Fig. 24. The power-feed unit feeds stock into the blade. It reduces operator fatigue and possible contact with the blade. Power-feed units are used primarily for ripping.

Fence The fence is an accessory that is standard equipment with all table saws (Fig. 16). The fence clamps to 1 or 2 table rails or is bolted to the table. The fence is used to control stock when ripping (cutting with the grain) solid stock or when cutting strips from a piece of sheet stock. The distance between the fence and the blade determines the size of the strips being cut.

Some fences may be tilted (Fig. 25) to accommodate pieces with bevelled edges. This feature is usually available only on expensive industrial saws. The same feature can be added to a common table saw with an angular wooden fence attachment. The unit attaches to the fence and will control stock with a bevelled edge.

Some woodworkers attach a piece of stock to the fence. This protects the fence from contact with the blade. This piece of stock must be true to assure that the fence remains parallel with the blade.

Fence Alignment.   There are many theories on fence alignment and fence length. Some experienced operators feel that the fence should be exactly parallel with the blade. Others feel that the fence should be angled away from the blade at the far end to minimize pinching and kickback. I have used table saws with both settings and found little difference.

If the fence is angled away on the right side of the blade, it will pinch when moved to the left side of the blade. Keep that in mind if you move the fence.

Fence length is also debatable. Some experienced operators use a short fence so there is no binding beyond the blade. The fence extends just beyond the blade's arbor. Other experienced operators prefer a fence that extends the entire length of the table. I prefer this type because it allows greater control over the wood.

Fence Adjustment.   Many fence-locking mechanisms do not always lock parallel to the blade or as they were adjusted. Periodically check the fence for correct alignment. Lock the fence and raise the blade to full height. Measure the distance to the fence at the front of the blade. Turn the blade so the same tooth is at the rear of the table, and measure the distance to the fence. If both measurements are the same, the fence is parallel. More information on table saw alignment can be found in Chapter 7.

Some easy-to-adjust fences (Figs. 26 and 27) are available for retro-fit to most table saws. These fences need much less adjustment and are usually accurate to 1/64 inch

Fig. 25. This fence locks to the table. It has a micrometre knob on the back for fine adjustment and a tilting mechanism that allows it to cut stock with bevelled edges.

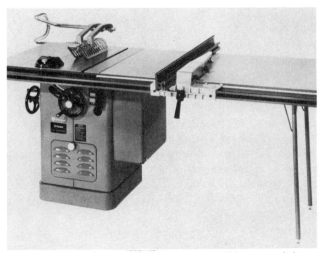

Fig. 26. This fence is a retro-fit to most table saws. It is easy to adjust and holds its accuracy quite well.

21

(.4 mm). This add-on fence locks only at the front of the table. It has a dependable gauge that allows measurement from the scale, not the blade. This makes fence adjustment safer and easier. This is especially true when a guard is used. The operator does not have to lift the guard or wait for the blade to stop to re-adjust the fence.

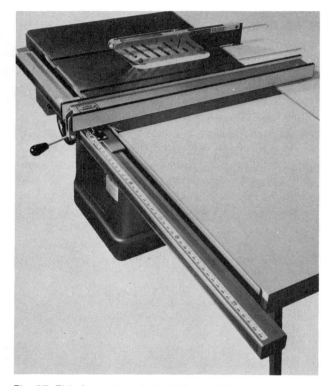

Fig. 27. *This fence is called a T-Square™ fence. It can be adapted to fit most table saws. It is easy to adjust and holds a setting quite well.*

Mitre Gauge The mitre gauge (Fig. 28) is also standard equipment with all table saws. The mitre gauge slides in the mitre slot. The mitre slot is cut into the table and runs parallel to the saw blade. Some mitre gauges have a control surface that can slide towards or away from the blade (Fig. 29). This allows greater stock control.

The mitre gauge controls solid stock when it is crosscut (cut across the grain). It is also used to trim small pieces of sheet stock, and can be turned to make angular cuts such as mitres on picture frame stock (Fig. 30). The mitre gauge has a protractorlike scale on it, but it is more accurate to measure the angle between the blade and the mitre gauge (Fig. 31).

Some woodworkers attach a piece of stock to the mitre gauge to increase stock control and accuracy (Fig. 32). It is important that this stock be true. To increase friction between the mitre gauge and the work, glue a piece of sandpaper or attach a piece of wood to the mitre gauge (Fig. 33). This reduces slippage when cutting mitres.

On some table saws, the mitre gauge comes with a stop rod (Fig. 34). The stop rod attaches to the mitre gauge. It can then be adjusted for cutting several pieces to the same length. A piece of wood may also be clamped to the mitre gauge for this purpose.

A clamping accessory is available for some mitre gauges (Fig. 35). The clamping accessory locks the stock to the mitre gauge so it will not slip. The clamping accessory usually is screwed to the mitre gauge in 1 or more places.

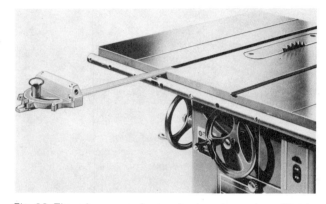

Fig. 28. *The mitre gauge is standard equipment on all table saws. It travels in a slot milled in the table. The slot runs parallel to the blade. Some mitre gauges engage in a track that keeps them from falling out when retracted.*

Fig. 29. *The control surface on this mitre gauge can slide towards or away from the blade. This allows greater control of the work. Note also the adjustable stop block. It is hinged so that it moves out of the way without changing the setting.*

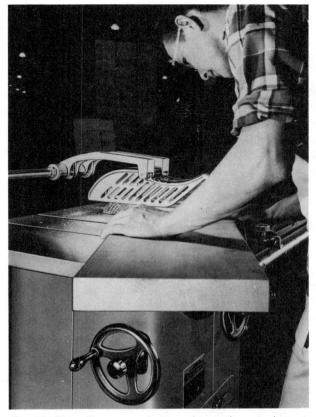

Fig. 30. The mitre gauge is turned to make angular cuts such as mitres. The mitre gauge controls the stock while the cut is made.

Fig. 31. Angular settings are more accurate when they are measured with a combination square or sliding T-bevel.

Fig. 34 (right). On some table saws, the mitre gauge comes with a stop rod. It attaches to the mitre gauge and can be adjusted to cut several parts to the same length.

Fig. 32. Some woodworkers attach a piece of stock to the mitre gauge. The stock increases control and accuracy and minimizes tear-out.

Fig. 33. Sandpaper has been glued to the stock attached to the mitre gauge. It reduces slippage between the mitre gauge and the work. This is helpful when making mitres on angular cuts.

23

Fig. 35. A clamping accessory is available for most mitre gauges. The clamp locks the stock securely to the mitre gauge.

Mitre Square When a large number of mitres must be cut for picture frames, door trim or window trim, a mitre square (Fig. 36) can be helpful. The mitre square has a right triangle oriented at 45° to the blade. This allows both mitres to be cut with 1 set-up. The 90° angle in the triangle assures that the included angle between the mitred parts is 90°. This eliminates the possibility of error when changing a conventional mitre gauge to cut mitres at the opposite end of the parts.

The mitre square also has a clamping device. The clamping device (Fig. 37) holds stock securely while the mitres are cut and eliminates the problem of creeping. The mitre square may also be used for cutting compound mitres. It is sold as an option.

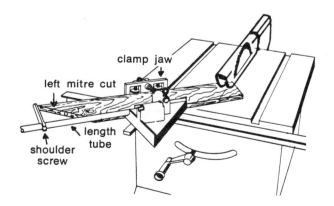

Fig. 36. The mitre square can be helpful when a number of mitres must be cut. The right triangle assures an included angle of 90° between the mitres.

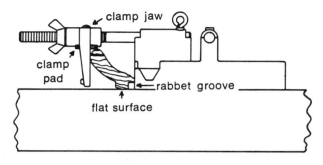

Fig. 37. The clamping device holds stock securely for cutting flat or compound mitres.

Tenoning and Universal Jigs The tenoning jig (Fig. 38) and the universal jig (Fig. 39) are designed to hold stock vertically. The universal jig will also hold irregularly shaped pieces. These jigs are used to guide pieces that cannot be controlled with the fence or mitre gauge (Fig. 40). Both jigs travel in the mitre slot and move in and out on a track in their base. They are commonly used for making mortise-and-tenon joints. Plans for a homemade jig appear in Chapter 8 (pages 234–255).

Fig. 38. The tenoning jig is designed to control stock that is cut or shaped on the end. The jig rides in the mitre slot.

Fig. 39. The universal jig is similar to the tenoning jig. It may be adjusted to make cuts on irregularly shaped pieces.

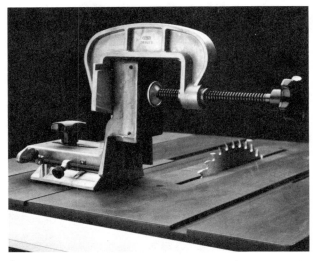

Fig. 40. This tenoning jig guides pieces that cannot be controlled with the fence or mitre gauge. The scale on the front is easy to read and adjust.

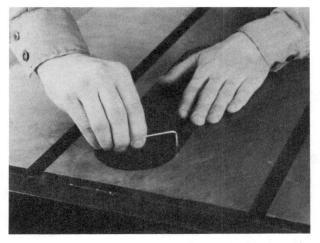

Fig. 41. The throat plate allows access to the blade, arbor and arbor nut. Some may be adjusted so they are in the same plane as the table.

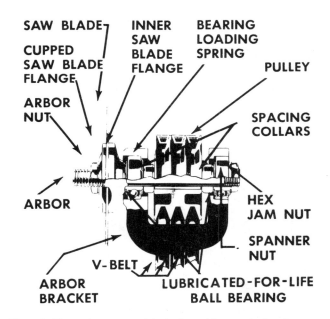

Fig. 42. The arbor assembly is found beneath the throat plate. The arbor nut must be removed to change blades.

Throat Plate The throat plate (Fig. 41) is an insert in the table that allows access to the blade, arbor, arbor nut and arbor washers (Fig. 42). Some throat plates can be adjusted. They can be levelled with the table top. Others snap into place and are not adjustable. The arbor nut is removed to change blades. Two arbor washers sandwich the blade, and the arbor nut holds them securely to the arbor. Arbor nuts may have right-hand or left-hand threads. Inspect the threads carefully to determine which way the nut must be turned.

Throat plates are usually made of metal (Fig. 43), but they may also be made of wood or plastic. In some cases, a throat plate is custom-made for the job.

The size of the opening in the throat plate varies according to what blade or attachment is being used. Be sure to select the correct or recommended throat plate for the operation you are performing. Avoid using a throat plate with an opening too large for the operation (Fig. 44). The workpiece could fall into the opening and cause a kickback or mishap.

Fig. 43. This metal throat plate is well-machined and is held securely with screws. Note the tight fit around the blade.

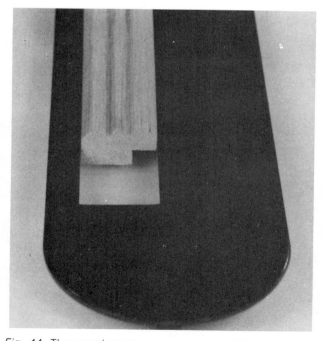

Fig. 44. The opening on some commercial throat plates may be too large for the work. This piece could easily fall into the cutter. A plywood throat plate was made to shape this stock.

When shaping stock with the moulding head or sawing with a specialized blade, it may be necessary to make your own throat plate. Auxiliary throat plates are usually made of wood or plastic. Wooden throat plates are the easiest to cut, but plastic throat plates will resist wear better than wood.

Use any throat plate that fits the saw as a model. Select stock as thick as the throat plate or slightly thinner. Veneer core plywood works well for throat plates. Rip the stock to the width of the throat plate. Lay out the curved ends with the throat plate (Fig. 45). Cut the curved ends with a band saw or sabre saw. Disc sand the curves to your layout line (Fig. 46).

Fig. 45. When making an auxiliary throat plate, use the metal throat plate as a template. Rip stock to throat plate width before laying out the ends.

Fig. 46. You can use the sanding disc to shape the ends of the wooden throat plate.

You may have to drill and tap holes to hold the throat plate in place (Fig. 47). Locate these holes in the lugs that support the throat plate. Drill the throat plate to match these holes. Anchor the throat plate with flathead machine screws. If the throat plate is too low, use tape, paper or veneer to raise it.

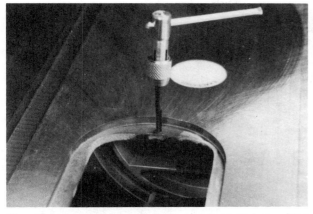

Fig. 47. Locate and tap holes in the support lugs of the table. These holes allow machine screws to hold the throat plate securely in place.

The hole in the throat plate is cut with the blade or shaper cutter. Mount the correct blade or shaper cutter and drop it beneath the table. Install the throat plate (Fig. 48), turn on the saw and slowly raise the moving blade or shaper head into the throat plate. The hole made (Fig. 49) in the throat plate will match the blade or cutter perfectly. If the arbor is to be tilted, the blade or cutter must be lowered beneath the table, tilted and then raised into the throat plate while moving.

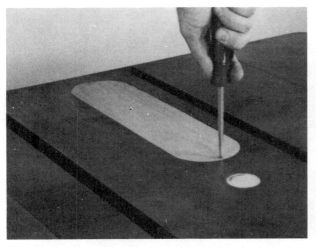

Fig. 48. Install the throat plate after the desired blade or shaper head is mounted on the arbor. Be sure to lower the arbor so the blade or cutter is beneath the throat plate.

Fig. 49. Slowly raise the turning blade or shaper head into the throat plate. The correct-size hole will be cut.

Guard The guard (Fig. 50) protects the operator from contact with the blade. Some guards are held in position by the splitter. The splitter (Fig. 51) holds the saw kerf open while a cut is made. This keeps the wood from pinching or binding against the blade. Other guards are suspended from arms mounted to the back or side of the table (Fig. 52). The splitter used with these guards is mounted beneath or to the back of the table.

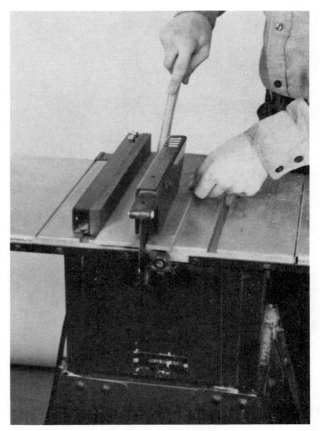

Fig. 50. The guard protects the operator from contact with the blade. This guard is made of metal.

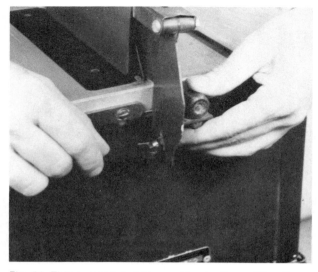

Fig. 51. This guard is held in position by the splitter. It can be removed easily for dado and rabbet cuts.

Fig. 52. This guard is suspended from a pair of arms. It may be mounted to the back or either side of the saw.

Guards are usually made of metal or clear plastic. Plastic guards offer more visibility, but they tend to scratch and become blurred. Solid metal guards limit vision. Woven wire guards protect the operator but increase the visibility of the work.

Most splitters also have anti-kickback pawls or dogs (Fig. 53). These pawls are made of sharpened steel. They are spring-loaded and ride on the work as it is cut. If the work should kick back, the pawls dig into the wood to stop the kickback. These pawls must be kept sharp to be effective.

Fig. 53. The anti-kickback pawls on this splitter are spring-loaded. They will dig into the wood if it begins to kick back. These pawls must be sharp to be effective.

Featherboard   A featherboard (Fig. 54) is a shop-made device used to help control stock. The featherboard is a piece of solid stock with several kerfs equally spaced along or with the grain. The end of the piece is cut at a 30–45° angle. The featherboard is clamped to the table or fence and is used to hold stock against the fence or table (Fig. 55). The featherboard acts like a spring. The feathers force stock against the fence or table. They help minimize kickback hazards.

Fig. 54. The featherboard is a shop-made device used to help control stock.

Fig. 55. This featherboard is holding the stock against the fence. If the piece were to kick back, the feathers would act like anti-kickback pawls.

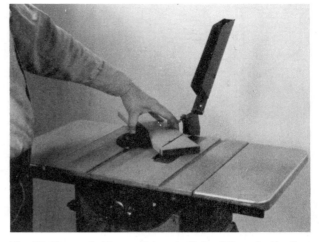

Fig. 57. The end of the work is cut off at a 45° angle. Feather length is then marked on the work.

The featherboard is an excellent table saw project. Use 2 spacer sticks (Fig. 56) and the fence to space the kerfs evenly. One stick is as thick as the desired "feathers," and the other is as thick as 1 feather and a saw kerf. Select a piece of stock 3–4 inches (76–102 mm) wide and 12–18 inches (30.5–45.7 cm) long. Cut off the end of the workpiece at a 45° angle before making any kerf cuts (Fig. 57). Mark the feather length on the workpiece with a pencil.

Set the distance between the blade and the fence with the thinner stick (Fig. 58). Adjust blade height to slightly above stock thickness and make the first cut. When the

blade reaches the layout line (Fig. 59), shut off the saw and let the blade coast to a stop. Do not move the workpiece.

With the work still over the blade, unlock the fence and insert the thicker stock between the fence and the work. Lock the fence in this position (Fig. 60). Lift the work off the blade and move it over so that it is touching the fence. The second kerf can now be cut (Fig. 61). Let the blade coast to a stop when it reaches the layout line. Use the thicker stick to space the fence again (Fig. 62). The last feather may be wider than the others. It can be eliminated by moving the fence with the thick stick and cutting off the entire edge (Fig. 63). Sand the featherboard lightly, and it is ready for use.

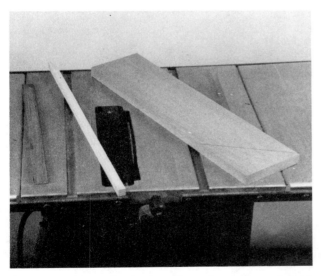

Fig. 56. Making a featherboard requires pieces of stock 3–4 inches (76 mm–102 mm) wide and 12–18 inches (30.5–45.7 cm) long. The 2 sticks space the kerfs in the featherboard. One is as thick as a feather (about ¼ inch [6 mm]); the other is as thick as a feather and a saw kerf.

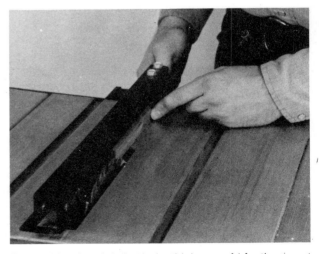

Fig. 58. Use the stick that is the thickness of 1 feather to set the fence for the first cut.

Fig. 59. Make the first cut. Set the blade slightly above the stock thickness and feed into the layout line. Hold the stock securely and shut off the saw. Do not release the stock until the blade stops turning.

Fig. 60. Leave the work in position on the blade and release the fence. Use the thicker spacer to set the fence. Lift the stock off the blade.

Fig. 63 (right). If the last feather is narrower or wider than the others, simply cut it off. The featherboard is now ready for use.

Fig. 61. Cut the second kerf. Stop the saw at the layout line. Do not release the stock until the blade stops.

Fig. 62. Continue moving the fence using the thicker stick to space the kerfs.

Push Stick   The push stick is a shop-made device (Fig. 64). It is used to feed stock through the blade of the table saw. The push stick keeps your fingers clear of the blade and allows you to cut thin or narrow pieces safely.

Push sticks take on many different sizes and shapes. They are cut for the job at hand. Since the push stick has many curves, it is not a good table saw project. Use a sabre saw or band saw to make a push stick.

Note: Before you do any sawing, cut several push sticks and keep them near the saw. Plywood scraps make good push sticks. Many serious accidents can be avoided by simply using 1 (or 2) push sticks. Several push stick patterns are furnished for your use (Figs. 65–68). Use these shapes or modify them to suit your needs. Be sure to round all edges and avoid sharp corners on the push sticks you make. Sharp edges and corners can easily split your skin if they are forced into your hand by a kickback.

Fig. 64. A push stick is a shop-made device used to feed stock into the blade. One or 2 push sticks can be used, depending on the job.

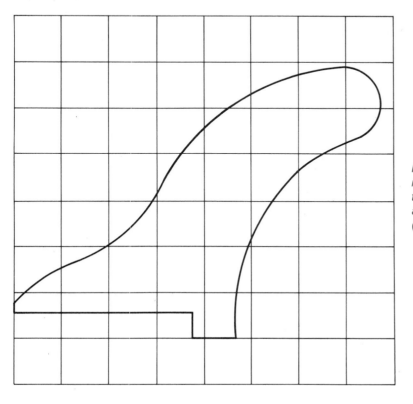

Figs. 65–68 (page 32). Use these patterns to make push sticks for your shop. Modify them to suit your needs, but avoid sharp corners and edges. These patterns are on a 1-inch (25-mm) grid. This pattern is half-size.

31

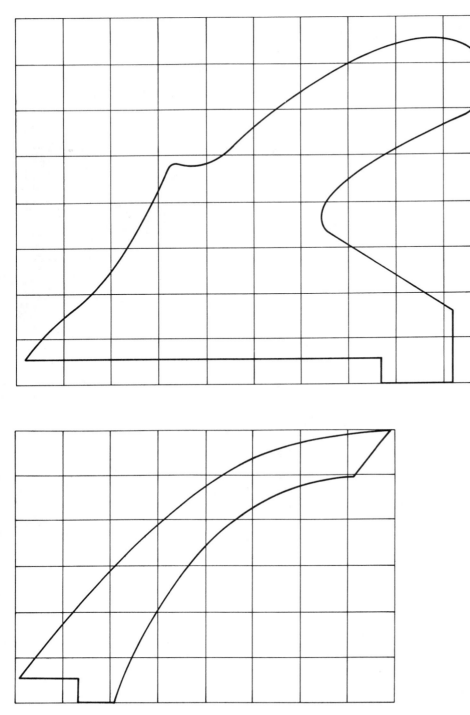

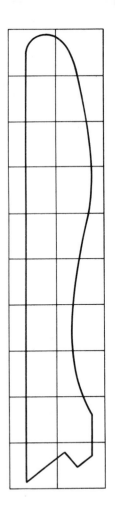

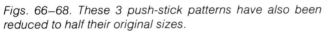

Figs. 66–68. These 3 push-stick patterns have also been reduced to half their original sizes.

Shooting Table A shooting table or board (Fig. 69) is a shop-made device that takes the place of the mitre gauge for cut-off work. The shooting board is usually set for a 90° cut. Shooting boards may be set at other angles, but they are usually not adjustable. The shooting board provides better control over the stock because it is larger than the mitre gauge.

The shooting board is a challenging table saw project. The base is made out of sheet stock ⅜–½ inch (10–13 mm) thick. The guides that fit in the mitre slots should be made from hardwood, so they resist wear (Fig. 70). The guides can be screwed to the board or dadoed into it. The vertical piece should be a true piece of stock about 1½ inch (38 mm) thick. Make this piece wide enough so that the blade does not cut it in half when elevated to full height. You may wish to put a piece at both ends of the plywood base for greater rigidity.

Fig. 69. The shooting board takes the place of a mitre gauge for cut-off work. Shooting boards are not usually adjustable.

Fig. 70. The guides that fit the mitre slots should be made from hard wood, so they resist wear.

Dead Man The dead man or roller support (Fig. 71) is a device used to support long or wide pieces of stock being cut on the table saw. There are many different types of supports. Some are commercial and others are shop-made.

Fig. 71. The dead man or roller support is used to support long or wide pieces cut on the table saw.

Commercial supports are usually metal. Their height is adjustable, and they have a rolling device to support the stock (Fig. 72). The rolling device makes travel smoother. Shop-made supports may also have a rolling device made of pipe, closet rod or a rolling pin. The shop-made dead man may be adjustable or fixed. Some shop-made dead man devices are much simpler. They use a portable workbench sawhorse with a piece of stock (Fig. 73) or a roller (Fig. 74) clamped to it. A sawhorse with a piece of stock clamped to it (Fig. 75) may also be used. The support or dead man is adjusted at the correct height to support the stock. For occasional use, the simple dead man is enough, but for frequent use a better one should be made or purchased.

33

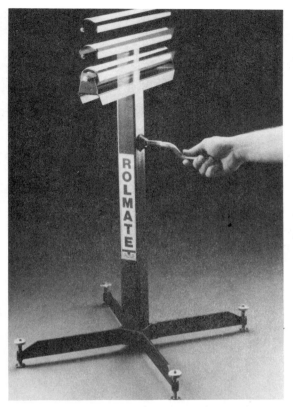

Fig. 72. The height on most commercial roller supports is adjustable. This one locks at the desired height.

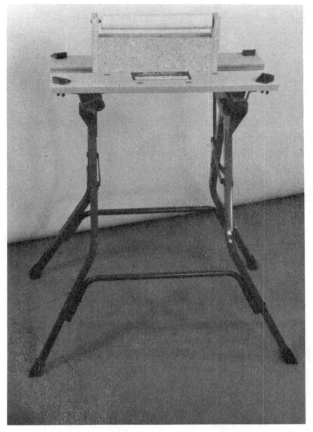

Fig. 74. The roller in this device is a piece of closet rod. It works well as a roller support and is easy to store and transport.

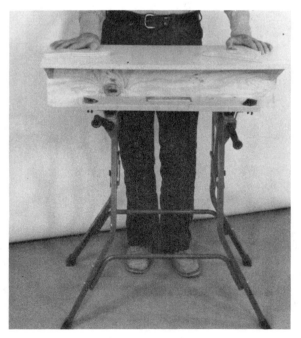

Fig. 73. A portable workbench sawhorse with a straight table clamped to it can be used as a dead man.

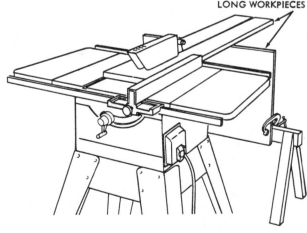

Fig. 75. A sawhorse with a piece of stock clamped to it can be used as a dead man. When a dead man is frequently needed, a commercial one should be purchased.

Accessory Storage

Table saw accessories must be stored conveniently and safely. The mitre gauge should hang on or near the saw when not in use (Fig. 76). This keeps it from being dropped or misplaced. The fence should also have convenient hanging storage (Fig. 77). Many fences are damaged because they are left on the floor when they are not in use. Damage to either the fence or mitre gauge encourages the operator to use the table saw without these accessories. This is dangerous and unnecessary!

At least one push stick should hang on the table saw at all times. This eliminates the temptation to work without a push stick. Keep several extra push sticks stored in a handy spot. When a push stick gets cut or damaged (Fig. 78), cut it in half and throw it away. This discourages the use of an unsafe push stick.

Extra throat plates, arbor nuts and arbor washers should be stored near or with the saw blades (Fig. 79). Mark the back of the throat plate so you can match it to the correct blade or accessory.

Fig. 78. When a push stick gets damaged, cut it in half and throw it away. This eliminates the temptation of using a hazardous push stick.

Fig. 76. These mitre gauges hang on the front of the saw when not in use. This protects them from being dropped or misplaced.

Fig. 79. Keep accessories stored close to the saw in an orderly manner.

Fig. 77 (left). This fence hangs on the side of the saw just below the table extension. It is out of the way and always ready for use.

3

Circular Saw Blades and Attachments

Wood is a stringy material. If you break a piece of wood, the stringy fibres make it difficult to get a clean break. If you split a piece of wood, the split is clean because the stringy fibres run parallel to the separation. When wood is crosscut (cut across the grain or stringy fibres), a crosscut blade is used (Fig. 80). The teeth are designed for crosscutting. Rip blades (for cutting with the grain or fibres) are designed for ripping only (Fig. 81). They do not crosscut efficiently.

The blade on a table saw is the most important link in the sawing process. It must be sharp and true. Blades should be checked frequently to be sure they are sharp and true.

A saw blade is subjected to extreme forces. Imagine a thin disc with the force of 1½ hp at 3450 rpm applied at the center, and the resistance of 2-inch (51-mm) oak applied at the periphery. There is great power at the center and great resistance at the outer edge. This generates the stress, heat and vibration that dull the blade. This is why many blades have small slots at the outer edge. These slots allow the blade to expand as the edge heats up. The slots prevent possible blade warpage.

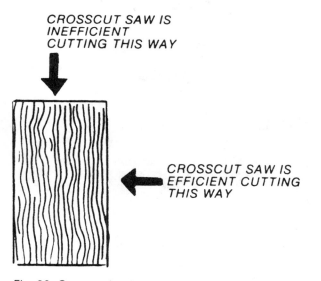

CROSSCUT SAW IS INEFFICIENT CUTTING THIS WAY

CROSSCUT SAW IS EFFICIENT CUTTING THIS WAY

Fig. 80. Crosscutting is done across the grain or stringy fibres. A crosscut blade with pointed teeth works best for this operation.

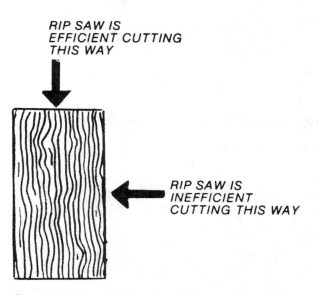

RIP SAW IS EFFICIENT CUTTING THIS WAY

RIP SAW IS INEFFICIENT CUTTING THIS WAY

Fig. 81. Ripping is done with the grain or stringy fibres. A rip blade with chisel-shaped teeth is best for ripping.

Circular Saw Terms

The cut made by a circular saw blade is called the *kerf* (Fig. 82). The kerf must be slightly larger than the saw blade thickness. The *tooth set* or *offset* is the bend in the tooth (Fig. 83). This set allows the blade to cut a kerf that is larger than the blade's thickness. The teeth on a circular saw blade are set in alternate directions.

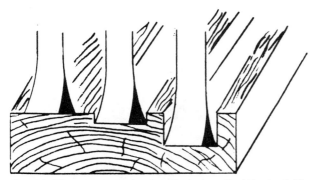

Fig. 82. The cut made by the blade is called the kerf. The kerf is slightly larger than the blade thickness due to the set of the teeth.

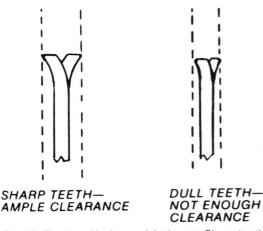

SHARP TEETH— AMPLE CLEARANCE

DULL TEETH— NOT ENOUGH CLEARANCE

Fig. 83. The bend in the teeth is the set. Sharp teeth have more set than dull teeth. Set allows clearance for the blade as it travels through the kerf.

The *gullet* is the area behind the cutting edge of the tooth (Fig. 84). It carries away the sawdust cut by the tooth. The larger the tooth, the larger the gullet.

The *hook angle* is the angle of the tooth's cutting edge as it relates to the center line of the blade. Rip saws usually have a hook angle of about 30° (Fig. 85). Crosscut saws usually have a hook angle of about 15°. The greater the hook angle, the bigger the tooth's bite (Fig. 86). Negative hook angles (Fig. 87) are sometimes used for tough cutting jobs. Some circular saw blades designed to cut used lumber have a negative hook angle. This allows them to cut nails or other metal in the wood.

Top clearance (Fig. 88) is the downwards slope of the back of the tooth. This slope keeps the back of the tooth from rubbing on the wood. Without top clearance, the blade cannot cut.

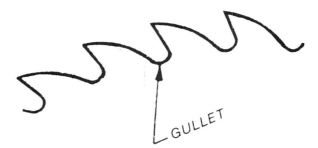

Fig. 84. The gullet is the area behind the cutting edge of the tooth. It is curved to reduce strain on the blade as it removes the chips or sawdust.

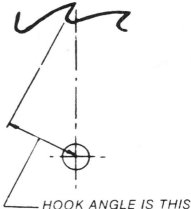

HOOK ANGLE IS THIS NUMBER OF DEGREES

Fig. 85. A rip tooth has a hook angle of about 30° This angle is measured between the center line of the blade and the face of the tooth.

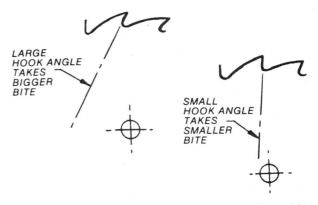

LARGE HOOK ANGLE TAKES BIGGER BITE

SMALL HOOK ANGLE TAKES SMALLER BITE

Fig. 86. The greater the hook angle, the bigger the tooth's bite. The larger the bite, the larger the gullet must be to clear the chips or sawdust.

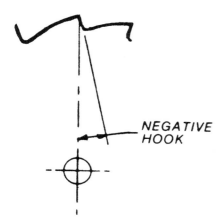

Fig. 87. Negative hook angles are sometimes used on blades used for tough cutting jobs.

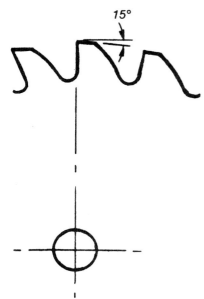

Fig. 88. Top clearance is the downward slope of the back of the tooth. This clearance angle keeps the back of the tooth from rubbing or pounding on the wood as the cut is made.

Common Blade Types

Rip Blades Rip blades have deep gullets and a large hook angle (Fig. 89). The tooth's cutting edge looks like a chisel. It has a straight cutting edge designed to cut with the grain. Rip teeth are usually quite large.

Crosscut Blades Crosscut blades have smaller teeth than rip blades (Fig. 89). The teeth on a crosscut blade come to a point, not an edge. This allows them to cut the stringy fibres in the wood.

Combination Blades Combination blades (Fig. 89) are designed for both ripping and crosscutting. They work very well for cutting wood fibres at an angle (mitre joints). Some combination blades have teeth that come to a point, but have a rip-tooth profile. Others have a chisel edge and a smaller hook angle. These blades do not produce smooth cuts, but they are well suited to general carpentry or rough construction (Fig. 90).

Smooth-cutting combination blades are sometimes called novelty combination blades. These blades have both rip and crosscut teeth. Novelty combination blades are preferred for cabinet and furniture work. This is because they cut smoothly with little tear-out (Fig. 90).

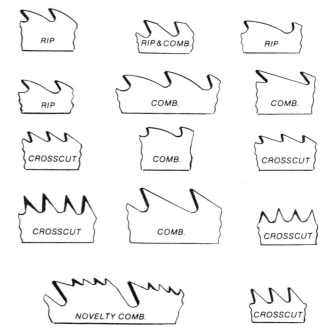

Fig. 89. Shown from left to right are the rip, crosscut and combination blades. Study the tooth shape so you can identify common saw blades. Note the plastic coating on the combination blade. Its purpose is to minimize pitch build-up.

Fig. 90. Tooth shapes of combination blades.

Hollow-Ground Blades Hollow-ground blades (Fig. 91) are blades with no set. The sides of the blade are recessed for clearance in the kerf. Some hollow-ground blades have sides that are recessed all the way to the hub (Fig. 92). Others are recessed only part of the way (Fig. 93). Blades with partially recessed sides cannot cut thick stock, but are more rigid.

Hollow-ground blades cause less splintering and tear-out in the wood they cut. The sides of the blade may burn and accumulate pitch (wood residue) if they are used for heavy cutting instead of finish cutting. Hollow-ground blades work best with very true stock.

Most hollow-ground blades have novelty combination teeth. Hollow-ground blades are sometimes called *planer blades*. This is because the wood is very smooth after being cut. It appears to have been planed. There are also blades with abrasives attached to the sides (Fig. 94). These blades sand the sides of the kerf after the blade cuts the wood (Figs. 95 and 96).

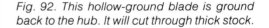

HOLLOW GROUND

Fig. 91. Hollow-ground blades have sides that are relieved or ground thinner than the teeth. The thinner sides provide clearance in the kerf. The teeth have no set and there is less tear-out.

Fig. 92. This hollow-ground blade is ground back to the hub. It will cut through thick stock.

Fig. 93. This hollow-ground blade is only ground part of the way back to the hub. It is designed to cut through sheet stock and solid stock less than 1¼ inch (32 mm). This blade has greater rigidity than those ground all the way to the hub.

Fig. 94. This carbide-tipped blade has abrasives bonded to each of its sides. It sands the kerf as the cut is made, and must be made to close tolerances to keep the abrasives from skipping. The blade may be resharpened and new abrasives can be bonded to it.

Fig. 95. The top cut here was made with the abrasive blade. The second cut was made with a carbon-steel combination blade. The bottom cuts were made with a carbide-tipped combination blade.

Fig. 96. The cut on the left represents the quality of the abrasive blade. The rebound of the wood fibres causes contact with the abrasives after cutting. The cut on the right represents the quality of a common carbide-tipped combination blade.

Plywood Blades Plywood blades, sometimes called panelling or veneer blades, are designed to cut hardwood plywood with cabinet-grade or furniture-grade outer veneers. These blades have very fine crosscut teeth with little set (Fig. 97). Some of these blades are hollow ground. The fine teeth and small amount of set allow very smooth splinter-free cuts. These blades should be used only when appropriate. Using them for other purposes can ruin them quickly. Certain types of plywood cores (particle or fibre) can dull these blades quickly. Carbide-tipped blades would be a better choice for particle or fibre core plywood or other sheet stock.

Fig. 98. Carbide-tipped blades have small pieces of carbide brazed to a steel rim. The carbide is located in an L-shaped seat. The carbide-tipped blade stays sharp much longer than a steel blade.

Fig. 97. This plywood blade has fine teeth and very little set. Use these blades for finish cuts only. General use will dull the teeth quickly.

Carbide-Tipped Blades Carbide-tipped blades have teeth made from small pieces of carbide. The carbide is brazed onto the circular blade (Fig. 98). Usually there is a little seat cut in the blade. This is where the carbide is brazed. Most carbide tips are wider than the metal blade, so no set is required. Carbide is much harder than the steel used for conventional blades. Carbide-tipped blades stay sharp 5 to 10 times longer than conventional blades.

Because of its hardness, carbide is also quite brittle. Carbide will fracture easily if struck against a hard object. Carbide-tipped blades must be handled with care.

Carbide-tipped blades are more expensive than steel blades, but they require much less maintenance. Carbide-tipped blades are preferred for tough materials such as hardboard, plastic laminates and particle board.

Carbide-tipped blades come in rip, crosscut, combination, hollow-ground and plywood categories. They do not always resemble their steel counterparts (Figs. 99–102). Usually the type of teeth, the number of teeth and the hook angle determine the blade's function. The teeth may be alternate top bevel, triple chip, rip, cut-off or combination (Fig. 103). Some carbide blades are called *control cut* blades. These blades have 8–12 teeth, which are set slightly above the blade's periphery. These teeth minimize the chance of a kickback or severe cut. Consult a manufacturer's catalogue for specifics and blade function.

Fig. 99. This carbide-tipped blade is a rip blade. It works well for ripping stock 1 inch (25 mm) or thinner. It has too many teeth (30) to rip 2-inch (51-mm) stock easily.

Fig. 100. This 40-tooth carbide-tipped combination blade is well suited to general cutting in stock up to 2 inches (51 mm) thick.

Fig. 101. This 48-tooth carbide-tipped blade is designed for crosscutting and trimming plastic laminates.

Fig. 102. This 60-tooth thin-rim carbide-tipped blade is designed for very fine cutting in sheet stock, plastic laminates and hardwood. Depth of cut is limited by the hub just below the expansion slots.

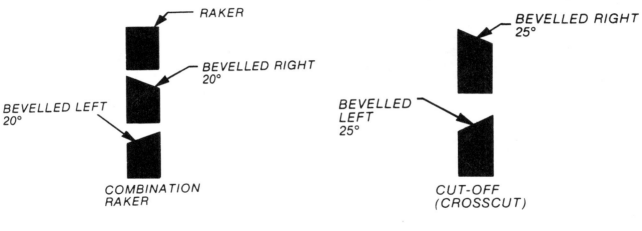

RAKER

BEVELLED RIGHT
20°

BEVELLED LEFT
20°

COMBINATION
RAKER

BEVELLED RIGHT
25°

BEVELLED
LEFT
25°

CUT-OFF
(CROSSCUT)

BEVELLED RIGHT
25°

BEVELLED LEFT
25°

ALTERNATE TOP BEVEL

Fig. 103. Some common carbide tooth shapes and groupings. Rip blades have flat raker teeth only. Combination blades have flat rakers ground slightly lower than the other teeth. This allows them to clean out the kerf. Cut-off blades are used for cross-grain trimming. Alternate top bevel blades are used for fine cutting of veneers where tear-out could be a problem.

Evaluating Carbide Blades. Not all carbide blades do the job equally well. Before buying any, look them over and evaluate them carefully. The size of the carbide tips is important. The larger the tips, the more times the blade can be sharpened. Look at the braze joint between the blade and the carbide tip. It often indicates blade quality. There should be no pits in the braze.

Inspect the teeth. They should be ground smooth. The smoother the surface of the carbide, the better the cut (Fig. 104). Keep the carbide blade sharp. Use a reliable sharpening service that polishes the teeth and leaves no coarse grinding marks.

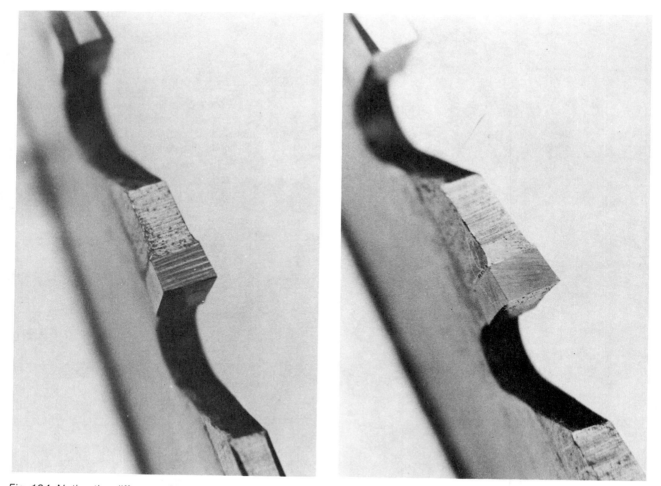

Fig. 104. Notice the difference in grinding quality from rough surface left to smooth surface right. Smoother surfaces mean sharper teeth and greater longevity.

Selecting Blades

One blade cannot perform all sawing operations. About 3 blades are needed for general sawing. For a 10-inch (25.4-cm) saw, select a rip blade with about 24 teeth. This will be coarse enough to handle any thickness the saw will accommodate. Choose a crosscut or cut-off blade with about 40 teeth. This blade will handle most general cut-off work. A finer-cutting hollow-ground blade with 60 to 80 teeth will complete the selection. Use it to cut finished pieces to length.

Select additional blades as needed. A general rule is that 3 teeth should be engaged with the work at any given time. Thicker pieces require less teeth than thinner ones. Consider what you are cutting, the desired finish and whether you are ripping or crosscutting before you select a blade.

Blade Collars Blade collars or stabilizers are used to increase saw blade rigidity. Some collars go on one side of

the blade, while others go on both sides of the saw blade. The blade collars go between the arbor washers, with the blade in the center (Fig. 105). The concave sides go against the blade.

By reducing vibration, circular saw blades stay sharp longer. True-running carbide-tipped blades have less stress on the sides, which reduces tip breakage and improves cutting. Reduced vibration also means reduced noise. The vibration causes resonant noise (singing or screaming) or pounding as the blade cuts the wood. Resonant noise or pounding causes an increase in the noise level that is quite noticeable. The excess noise increases operator fatigue and is distracting.

If you install blade collars, some readjustment of the saw will be necessary. Blade collars change the relative position of the blade on the arbor. This requires readjustment of the splitter, and may require enlargement of the hole in the throat plate.

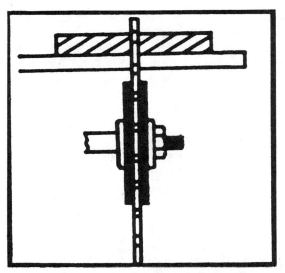

Fig. 105. The blade collars or stabilizers go between the arbor washers. They reduce blade vibration and noise, and also increase accuracy.

Blade Maintenance

Blades should be protected from damage when not in use. The teeth of blades in storage should not touch. Such contact can dull or break carbide teeth, and will dull steel blades. Hang blades individually or with spacers between them. This will keep them sharp. Protect blades from corrosion. Corrosion will deteriorate a sharp cutting edge.

Handle circular saw blades carefully. A sharp (or dull) blade can cut you. Never lay a blade on the cast-iron surface of your table saw. The set of the teeth causes them to scratch the table and become dull. Lay the blade on a scrap of stock when changing blades (Fig. 106).

Fig. 106. When changing blades, lay the blade on a scrap of wood. Contact with the metal table can dull the blade quickly.

Pitch   When a circular saw blade becomes hot, pitch will accumulate on it. Pitch is a brown sticky substance (wood resin) that looks like varnish (Fig. 107). As pitch accumulates on the blade, it acts as an insulator. This keeps the blade from dissipating heat and causes it to become dull faster.

Pitch is usually a sign of a blade with too little set for the job. It can also mean that the blade is too dull to cut. In some cases, the blade accumulates pitch and smokes when it is installed backwards (teeth pointing the wrong way). Some blades are Teflon®-coated to resist pitch accumulation, but the Teflon® wears off after 2 or 3 resharpenings. Commercial pitch removers can be used to clean blades. Kerosene, hot water and oven cleaner also work well. Avoid using abrasives to remove pitch. Abrasives leave scratches that make it easier for pitch to anchor itself to the blade. Pitch accumulation does not always mean the blade is dull.

Fig. 107. Pitch is a brown sticky substance that looks like varnish. Here it is accumulating behind the carbide tips on this blade.

Dull Blades   Some indications of a dull blade include:
1.   Stock tends to climb over the blade
2.   Blade smokes or gives off a burnt odor
3.   Increased effort is needed to feed the stock into the blade
4.   The saw no longer cuts a straight line

Dull blades can also be identified by visual inspection. Look at the teeth. Rip teeth should come to an edge (Fig. 108). The edge should be a straight line and not rounded. Crosscut teeth should come to a point. The 2 cutting angles should form a straight line to the point of the tooth (Fig. 109).

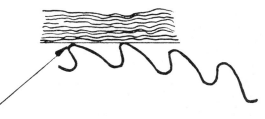

←MORE PRESSURE NEEDED TO CUT

Fig. 108. The rip teeth shown here have rounded ends. This means they are dull. They should form a straight line or edge. More energy and feed pressure is needed to make a rip with a dull blade.

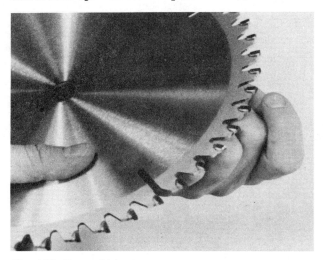

SHARP   DULL

Fig. 109. Crosscut teeth also become rounded or flat on the end. Sharp teeth come to a point.

Carbide teeth stay sharp longer than steel teeth, but they also become dull. If a dull carbide blade is left on the saw, the brittle teeth will crack or shatter. Drag your fingernail across the carbide tip (Fig. 110). It should cut a chip (remove a curl from your fingernail). If it does not (fingernail slides across the tip), it is too dull to cut properly. Disconnect the saw to check a blade that is mounted. Replacing broken carbide tips is much more expensive than sharpening. Keep carbide blades sharp, and broken tips will not be a problem.

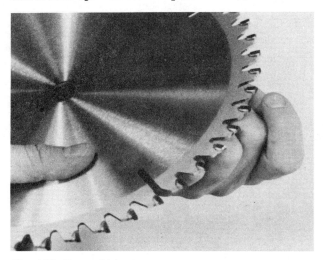

Fig. 110. If a carbide-tipped blade is sharp, it will raise a chip on your finger (you can see one on my index finger). If it is dull, your fingernail will slide across the tip.

Getting Blades Sharpened In most cases, it is best to have your blades sharpened by a professional. The equipment they use is very accurate, but too expensive for the

individual (Fig. 111). Find a reliable service and develop a good working relationship. Not all sharpening services are equal. Some do better work than others. When trying a new service, do not send them your best blades. Have them sharpen 1 or 2 general-duty blades first. Inspect the blades carefully (Fig. 112) If the results are not satisfactory, try another sharpening service.

Make a board for transporting blades (Fig. 113). Put cardboard spacers between the blades. This will make the blades safer and easier to transport. It will also keep them well protected and sharp.

Selecting the Correct Blade for the Job Blade performance is best when the blade is matched to the job. The following general rules will help you select the correct blade:

1.   Three teeth should be in the work at all times.
2.   Larger teeth are best for ripping.
3.   Use a rip blade when the job is strictly ripping.
4.   Small teeth mean a smoother cut and a slower feed rate.
5.   Use the largest tooth blade that will produce satisfactory results.
6.   Hollow-ground blades and panelling blades should be used only for true, dry cabinet-grade lumber.
7.   Remove high quality or specialty blades as soon as the job is done.
8.   Green lumber and construction lumber require blades with more set than dry hardwood lumber. This is due to the increased moisture content.
9.   Never use a dull blade. It is unsafe and produces poor results.

Always analyze the job using the general rules listed and any other information you may have. The time spent changing blades is time well spent. The correct blade does the most efficient and safest job. Dull blades waste time and energy.

Trial-and-error experience will help you select the best blade for every job you do. Make note of which blade does the best job. This provides a ready reference for future use.

Some blades have a knock-out arbor hole so that they may be used with more than 1 size of arbor. Be sure the knock out is in securely when it must be used. The blade's arbor hole should just fit the arbor. A sloppy fit means the blade is incorrect for the arbor. Extra knock outs or spacers can be purchased at most hardware stores (Fig. 114).

A prick punch may be used to offset metal around the arbor hole (Fig. 115). This holds the knock out in more securely. Knock outs are frequently removed when the blade is sharpened. Always check the arbor hole after your blades have been sharpened.

Fig. 111. Professional sharpening equipment is very accurate, but too expensive for the average woodworker. A quality sharpening job is a bargain.

Fig. 112. Inspect blades after sharpening. Carbide-tipped blades ground as smoothly as the one shown here will stay sharp a long time.

Fig. 113. A sharpening or transportation board like this will keep blades sharp. Use a cardboard spacer between blades to keep them separated and sharp.

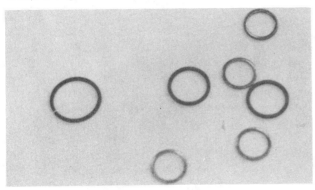

Fig. 114 (left). Extra knock outs or arbor spacers are available at most hardware stores. They are used to reduce the size of the arbor hole.

Fig. 115. A prick punch may be used to offset metal around the arbor hole. This holds the knock out in more securely.

Dado Heads

A dado head is used to cut dadoes and rabbets. Dadoes are square or rectangular channels in wood. Rabbets are L-shaped cuts along the edge of a piece of stock. The dado head is used for joinery cuts. There are 2 types of dado heads, the wobble type and the blade and chipper type. Both types require a special throat plate when they are used.

Wobble Types Wobble-type dado heads form a dado with a single wobbling (oscillating) blade. The oscillation of the blade causes it to cut a dado of the desired shape. Offset washers make the blade oscillate. One is mounted on either side of the blade. Both washers have registration marks. These marks serve as guides to the width of dado that will be cut at that setting.

Some wobble dado heads consist only of a pair of offset washers (Fig. 116). These washers are then used with a

Fig. 116. This pair of dado or wobble washers is used with a conventional saw blade. By turning the washers on the arbor, various dado widths can be cut.

circular saw blade that fits the saw. Most blades will work with these washers. Experimenting with various blades on scraps will determine which blade is best for cutting dadoes.

Other wobble dado heads consist of a heavy carbide-tipped blade and a pair of offset washers (Fig. 117). This wobble dado works only as a unit. The heavy carbide-tipped blade makes this unit suitable for particle board and other wood composition products. This wobble dado set (blade and washers) is available with a varying number of carbide tips on the blade. The one with the largest number of carbide tips cuts the smoothest dado. It also is less likely to tear out the wood next to the dado.

Fig. 117. This wobble dado is sold as a set. The washers and blade work as a unit to cut dadoes. This blade has carbide-tipped teeth, which makes it suitable for cutting particle board and plywood.

Blade and Chipper Types Blade and chipper dado heads come as a complete set. The 2 blades or cutters resemble a combination blade (Fig. 118). Each blade or cutter is designed to cut a ⅛-inch (3-mm) kerf. The chippers have 2 cutting edges. They are mounted between the blades. Chippers are designed for ⅛-inch (3-mm) or 1/16-inch (1.5-mm) spacing. Blade and chipper dado sets may be carbide tipped (Fig. 119) or tool steel.

A complete dado set will cut dadoes from ⅛ inch (3 mm) or ¼ inch (6 mm) to 13/16 inch (20 mm) by varying the number of chippers between the blades. Two blades or cutters must be used for all dadoes except ⅛ inch (3 mm). This requires 1 cutter. A ¼-inch (6-mm) dado would be made with 2 blades. A ⅜-inch (10-mm) dado would be cut with the 2 ⅛-inch (3-mm) blades and 1 ⅛-inch (3-mm) chipper.

A blade and chipper type of dado head cannot be adjusted to odd-sized dadoes as easily as a wobble type. With the use of paper or cardboard rings (Fig. 120), the dado head can be adjusted somewhat. The rings are slipped over the arbor between the cutters and chippers. This allows extended spacing and an oversized cut. As the dado becomes dull, some paper spacing is needed to compensate for wear.

Fig. 118. This steel cutter (right) and chipper (left) are the 2 components of a dado head. Chippers are used with the cutters to make dadoes over ¼ inch (6 mm) wide.

Fig. 119. This carbide-tipped cutter (right) and chipper (left) are best suited to particle board and plywood. The 2 missing teeth on the cutter make room for the chipper when it is mounted between 2 cutters.

Fig. 120. Cutter and chipper dado heads can be spaced with paper washers to make an odd-sized dado.

Moulding Heads

Moulding heads (Fig. 121) are used to shape stock on the table saw. Stock can be shaped into moulding, lipped doors and joinery. The moulding head mounts on the saw arbor. It has slots into which the moulding cutters are fastened. A special throat plate is used with the moulding head. Some moulding heads have only 1 or 2 cutters, but most have a set of 3 cutters for each shape that is cut. The moulding heads that use a set of 3 cutters are safer and cut smoother moulding.

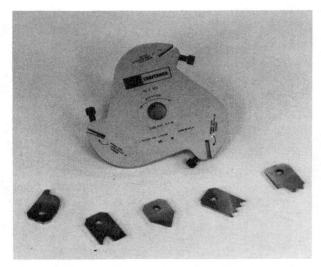

Fig. 121. The moulding or shaper head is used to shape stock. There are many different cutters that can be used in the moulding head.

There are many moulding cutter types and shapes. They are ground from flat steel and usually have a mounting hole. The mounting hole is used to attach them to the moulding head. Moulding cutter manufacturers have their own mounting designs. This means that cutters of different brands are not interchangeable. Follow manufacturer's directions for mounting moulding cutters in the moulding head (Fig. 122). Check them periodically during operation to be sure they are tight. Be sure the cutters all face forward. The flat side of the cutter does the cutting.

When the cutters become dull, the flat side can be honed on an oilstone or waterstone (Fig. 123). Honing the flat side will cause the clearance angles to form an edge with the flat side. Never hone the clearance angles on the cutters. This could change the shape of the cut. If cutters have large nicks, discard them and buy a new set. It is important to keep shaper cutters sharp. Dull cutters tend to tear the wood and may cause a kickback.

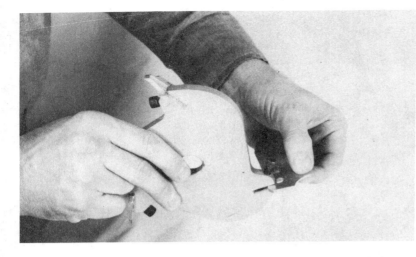

Fig. 122. When installing cutters in the shaper head, follow the manufacturer's instructions. Be sure the cutters are tightened securely; check them periodically.

Fig. 123. Dull cutters can be honed on an oilstone or waterstone. Hone the flat side only. Keep the cutters sharp and free of rust.

Sanding Discs

Sanding discs for table saws are made from tempered steel or cast aluminum. They vary in size from about 6–10 inches (15.2–25.4 cm) in diameter. When a sanding disc is mounted on the arbor, the table saw can be used to disc sand outside curves and straight edges. The disc can be tilted to sand chamfers and bevels. Some discs are designed to be used in conjunction with the fence. They have a 2° bevel on the face (Fig. 124). When they are used to sand edges of stock fed between the disc and the fence, they leave sanding marks that are parallel with the grain.

The most common mistake made when disc sanding is to use too fine an abrasive. Because of the high rpms of the disc, fine abrasives cannot clear the wood chips fast enough. This causes heat and ultimately burns the abrasive. For general-duty sanding, 60-grit or 80-grit abrasives work best. Rougher work can be done with 40-grit abrasives, and finer work can be done with 100-grit or 120-grit abrasives. Avoid heavy feed or large cuts when

using fine abrasives. Remove most of the stock with coarse abrasives. Then progress to a finer abrasive. Some discs carry abrasives on both sides. This makes it easy to go from a coarse abrasive to a fine abrasive in a hurry.

When abrasives wear out (Fig. 125), they must be replaced. If contact-type cement is used, the abrasive sheet peels off easily (Fig. 126). Other disc cements make disc removal more difficult (Fig. 127). If residue remains on the disc, it can be removed with a sharpened piece of hardwood.

Mount the disc on the table saw using the correct throat plate. Turn the saw on with the disc at full height. Use the sharpened piece of hardwood to scrape the disc. Press the wood lightly against the disc (Fig. 128). Work from the outside edge towards the center. Repeat the process until the disc is clean. Attach the new disc according to the directions furnished with the disc cement (Figs. 129–132). Cement and precut discs are available from most hardware dealers. Discs can also be made from heavyweight abrasive paper.

FENCE

ENTIRE
SANDING SURFACE
OF TAPERED SIDE
SANDS WORKPIECE

TABLE

SAW ARBOR
TILTED 2°

2° TAPER AND
2° ARBOR TILT
EXAGGERATED
FOR CLARITY

Fig. 124. Some sanding discs are tilted 2° for edge sanding. These discs leave sanding marks parallel with the grain.

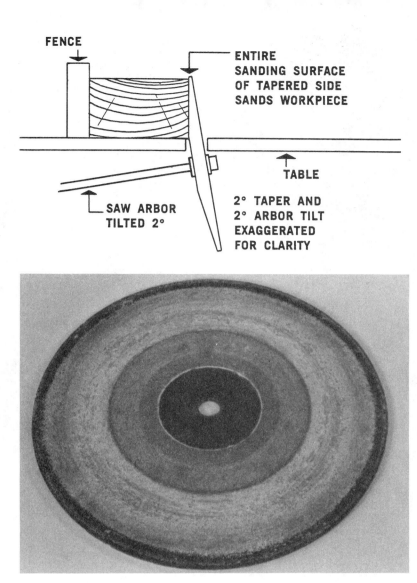

Fig. 125. When abrasives become worn or burned, they must be replaced.

Fig. 126. Discs anchored with contact cement peel off easily.

Fig. 127. Residue left on this disc can be removed with the sharpened piece of stock behind the disc.

Fig. 128. Press the piece of stock against the turning disc. Work from the outside towards the center.

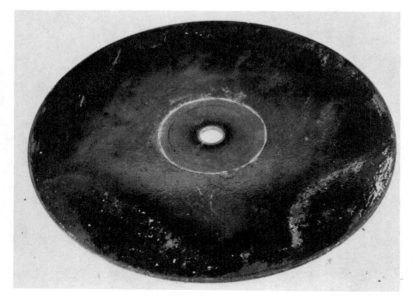

Fig. 129. The disc should be completely clean before new abrasives are applied.

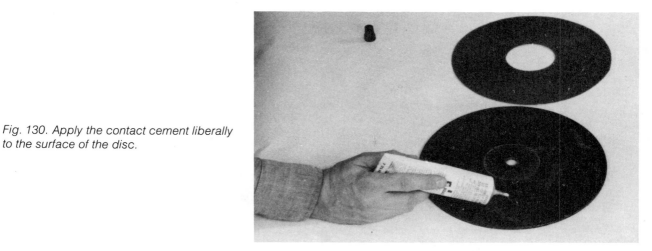

Fig. 130. Apply the contact cement liberally to the surface of the disc.

Fig. 131. Press the disc into the cement and lift up to allow the solvents to evaporate.

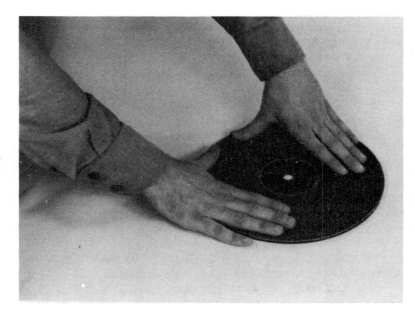

Fig. 132. After 30 seconds, lay the abrasive down on the disc and smooth out any bubbles.

4
Safety Procedures

Factors Contributing to Accidents with the Table Saw

Accidents on the table saw can occur to both the novice and the experienced operator. The novice operator's accident is usually caused by a lack of knowledge of table saw safety. The novice operator may not be able to identify an accident-producing situation.

The experienced operator's accident is usually caused by carelessness or an outright violation of the safety rules. When an experienced operator attempts and gets away with safety rule violations, they soon become common practice. This is when the accident is likely to occur.

All accidents have other contributing factors (Fig. 133), among which are the following:

1. *Working while tired or taking medication.* Whenever you are tired, stop or take a break. Accidents are most likely to happen when you are tired. Medication and alcohol can affect your perception and reaction time.

2. *Rushing the job.* Trying to finish a job in a hurry leads to errors and accidents. The stress of rushing the job also leads to early fatigue.

3. *Inattention to the job.* Daydreaming or thinking about another job while operating the table saw can contribute to accident potential. Repetitive cuts lend themselves to daydreaming. Be doubly careful when making them.

4. *Distractions.* Conversing with others, unfamiliar noises and doors opening or closing are all distractions in the shop. Shut off the table saw before you converse or investigate an unfamiliar noise.

5. *General housekeeping.* A dirty or cluttered work area provides tripping hazards and excess dust that can be a breathing hazard. Keep the shop neat and clean (Fig. 134). It is more pleasant and safer to work in a clean area.

It's the RIGHT TIME for Safety...

When it's light, not dark
When you're dressed for the job
When soil or surface is dry, not damp
When the work area is clean, not cluttered
When you take time to "know" a new tool
When you use your most productive hours
When you're vigorous, not vanquished
When you're smiling, not angry
When you're relaxed, not hurried
When you get the help you need
When tools are in top condition
When you take a break

power tool institute, inc.

Fig. 133. If the factors listed above are not observed, accidents can occur. Any negative factors should be a warning to stop working.

Fig. 134. Housekeeping is an important aspect of accident prevention. Pieces left on the table can be thrown by the blade or pinched between the blade and guard, causing a kickback. Scrap that accumulates on the floor can also be a tripping hazard.

Kickbacks

A kickback occurs when a piece of stock is forced towards the operator at great speed. Usually the stock becomes trapped·between the rotating blade and a stationary object such as the fence or guard. In some cases, the saw kerf closes around the blade. This traps the blade and may also cause a kickback. Stock that is kicked back can have the velocity of an arrow. This is a serious hazard. Another hazard of the kickback is the fact that the operator's hand may be pulled into the blade as the stock kicks back.

Kickback hazards can be minimized by observing the following precautions:

1.   Cut only true, smooth stock that will not become twisted and pinched in the blade.

2.   Use a guard equipped with a splitter. The splitter keeps the kerf open when cutting stock (Fig. 135).

3.   Keep the anti-kickback pawls sharp. This allows them to dig into the wood if it begins to kick back.

4.   Use only sharp, true blades. Dull or pitch-loaded blades lend themselves to kickbacks. Warped blades also tend to pinch in the kerf and cause kickbacks.

5.   Avoid using the fence for crosscutting. Stock can get trapped between the blade and fence, and will kick back or kick up as the cut is completed.

6.   Control all cuts with a mitre gauge, fence or jig. Never attempt to cut freehand (without any stock control). The stock will become twisted and kick back.

7.   Make sure the rip fence is parallel to the blade. When the fence is not parallel, stock may be pinched.

8.   Always feed the piece being cut completely through and past the blade when ripping. Never release the stock while it is still touching the blade and fence. A kickback may result. Use a push stick or push block for thin rips.

9.   Stand to the side of the saw when ripping. If you stand behind the piece being ripped, you become the target of a kickback (Fig. 136).

Fig. 135. The splitter keeps the kerf open when a piece is ripped. This minimizes the chance of pinching and kickback.

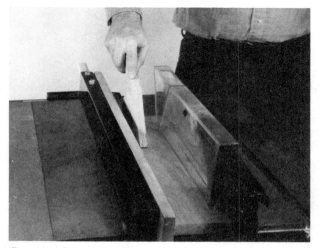

Fig. 136. Standing to the side of the work when ripping keeps your body out of the kickback zone.

55

General Working Environment

The working environment can also be a factor in the safe operation of the table saw. The saw should be set at a comfortable height. Most operators prefer a height of 34–36 inches (86.4–91.4 cm). Be sure the saw does not rock and has been levelled properly (Fig. 137). When possible, it is good practice to anchor the saw to the floor.

Be sure a grounded outlet of the correct amperage is close by. This outlet should be below the saw so the cord does not interfere with stock being cut. Adequate lighting makes operation of the saw much safer. Shadows and dim lighting increase operator fatigue and measurement errors.

The area surrounding the table saw should be ample enough to handle large pieces of stock. Traffic should be routed away from the back of the saw. In the event of a kickback, this is where the stock is most likely to go. Keep the floor around the saw free of cut-offs and debris. Cut-offs and other debris can be a tripping or slipping hazard.

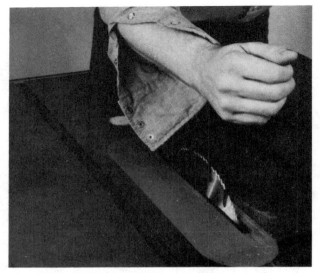

Fig. 138. A loose sleeve can cause you to get "wrapped up" in your work. Avoid loose sleeves and clothing.

Fig. 137. Levelling the saw before use will keep it from rocking. An unstable saw is dangerous.

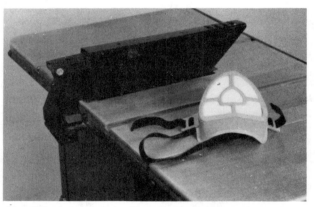

Fig. 139. A dust mask will protect your lungs when you use a fine-tooth blade.

Table Saw Operating Rules

1. *Protect yourself.* Always wear protective glasses when you operate the table saw. If the area is noisy, wear ear plugs or muffs to preserve your hearing and minimize fatigue. Gloves are all right for handling rough lumber, but never wear gloves (or other loose clothing) when operating the table saw (Fig. 138). Your hand could easily be pulled into the blade if the blade caught the glove (or other loose clothing). When using a fine-tooth blade, wear a dust mask to protect your lungs (Fig. 139).

2. *Use the guard.* Whenever possible, use the guard. The guard minimizes the chance of kickbacks with the splitter and anti-kickback pawls. It also makes contact with the saw blade very difficult (Fig. 140).

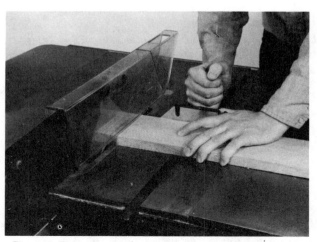

Fig. 140. The guard will minimize the chance of a kickback and make contact with the blade difficult.

3.   *Keep the blade low.* Set the blade height no more than ¼ inch (6 mm) higher than stock thickness (Fig. 141). This minimizes exposed blade. Less blade in the stock also reduces the possibility of kickback caused by pinching.

4.   *Keep the blade sharp.* A sharp blade makes the table saw much safer to use. A dull blade or an incorrect blade increases the chance of kickback. They also require more cutting force. This excess force can throw the operator off balance and lead to an accident.

5.   *Inspect your stock.* Before sawing any stock, look it over. Loose knots, twists, cupping (Fig. 142) and rough or wet lumber can mean trouble. Loose knots can be ejected by the saw blade. Rough, warped or wet lumber can cause kickbacks. Small pieces can also mean trouble. Machining them puts your hands too close to the blade. If possible, machine large pieces and cut them into smaller pieces.

6.   *Position yourself.* Stand to the side of the blade to avoid kickbacks. Be sure you have firm footing and balance when operating the table saw. Avoid overreaching and reaching over the blade.

7.   *Guard against accidental starting.* When making adjustments to the table saw, do so with the power off. It is too easy to make an adjustment error that could cause an accident when the power is on. Make repairs, change blades and install dado and moulding heads with the power disconnected (Fig. 143). Otherwise a serious accident could occur.

8.   *Use control devices.* Devices like push sticks and featherboards make handling stock safer. These devices get in close and control the stock. Your hands are well away from the blade in a safe position (Fig. 144). Keep these control devices near the saw at all times. Patterns for push sticks can be found in Chapter 2.

9.   *Keep a safe margin.* By keeping your hands a safe distance (4–6 inches [10.2–15.2 cm]) from the blade, you allow a margin for error. When your hands are a safe distance from the blade, there is always time to react to a hazardous situation.

10.   *Think about the job.* When performing a new operation, think about the job before you begin. Ask yourself, "What could happen when I . . .?" Questions of this nature help you identify and avoid an accident-producing situation. If you have a premonition of trouble, stop! Avoid any job that gives you a bad feeling. Try setting up the job another way, or ask some other experienced operator for an opinion.

11.   *Know your saw.* Read the owner's manual and understand it before you operate the saw. All saws are different; make sure you understand the one you are using.

Fig. 141. A low-set blade (¼-inch [6 mm] above the work) is important. This minimizes your chance of contact with the blade and reduces the kickback hazard.

Fig. 142. Notice the cup in this piece. If it were ripped, the piece would pinch against the blade when the cut was completed. This can be a potential kickback hazard.

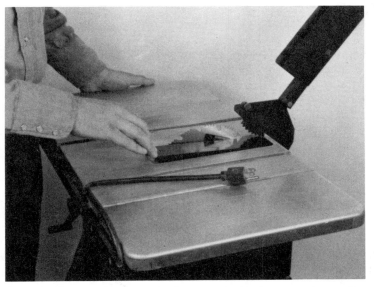

Fig. 143. Be sure the power is disconnected before you change the blade or make adjustments. Placing the plug on the table assures you that the power has been disconnected.

Fig. 144. The featherboards and push stick make contact with the blade or a kickback almost impossible. Strive for a safe set-up whenever you operate the saw.

Part II:
Basic, Intermediate and Advanced Operations

5

Basic Operations on the Table Saw

Basic operations include common table saw cuts and maintenance. Careful planning and accurate measurement are a part of every table saw operation. Always plan ahead. Think about the job before you begin. The job will be safer, and the results better.

Changing the Blade

Changing the blade is 1 of the most common table saw operations. Select the correct blade for the job you are doing. Before you change the blade, disconnect the power. Unplug the saw or shut off the power at the main junction box.

Raise the guard and lift out the throat plate (Fig. 145). On some saws, it is easiest to change the blade when it is raised to full height. Look at the threads on the arbor. If they are right-hand threads, remove the arbor nut by turning it counter-clockwise. Remove a left-hand arbor nut by turning it clockwise. It may be necessary to hold the blade stationary while the arbor nut is loosened. This

is done by wedging a push stick or scrap against the blade (Fig. 146). Remove the outer arbor washer (and blade stabilizer if one is used), and lift the blade off the arbor.

Inspect the arbor washers (and blade stabilizers, if used) for pitch or wood chips (Fig. 147). The bearing surfaces of the arbor washers should be clean. They should bear against the saw blade uniformly at their outer edge. Remove any pitch before replacing the arbor washers (and blade stabilizers).

Replace the inner blade washer (and blade stabilizer). Install the desired blade over the arbor. The blade's teeth should point towards the front of the machine. The outer arbor washer (and blade stabilizer) is now placed on the arbor. Replace the arbor nut. Tighten it snugly against the blade, but do not overtighten it (Fig. 148). This can make removal very difficult.

Replace the throat plate (Fig. 149). Check the blade to be sure it is square with the table. Adjust the blade tilt if necessary. Replace the guard and proceed.

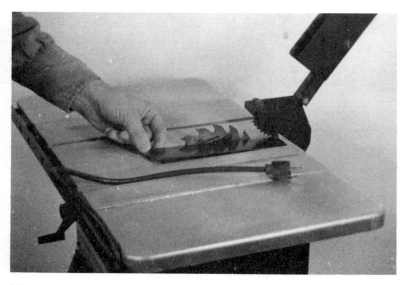

Fig. 145. Disconnect the saw and remove the throat plate. Some throat plates can be removed only one way, so do not force them. The cord in clear view assures you that the saw is disconnected.

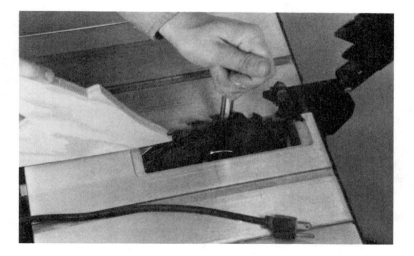

Fig. 146. Inspect the threads to determine which way to turn the arbor nut. Wedge a scrap or push stick between the blade and saw to hold the blade while the nut is turned. Do not force the arbor nut; you could be turning it the wrong way.

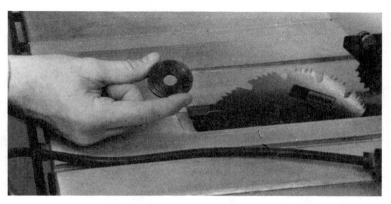

Fig. 147. Replace the blade. Be sure the teeth are pointing in the right direction. Inspect the arbor washers (and blade collars if used) for pitch or wood chips. They can cause the blade to wobble instead of running true.

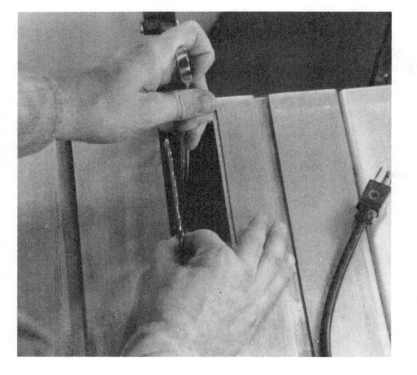

Fig. 148. When tightening the blade, pinch the blade between your thumb and index finger. Tighten the arbor nut until you can no longer hold the blade still. This is usually tight enough. Overtightening the blade makes removal difficult.

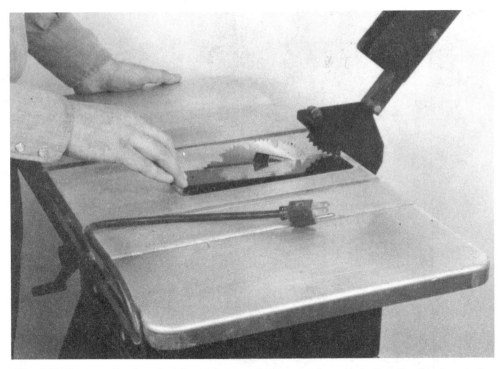

Fig. 149. Replace the throat plate. Make sure it is secured properly. Turn the blade over by hand to be sure it does not hit the throat plate.

Common Table Saw Cuts

The 2 most common table saw cuts are rip cuts and crosscuts. Rip cuts are made with the grain, and crosscuts are made across the grain.

Ripping   Ripping is done using the fence as a guide. Set the distance between the fence and blade at the desired stock width. For finished work allow extra width for planing off saw marks. Measure the desired width from the face of the fence to a tooth on the blade (Fig. 150). The tooth should be one that is set towards the fence. This produces the most accurate measurement.

Set the blade height about ¼ inch (6 mm) above the stock and replace the guard and splitter. Inspect your stock. Place the truest edge against the fence. If the rip is narrower than 5 inches (12.7 cm), be sure to use a push stick to guide the wood.

Turn on the saw and position yourself comfortably to the side of the blade. Right handers usually stand to the left of the blade, and left handers usually stand to the right of the blade. Guide the wood into the blade at a uniform speed (Fig. 151). If the blade slows down, you are feeding too fast. If the edges of your stock appear burned, you may be feeding too slowly. This may also indicate a dull blade or blade binding. Check the fence to be sure it is parallel to the blade. Some commercial devices can be used to hold stock against the fence (Figs. 152 and 153).

Guide the entire length past the blade. Do not stop feeding the stock until the entire length is past the blade. If the piece stops while in contact with the blade and fence, a kickback could occur.

When ripping long pieces, use a dead man to support the wood (Fig. 154). Large, heavy pieces may require an extra person to handle and guide them safely (Fig. 155). Never try to rip stock that is too heavy for you to handle. When ripping strips off a piece of sheet stock, make the widest rip first. This allows most of the weight of the panel to balance on the table saw. This also minimizes the flexing in thin, lighter sheets and allows truer cuts. It may also be beneficial to cut the length of the panel in half before ripping. This can be done on large table saws. It may also be done with a portable circular saw.

A stock-cutting sheet allows you to plan your cuts before you do any cutting. Graph paper makes the layout simple. Mark off an area 4 squares by 8 squares. Sketch in the grain direction if your stock has a grain pattern. Draw all the needed parts onto the graph paper, so that all cuts are organized. Number the cuts for more efficient cutting. Remember, the outer edges of the sheet stock are true and square. These edges can always be used as control surfaces for accurate cutting.

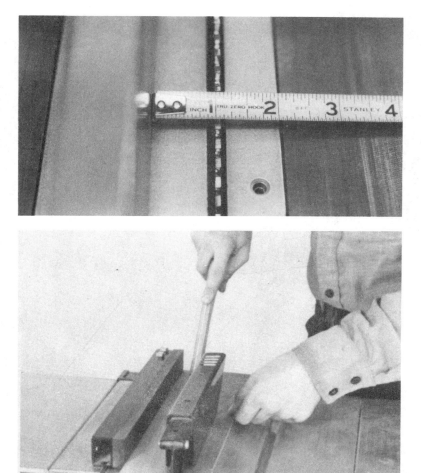

Fig. 150. Set the distance from the fence to a tooth that points towards the fence. This distance determines the rip dimension. The set-up shown is set for a 1-inch (25-mm) rip.

Fig. 151. When ripping, guide the work into the blade at a uniform speed. If the blade slows down, you are feeding too fast. Burned edges can mean the blade is dull or you are feeding too slowly.

Fig. 152. This commercial device pulls stock towards the fence and acts as a guard on narrow rips.

Fig. 153. On wider rips, any common guard can be used with this ripping device. There is also a locking device built into the wheels, so they only turn one way. This minimizes the chance of a kickback.

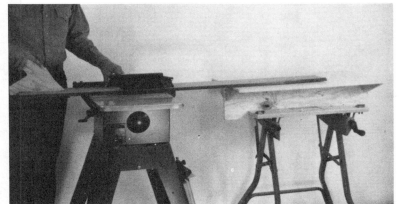

Fig. 154. When ripping long pieces, use a dead man to support the work. Other types of dead man supports are shown in Chapter 2 (Figs. 71–75).

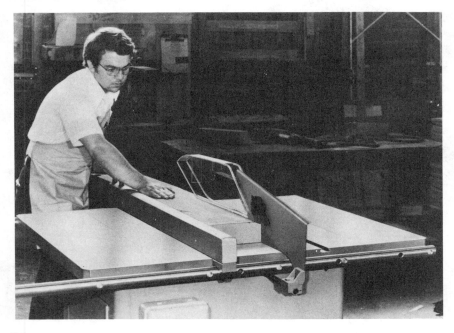

Fig. 155. Large, heavy pieces may require an extra person to support the stock on the way in or out. Avoid ripping heavy pieces of stock alone. It is difficult to handle, control and guide them safely.

Ripping Narrow Pieces. Ripping narrow pieces can be dangerous if not done carefully. Narrow pieces cannot usually be cut with the guard in position. This is because the push stick will not go between the fence and the guard. In addition, thin stock tends to climb the blade and kick or bounce.

A plywood fixture can be made to rip narrow pieces using the guard (Fig. 156). A notch cut along the edge leaves a heel that will grip the work. The fixture rides along the fence and allows clearance between the guard and fence (Fig. 157). Use a push stick to hold the stock against the fixture. Strips will be uniform in size (Fig. 158), and the operation will be much safer.

Thin stock that must be ripped into narrow pieces can be cut with the help of a featherboard. The guard is removed, and the fence is positioned. The featherboard is clamped to the fence. The blade must be beneath the table when this is done (Fig. 159). The blade is then turned on and raised into the featherboard. Stock may now be ripped. The featherboard acts as a guard and a hold-down (Fig. 160).

Fig. 156. For ripping narrow strips, a plywood fixture can be made. It has a notch cut along one edge to grip the work.

Fig. 157. This fixture allows use of the guard when ripping narrow strips.

Fig. 158. The notch on the fixture grips the work for feeding, but it also minimizes the chance of a kickback. Often, the anti-kickback pawls will not ride on a narrow strip of wood and function correctly.

Fig. 159. Thin, narrow strips tend to rattle and flutter when ripped. A featherboard can eliminate this problem. The featherboard is clamped over the blade's path. The blade is dropped below the table and elevated into the featherboard (while running).

Fig. 160. As the thin strips are ripped, the featherboard eliminates rattle and acts as a guard by covering the blade.

Crosscutting Crosscutting is usually done with the mitre gauge. A shooting table or board may also be used (Fig. 161). When crosscutting an individual piece, usually mark and cut it along the layout line. A pencil line is most common, but a utility knife is sometimes used. The utility knife cuts the wood fibres and minimizes tear-out along the cut (Fig. 162).

To assure a square cut, make sure the mitre gauge is perpendicular to the blade (Fig. 163) and the blade is perpendicular to the table (Fig. 164). Use a square to check the angle. Raise the blade to full height and position the mitre gauge across from the blade. Place the head of the square against the blade and the blade of the square against the mitre gauge. Check the angle, and adjust the mitre gauge if necessary. Make sure the set of the blade does not tilt the square for an incorrect adjustment. Keep the square off the blade's teeth.

To make a crosscut, place the stock against the mitre gauge and move up to the blade. Your layout line should line up with a tooth that points towards the layout line (Fig. 165). *Note*: The saw blade should be on the waste or scrap side of the line.

Move back from the blade with the stock held firmly against the mitre gauge and replace the guard. Turn on the saw and advance the mitre gauge, holding the stock firmly (Fig. 166). Feed the stock into the blade at a uniform speed. When the piece is cut, retract the mitre gauge. Keep a firm grip on the stock until it is clear of the blade.

Note: When crosscutting, keep the fence well away from the blade. Any cut-off stock trapped between the blade and fence could kick back. Keep the table clear of scraps as you work; accumulated scrap can also be a hazard. Clear the scrap with the saw turned off.

When crosscutting large panels, it may be necessary to reverse the mitre gauge (Fig. 167) in the slot. This is because the tongue on the mitre gauge is too short to reach the slot when located behind the stock. If the tongue will not stay engaged in the slot for the entire cut, shut the saw off midway into the cut. After the blade stops, reverse the mitre gauge (Fig. 168), and proceed. It is also possible to clamp a straightedge on the panel (Fig. 169) and allow it to ride along the table edge. The straightedge becomes the control surface for the cut.

Fig. 161. A shop-made shooting board can be used for crosscutting. The shooting board cuts stock at a fixed angle, while the mitre gauge can be adjusted to different angles.

Fig. 162. Marking the layout line with a utility knife will reduce tear-out of the wood fibres when the cut is made. A pencil may also be used for less exact work.

Fig. 163. While making a square cut, make sure the blade is perpendicular to the mitre gauge.

Fig. 164. In addition to being perpendicular with the mitre gauge, the blade must also be perpendicular to the table.

Fig. 165. The layout line should line up with a tooth that points towards it. The rest of the blade should cut into the waste or scrap side of the work.

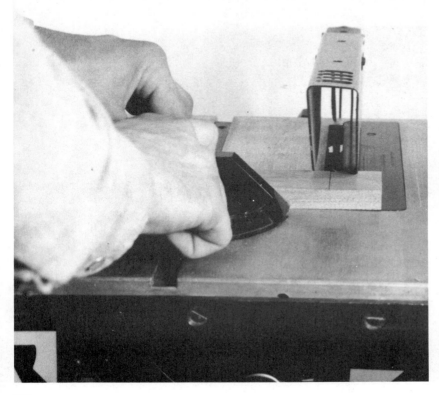

Fig. 166. Advance the mitre gauge into the blade at a moderate speed when crosscutting. Feeding too slowly wastes time, and feeding too quickly increases tear-out. Keep the good or exposed face of your work up so that any tear-out occurs on the back or unexposed side of the work.

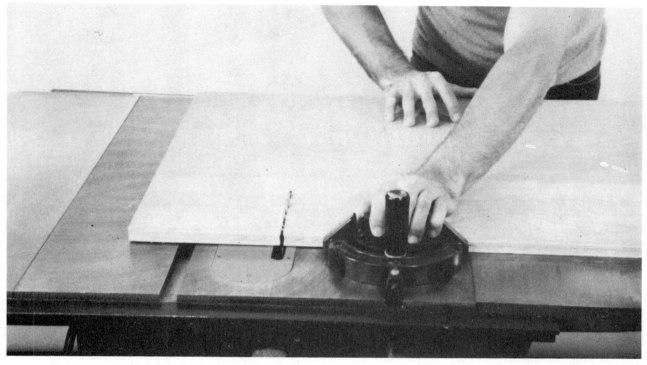

Fig. 167. Sometimes the mitre gauge has to be reversed when crosscutting wide panels. This is because the stock is wider than the tongue on the mitre gauge. The mitre gauge has to be reversed in the middle of the cut.

Fig. 168. When the stock is on the table, shut off the saw. Allow the blade to come to a complete stop. Reverse the mitre gauge and proceed with the cut.

Fig. 169. A straightedge clamped to the work can be used as a fence on large pieces. The straightedge rides along the end of the table.

It is frequently necessary to crosscut several pieces to the same length. To eliminate layout of individual pieces, a stop rod or a stop block may be used. A stop block is a true piece of stock that is clamped to the table, fence or mitre gauge. It locates one end of the part. This end should already be square. The distance from that end to the blade is the desired-part length. When the stop block is clamped to the fence (Figs. 170 and 171) or table (Fig. 172), it should not be near the blade. Keep the stop block towards the front of the table. This will eliminate a pinching problem and prevent kickbacks.

A stop block may be clamped to the shooting board (Fig. 173) or the mitre gauge (Fig. 174). It can also be clamped to a piece of stock attached to the mitre gauge (Fig. 175). The clamp should be adjusted so that vision or movement is not impaired. A clamp of the correct size will minimize this problem.

The stop rod is an accessory made for the mitre gauge.

It attaches to either side of the mitre gauge. The stop rod is adjusted to correct stock length and locked in position. The stock is held against the mitre gauge. One end of the stock touches the stop rod (Fig. 176). The other end is then cut to the desired length. Be sure the end that touches the stop rod has been squared before you make the cut. A precision set-up does little good when the stock is not square.

Note: The most common mistake made with the stop rod is to run the stop rod into the saw blade. Double-check stop-rod position and blade height before you make a cut. Failure to do so could damage the stop rod or the saw blade.

When cutting several pieces, work carefully. Do not feed too fast, or grain tear-out will increase. Keep extra pieces well away from the blade (Fig. 177), and do not allow scrap to accumulate.

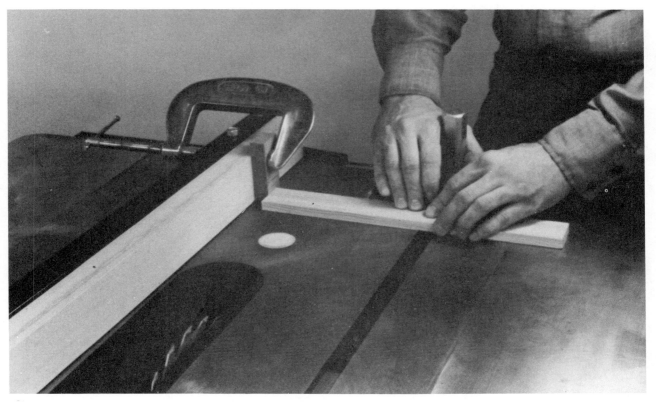

Fig. 170. The stop block clamped to the fence makes all pieces equal in length and keeps stock from being pinched between the fence and blade. The stock is butted to the stop block and then cut.

Fig. 171. Notice how all parts are cut uniformly. By keeping the stop block well away from the blade, no chance for a kickback exists.

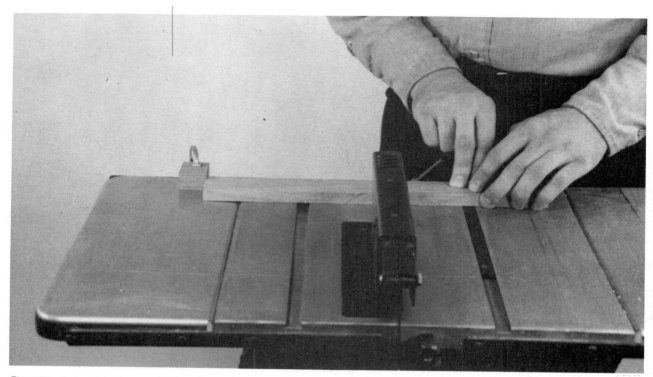

Fig. 172. A stop block can also be clamped to the table. **Keep** it well away from the blade so there will be no chance for a kickback to occur.

Fig. 173. A stop block is being clamped to the shooting board to control the length of the parts being cut. The square end of the part is butted to the stop block.

74

Fig. 174. The stop block is clamped directly to the mitre gauge in this set-up. This works well for shorter pieces. Be sure to use a clamp that is not too large. It could hamper the operation.

Fig. 175. For longer parts, the stop block can be clamped (or screwed) to a piece of stock that has been attached to the mitre gauge.

Fig. 176. A stop rod can also be used for crosscutting parts to length. The square end of the part is butted against the hook and the cut is made. Be sure to keep the stop rod out of the blade's path.

Fig. 177. Notice how all parts not being cut are stacked well away from the work area. All scrap has also been cleared away. This is a safe work area. Note the rolling table on this production saw.

Cutting Mitres

Mitres are rips or crosscuts made to any angle other than 90°. The most common mitring jobs are crosscuts on picture frames and door or window trim. These jobs require a mitre gauge angle of 45°. Rip-cut mitres are discussed under the section on cutting chamfers and bevels (pages 84–88).

When cutting mitres, begin by squaring the saw blade to the table. Any tilt in the blade can make mitres more difficult to fit. The angle between the blade and mitre gauge can be read off the protractor scale on the mitre gauge. It is more accurate to set the desired angle with a drafting square (Fig. 178), combination square (Fig. 179) or a sliding T-bevel. For angles other than 45°, copy the angle with the sliding T-bevel and adjust the angle between the blade and mitre gauge to this setting. The included angle is the desired angle, regardless of the angle indicated on the mitre gauge. The mitre gauge's protractor is not always accurate.

If the stock you are mitring has the angle laid out, use it to adjust the mitre gauge. Turn the mitre gauge upside down and adjust it so the head is touching the edge of the stock (Fig. 180). Adjust the tongue so that it is parallel to the layout line. The mitre gauge will now cut the desired angle.

A mitre is cut in the same manner as a crosscut (Fig. 181). Because of the incline of the mitre gauge, the stock may slide or creep as the mitre is cut. The stock can be held with a clamp if this happens (Fig. 182). A stop rod can also be used to control sliding (Fig. 183).

A shop-made (Figs. 184 and 185) or commercial (Figs. 186 and 187) mitre jig can be helpful when cutting several mitres. The jig travels in the table slot or slots. The jig is inclined 45° in both directions, and the included angle is 90°. This assures a 90° corner even when the 45° angles are not perfect. One end of every part is cut on the left side of the jig. The complementary angle is cut on the right side of the jig. This angle is on the other end of every part. As the 2 parts are fitted, the result is a 90° corner.

The same result can be achieved using 2 mitre gauges. Set the mitre gauge in the left slot to 45°. Set the mitre gauge in the right slot perpendicular to it with a framing square (Fig. 188). One blade of the square is placed against each mitre gauge. The result is a 90° included angle. Complementary mitres will be cut (Fig. 189) if the set-up is accurate. A stop rod can be added to this set up to control length. Check your framing square before this set-up. Be sure the blades are perpendicular to each other. It is common to find new framing squares on the shelf that do not have perpendicular blades.

Fig. 178. A drafting square is one of the most accurate tools for setting the mitre gauge or blade for mitre cuts. Make sure that blade set does not affect your set-up.

Fig. 179. A combination square used in this fashion produces a very accurate mitre. Be sure to keep the square off the blade's teeth.

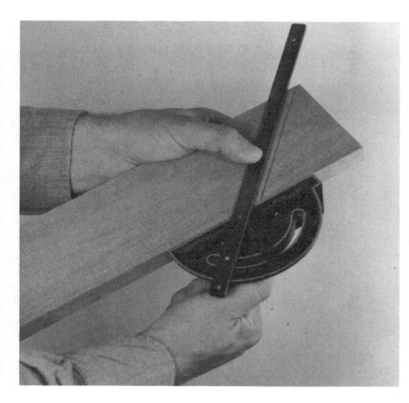

Fig. 180. The mitre gauge can be used to copy a layout line on your work. The head touches the edge of the work and the tongue is turned to the desired angle. Copying the angle directly off the work reduces the chance of error.

Fig. 181. A mitre is cut in the same manner as a crosscut. Hold the stock firmly so that it does not creep.

Fig. 182. Using a mitre gauge with a clamp will reduce creeping or sliding problems.

Fig. 183. A stop rod will control stock length when mitring. It will also reduce creeping or sliding problems.

Fig. 184. A shop-made jig can be used to cut mitres. The first mitre is cut on one side of the jig.

Fig. 185. The complementary mitre is cut on the opposite side of the jig. Note the stop block clamped to the jig. It controls stock length.

Fig. 186. This commercial mitre jig is used to cut both ends of a mitred piece. The right mitre slot is used to cut the first mitre.

Fig. 187. The left slot is used to cut the complementary mitre. The jig is reversed and a stop rod is used to control stock length. This jig also has a clamping device to control creep.

Fig. 188. With 2 mitre gauges, you can cut complementary mitres. The mitre gauge in the left slot is set at 45°. The mitre gauge in the right slot is set perpendicular to it. A framing square is used to adjust the mitre gauge in the right slot.

Fig. 189. These 2 mitres will have an included angle of 90° even if the 2 mitres are not exactly 45°. A stop rod may also be used to control stock length.

Fitting mitres can be more difficult than cutting them. When the angles are all correct, the frame can still appear to have poorly fitted mitres. Some causes are the following:

1. A thin blade that flutters while cutting. This causes the cut or mitre to have some dips.
2. One piece of the frame is too long (or short).
3. The blade is not perpendicular to the table.
4. The blade is dull and is tearing the mitre.
5. The object being framed is not square—thus affecting the fit of the mitres.
6. The framing stock does not have parallel edges.
7. There is slop in the mitre gauge slot, which causes the gauge to wander while the mitre is cut.

Minor adjustments in a mitre cut can be made by placing a piece of paper or veneer at one end of the mitre gauge (Fig. 190). This changes the mitre angle slightly. It may be enough to improve the fit. When fitting mitres, work patiently and carefully. Make test cuts on a scrap to be sure of a proper fit. Well-fitted mitres are the sign of a high-quality job.

Cutting Chamfers and Bevels

Chamfers and bevels (Fig. 191) are cut with the blade tilted. Chamfers are inclined surfaces that go from a face to an edge. Bevels are inclined surfaces that go from face to face. End and edge mitres are bevel cuts made at 45°.

The blade, instead of the mitre gauge, is tilted for end and edge mitres.

When chamfers and bevels are cut with the grain, the rip fence is used to guide the wood. Chamfers and bevels cut across the grain are guided with the mitre gauge. The blade is tilted to the desired angle by turning the blade-tilting handwheel on the side of the saw (Fig. 192). Use the scale on the front of the saw or a sliding T-bevel (Fig. 193) to set the blade angle. A sliding T-bevel is the most accurate.

Once the desired angle is set, lock the blade tilt in position. Set the blade height to no more than ¼ inch (6 mm) above the work. Be sure the guard works properly with the blade tilted (Fig. 194). Adjust it if necessary. Remove it if it is not designed to be used with the blade tilted.

When cutting with the grain, adjust the fence to the desired stock width. The piece being cut should be between the blade and fence. The cut-off should fall free on the other side of the blade (Fig. 195). Avoid cuts that pinch a triangular-shaped piece between the fence and the blade. A kickback is certain to result.

Make edge chamfer cuts or bevel cuts the same way you would make a rip cut. Push the stock completely clear of the blade at the end of the cut.

Make end chamfer cuts and bevel cuts the same way you would make a crosscut (Fig. 196). Thicker stock (Fig. 197) will require slower feeding than thin stock. If several pieces are being cut, set up a stop block or stop rod.

Fig. 190. Small adjustments in a mitre joint can be made with a piece of paper or veneer. The paper or veneer is placed between the work and the mitre gauge. This alters the angle of the mitre slightly, and may improve the fit.

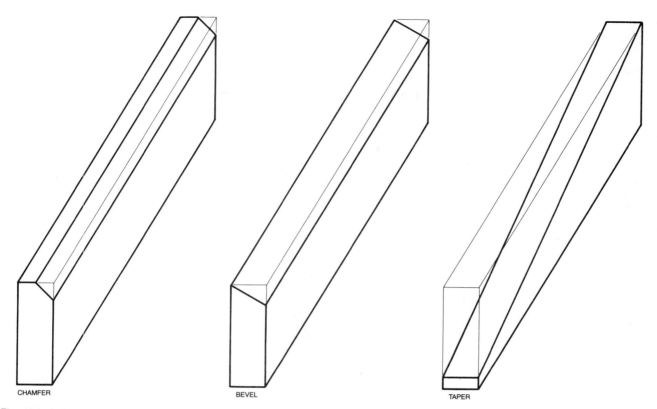

CHAMFER BEVEL TAPER

Fig. 191. A chamfer is an inclined surface that goes from a face to an edge. A bevel is an inclined surface that goes face-to-face. A taper is an inclined surface that goes from end to end.

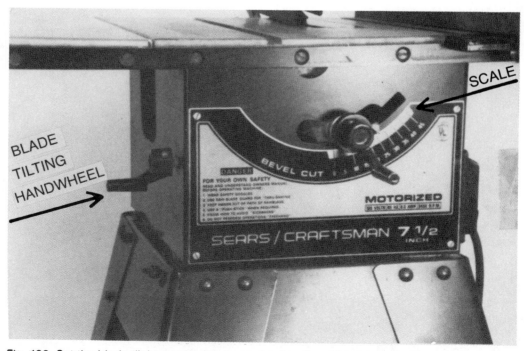

Fig. 192. Set the blade tilt by turning the handwheel on the side of the saw. Be sure any locking device has been released before you turn the handwheel. The scale on the front of the saw will help you determine the blade's angle.

Fig. 193. A sliding T-bevel will give you a more accurate setting than the scale on the saw. Use a protractor to set the sliding T-bevel.

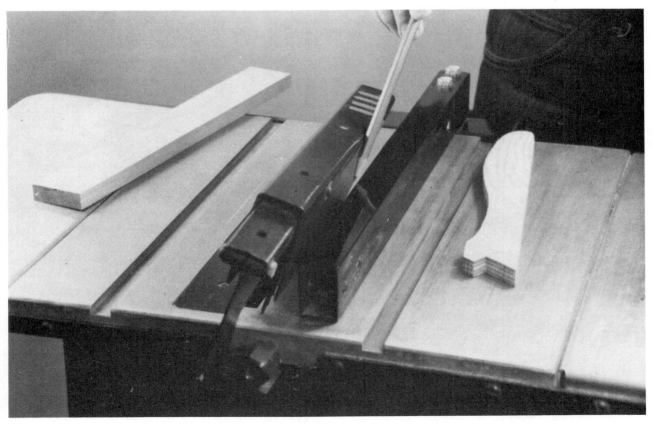

Fig. 194. Be sure the guard works properly with the blade tilted. Here the push stick will not go between the guard and fence.

Fig. 195. Be sure the cut-off falls free when the cut is complete. When a scrap is pinched between the blade and fence, a kickback could result.

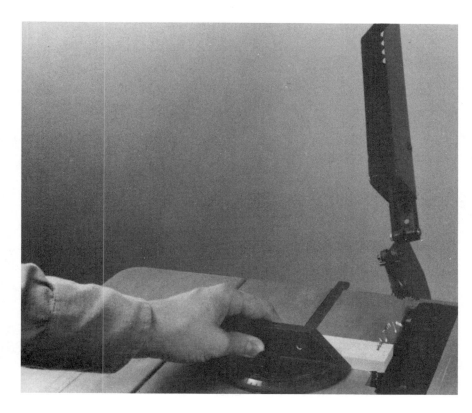

Fig. 196. A bevel or chamfer cut on the end of your work is made in the same way as a crosscut.

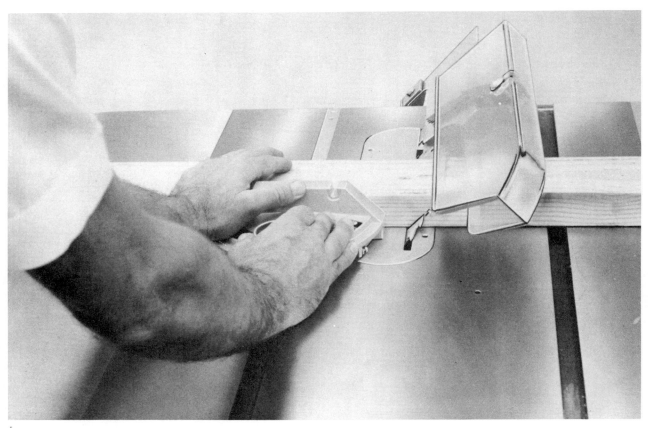

Fig. 197. When inclined cuts are being made in thick stock, the feed rate will be slower.

Cutting Compound Mitres

Compound mitres are usually made with both the blade and mitre gauge tilted. A compound mitre is cut when the mitred stock is angled or inclined from the true plane. The following charts give some of the common inclines and the correct settings for the blade and mitre gauge. Practice these cuts on scrap until you master them.

Four-Side Mitre

Incline of Work	Blade/Angle	Mitre Gauge Angle
5°	44¾°	85°
10°	44¼°	80¼°
15°	43¼°	75½°
20°	41¾°	71¼°
25°	40°	67°
30°	37¾°	63½°
35°	35¼°	60¼°
40°	32½°	57¼°
45°	30°	54¾°
50°	27°	52½°
55°	24°	50¾°
60°	21°	49°

Four-Side Butt

Incline of Work	Blade/Angle	Mitre Gauge Angle
5°	½°	85°
10°	1½°	80¼°
15°	3¾°	75½°
20°	6¼°	71¼°
25°	10°	67°
30°	14½°	63½°
35°	19½°	60¼°
40°	24½°	57¼°
45°	30°	54¾°
50°	36°	52½°
55°	42°	50¾°
60°	48°	49°

When the blade tilts towards the left mitre slot, the mitre gauge has to be tilted clockwise for right-hand mitres (left mitre slot) (Fig. 198) and counterclockwise for left-hand mitres (left mitre slot) (Fig. 199). The setting remains the same. If the blade tilts towards the right mitre slot, use the same procedure with the right mitre slot. Some mitre gauge angles with ¼-degree increments are difficult to set. Be sure to test the set-up on scrap or oversized parts. Minor adjustments may be needed.

A stop block or stop rod can be clamped to the mitre gauge when you cut the second compound mitre. This will assure uniform length. A mitring jig may also be used. Be sure to measure picture frame length along the rabbet (Fig. 200). The picture frame must accommodate a piece of glass. The standard-size glass fits the frame's rabbet. If you measure the inner edge of the frame, the frame may be too small for the glass.

If the work is tilted to the desired angle, the blade may be set at 90° and the mitre gauge is set at 45°. When the work is tilted (Fig. 201), the set-up is easier to make and more accurate. On wide stock, the blade may not go high enough to cut through the stock. With extra blade exposed, this set-up is not as safe as one with the blade and mitre gauge inclined. Work carefully, and be sure the stock is tilted to the exact angle at which it will be used.

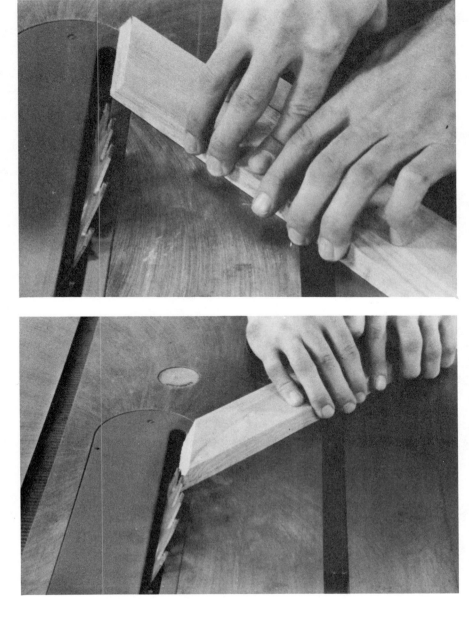

Fig. 198. The right-hand compound mitre is cut in the left mitre slot. The mitre gauge is tilted clockwise.

Fig. 199. The left-hand compound mitre is also cut in the left mitre slot. The mitre gauge is tilted counter-clockwise.

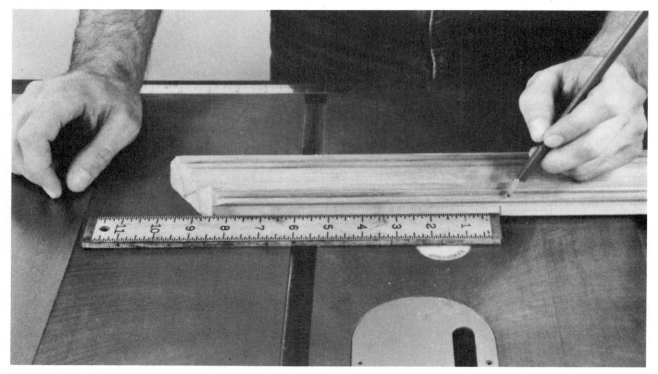

Fig. 200. When making a picture frame, be sure to measure the frame length along the rabbet. The frame has to be cut to the desired glass size, and the glass fits in the rabbet.

Fig. 201. Compound mitres are sometimes cut with the work inclined to its intended angle. When cut this way, the blade is set at 90° and the mitre gauge at 45°. More blade is exposed with this method, and it will not work on wide pieces.

Cutting Dadoes

When cutting dadoes, disconnect the power and remove the blade from the arbor. Replace the blade with a dado head. Wobble types are adjusted to the desired width, and bolted to the arbor. With the blade and chipper types, the correct combination of blades and chippers is selected (Figs. 202a–202e). One or 2 blades (cutters) are always used. Chippers make up the rest of the combination sandwiched between 2 blades. A ½-inch (13-mm) dado would use two ⅛-inch (3-mm) blades and two ⅛-inch (3-mm) chippers.

Mount the dado head carefully; make sure the teeth point towards the front of the saw. The wobble dado should be tightened carefully so the setting is not changed (Figs. 203). The chippers in the blade and chipper set must be staggered so the head is balanced. The chippers closest to the blades should rest in the gullets of the blades. This keeps them from rocking.

Make sure the correct throat plate is used with the dado head (Fig. 204). It is good practice to turn the dado over by hand to make sure it does not hit the throat plate. All set-up and preliminary checks should be made with the power disconnected.

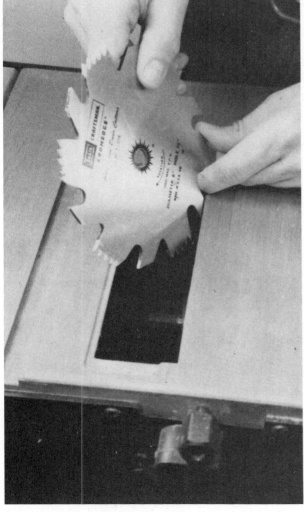

Fig. 202a. A dado size is selected, and the cutter is placed on the arbor. Cutter teeth should point towards the front of the saw. Be sure the power is disconnected before you begin.

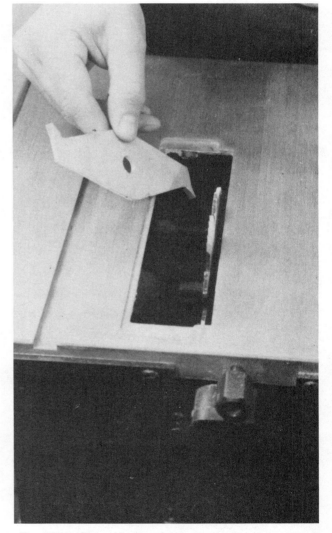

Fig. 202b. The chippers are added after the cutter is mounted. Be sure to stagger the chippers so the dado head is balanced.

Fig. 202c. Paper washers may be added for slight adjustments in dado width.

Fig. 202d. The dado head is set up and ready to be tightened. Chippers are in the gullets of the cutters and staggered around the head. Be sure the dado head does not hit the throat plate.

92

Fig. 202e. A test cut is made after the dado head is set up.

Fig. 203. Be consistent in how you tighten the dado head. It can affect dado width slightly.

Fig. 204. A throat plate must be used with the dado head. Turn the dado head over slowly to be sure it does not hit the throat plate. Make this check again if you tilt the dado head.

A ⅜-inch (10-mm) dado depth is suggested for each pass or cut. If a ¾-inch (19-mm) dado depth is required, make 1 cut at ⅜ inch (10 mm) deep (Fig. 205) and 1 cut at ¾ inch (19 mm) deep (Fig. 206). The species of wood, horsepower of the saw and dado type will determine the appropriate dado depth. As you become familiar with dado operations, you will know the limits of your table saw and dado head. Generally, harder woods like oak and beech require lighter cuts than softer woods like pine or basswood.

Cut a dado in scrap stock and check the dado width (Fig. 207). If the width is correct, set the depth. Turn the elevating handwheel to adjust dado depth.

To change the width of a wobble dado, turn the offset washers. Disconnect the saw, remove the throat plate and loosen the arbor nut. Turn the offset washers and tighten the arbor nut. To change the width of the blade and chipper, dado-head chippers or spacers must be added (or subtracted). To make the dado head ¹⁄₁₆ inch (1.5 mm) larger, add a ¹⁄₁₆-inch (1.5-mm) chipper. For smaller adjustments, paper or cardboard spacers can be placed between the cutters and chippers (Fig. 120).

Remove the throat plate and arbor nut with the power disconnected. Add (or subtract) chippers and spacers. Replace the arbor nut and tighten securely. Be consistent in how you tighten the arbor nut; this can affect dado width (Fig. 203). *Note*: Most dado heads are used without the outer arbor washer. The extra width makes it impossible to fasten the arbor nut when the outer washer is used.

Not all dadoes are cut perpendicular to the stock. The dado head (Fig. 208) and/or mitre gauge can be tilted to cut the desired dado. Make sure the dado head does not hit the throat plate when tilted. When working with dado heads, several problems can occur. Common problems are tear-out and dadoes of irregular depth. Tear-out can occur at the end of the cut or on the face of the cut.

Tear-out on the face of the cut can be caused by a lack of set or clearance on the outside cutters. This pinches the dado head and tears out the face of the stock. A dull dado head will also cause face tear-out.

Feeding the stock across the dado head too fast can also cause tear-out. Vary your speed and compare the results. Cutting a dado too deep in 1 cut may also cause tear-out. Take a lighter cut to see if the tear-out stops.

Fig. 205. The first cut in this dado is ⅜ inch (10 mm) deep and ⅝ inch (16 mm) wide.

Fig. 206. The second cut in this dado is ¾ inch (19 mm) and ⅝ inch (16 mm) wide. Light cuts produce better dadoes and reduce the chance of kickback.

Fig. 207. Always check your set-up in scrap stock. If the width is correct, set the desired depth of cut. Note the piece of stock backing up the work. This eliminates tear-out.

Fig. 208. The dado head can be tilted for an inclined dado. The mitre gauge can also be tilted for a dado cut at an angle.

Tear-out at the end of the cut is caused by the force of the dado head pushing against the stock. A piece of stock attached to the mitre gauge can be used to back the cut (Fig. 207). The tear-out then occurs in the stock attached to the mitre gauge. It is also possible to cut the dadoes in oversized stock. Trim away the tear-out as you cut the piece to finished size.

Dado heads with cutters and chippers are designed to cut the dado slightly deeper under the cutters. The cutters scribe the 2 sides of the dado, and the chippers remove the stock in between. The extra dado depth at the cutters allows the stock cut by the chippers to break off evenly. With large-diameter wobble dado heads, the bottom of the dado may appear concave or convex. This is a result of the wobble in the blade. On wider dadoes, it cuts deeper in the center of the dado than at the edges (Fig. 209). Blade and chipper types may also have an irregular bottom (Fig. 210).

A sharp chisel (Fig. 211) or router plane may be used to true up the dado. If the dado is not visible, the slight irregularity will not affect gluing. Work carefully when trimming a dado. Take light cuts. Heavy cuts can leave the bottom of the dado more irregular than it was.

Keep the dado head sharp. A dull dado head produces poor results. Extra force is needed to cut with a dull dado head. This makes it unsafe. Make sure that all sheet stock is dadoed with a carbide dado head. Steel dado heads become dull rapidly in all materials except solid wood. The glue and other additives are hard. They take the edge off steel tools quickly.

TYPICAL PATTERN OF CUT WITH ADJUSTABLE DADOES AT DIFFERENT WIDTHS

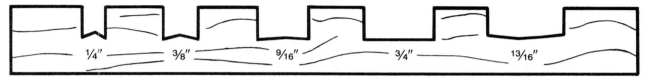

Fig. 209. Dadoes cut with a wobble head may have a concave or convex bottom.

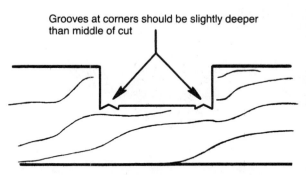

Grooves at corners should be slightly deeper than middle of cut

Fig. 210. Dadoes cut with a cutter and chipper dado head will be slightly deeper under the cutters. This allows the chippers to break out the center of the dado evenly.

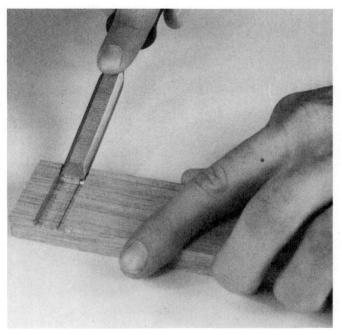

Fig. 211. A chisel can be used to clean up a dado. A router plane may also be used.

Cutting Moulding

Moulding cut on the table saw requires careful attention to detail. Light cuts must be taken, and all adjustments and set-ups must be carefully checked before you begin. Install the desired cutters in the moulding head (Fig. 212). Follow the manufacturer's instructions for their installation. Be sure the fasteners are locked securely and the cutters are pointing in the same direction (Fig. 213).

Disconnect the power to the saw and mount the cutter head. The flat side of the cutters should face the front of the saw (Fig. 214). Select the correct throat plate for the moulding head and set it in position. Turn the cutter head by hand to be sure it does not hit the throat plate. Also be sure that the stock will not drop into the hole in the throat plate (Fig. 215). Make a new throat plate if necessary (Fig. 216).

Mount an auxiliary fence against the table saw fence. It should be made of dense solid stock with no knots (Fig. 217). The auxiliary fence allows you to use only part of the cutter head. The remainder is cut into the auxiliary fence. Make the cut-out in the fence with the planer (flat) cutters. The saw is turned on, and the cutter head is elevated slowly to make the cut-out (Fig. 218).

Adjust the fence and the cutter height. Cuts of ⅛–¼ inch (3–6 mm), depending on species hardness, are best. Deeper cuts should be made in 2 or more passes. Keep the final pass light (¹⁄₁₆ inch [1.5 mm]) for best results. Use featherboards to help hold and guide the stock (Fig. 219). Use a push stick or push sticks to feed the stock. All shaping should be done with the cutter under the auxiliary fence or right next to the fence. This allows greater control of the stock and minimizes the chance of kickback.

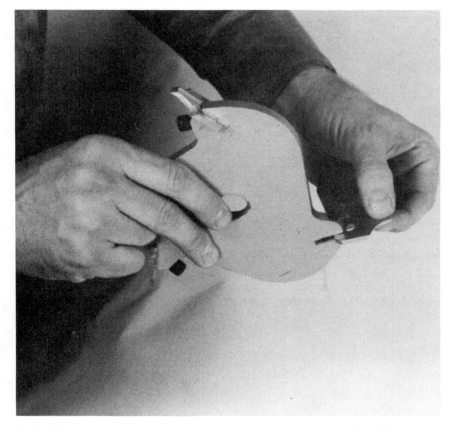

Fig. 212. Install the cutters in the moulding or shaper head with the flat side pointing towards the operator or direction of rotation.

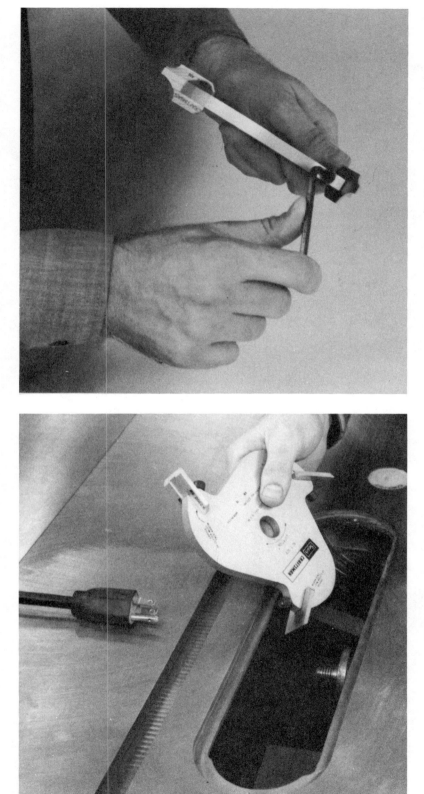

Fig. 213. Make sure the fasteners holding the cutters are locked securely. Check them periodically to be sure they remain tight.

Fig. 214. Install the shaper head so the flat side of the cutters faces the operator. Be sure to use the appropriate spacers and bushings with the shaper head.

99

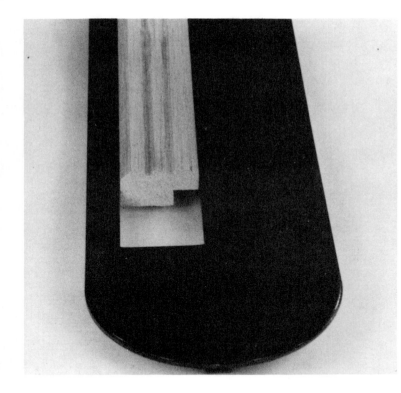

Fig. 215. Be sure the throat plate used with the shaper head is the correct size. If not, the work would fall into the throat plate shown here.

Fig. 216. The wooden throat plate shown here is better suited to the work than the standard throat plate. The method for making auxiliary throat plates is discussed in Chapter 2 (pages 25–27).

Fig. 217. A wooden auxiliary fence is attached to the metal fence. Use a straight-grained hardwood for this purpose. Part of the fence will be cut away by the shaper cutter pictured.

Fig. 218. The fence has been cut away by the shaper cutter. The moving cutter was raised into the fence. The cut-away portion allows you to use only part of the shaper cutter.

Fig. 219. *Light cuts with the help of a featherboard and push stick are safest. Avoid heavy cuts. They tear the wood and cause kickbacks.*

When shaping, always control your stock. Use the fence for edge shaping. The mitre gauge (Fig. 220) or a tenoning jig (Fig. 221) can be used for end shaping. The guard cannot be used for shaping operations. Work carefully. Keep your hands clear of the cutter head and kickback zone. Stand to the side of the stock as you feed it into the cutter. Take light cuts for smoother shaping and less chance of kickback. Feed stock slowly when shaping. This minimizes surface tear-out. If the motor slows down, take a lighter cut. Make sure the stock is true and free of defects. Shaping operations can destroy pieces containing loose knots, shakes and honeycombing. When in doubt, do not shape the piece.

Back the piece with scrap stock to minimize tear-out. You can also shape oversized pieces and saw off the tear-out in some applications. Shape end grain first when doing all 4 sides of a piece. (Fig. 222). Any tear-out at the ends will be removed when the edges are shaped (Fig. 223)

Fancy pieces of moulding can be made by shaping stock with 2 or more cutters. Remember to retain 2 true surfaces to control the stock. One surface should rest on the table, and the other should be held against the fence or mitre gauge.

When the arbor is tilted, additional shapes can be cut. After tilting the arbor, make sure it does not touch the throat plate. Before you turn on the power, turn the shaper head over by hand. Change the set-up if it touches the throat plate. *Note:* This check should be made with the power disconnected.

Some small pieces of moulding are safer and easier to cut when they are part of a larger piece. Both edges of a wider piece of stock are shaped. The moulding is then ripped from both edges of the wider piece (Fig. 224). Use a fine-cut rip or hollow-ground combination blade to rip the moulding from the wider piece. This will keep the edge smooth. No planing should be needed.

Fig. 220. The fence controls depth of cut and the mitre gauge controls the work. Shaping is safest when the cutter is next to the fence.

Fig. 221. Here the tenoning jig controls the work. Depth of cut is controlled by cutter height.

Fig. 222. End grain is shaped first when all 4 edges are shaped. This tear-out will be removed after edge-grain shaping.

Fig. 223. Note how the tear-out was removed when the edge was shaped.

Fig. 224. Small pieces of moulding should be ripped away from a larger piece. Small pieces tend to break or shatter when shaped.

Disc Sanding

Disconnect the power and remove the blade. Mount the sanding disc and replace the throat plate. Raise the disc to full height. Remove the fence and mitre gauge. The table saw is now set up for sanding outside curves.

An outside curve is sanded against disc rotation. Turn on the power and feed the work into the disc (Fig. 225). Let the abrasive do the cutting. Take a light cut and keep the work moving. This will keep the abrasive from burning the wood. Always work on the half of the disc that is moving downwards towards the table. If you work on the half of the disc moving upwards, the disc has a tendency to lift the work.

If the edge of the curve is chamfered or bevelled, the arbor or the stock can be tilted. This allows the disc to sand at the exact angle of the bevel or chamfer (Fig. 226). A mitre gauge may be used for control, if desired (Fig. 227).

A circle-sanding jig can be used on the table saw (Fig. 228). The jig allows you to sand a perfect circle. The stock is first rough cut to a slightly oversized circle. The rough-cut blank is then placed over the center pin on the jig. The blank is advanced into the moving disc (Fig. 229). When it touches, the disc is spun around the center pin until the entire edge is sanded.

Continue advancing the blank until you hit the stop on the jig. Back the circle away from the disc and remove it from the center pin. The edge of the disc is sanded to desired size. The circle-sanding jig works well for wheels,

clock faces and other circular objects. Straightedges may also be disc sanded. Some are sanded free-hand, and others are sanded with a guide such as the fence, mitre gauge or tapering jig.

When pinching a piece of stock between the fence and disc, take a light cut (Fig. 230). A heavy cut can burn the wood and cause a kickback. Some discs require a slight offset (2°) for edge sanding with the fence. This reduces the stress on the disc and makes the sanding marks run parallel to the edge.

The most common error made when disc sanding is to burn the disc. The disc gets hot and fills up with sawdust and pitch. A burned disc will not cut. Burning is caused by 1 of 2 things. The first is using too fine an abrasive for the job. The second is not moving the part as it is sanded. Keeping the part stationary causes heat buildup on the disc and the wood. Move the wood and use the entire downwards moving half of the disc. This spreads the heat over the wood and disc.

Remember, sanding operations cause a lot of dust to fly. Wear a dust mask, and make provisions for dust collection at the table saw. Because a sanding disc does not have teeth, some people feel that it is not as dangerous as a sawblade. A sanding disc is full of abrasive particles, which are small teeth. These teeth make smaller bites, but cut just the same. Keep your hands clear of the disc and throat plate. If your finger becomes pinched between the disc and throat plate, a serious injury can occur.

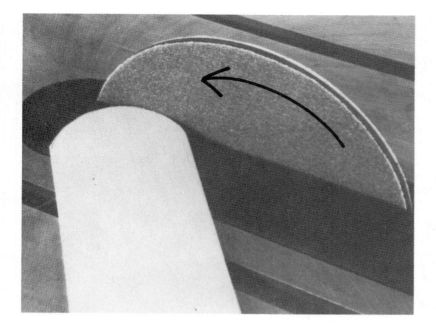

Fig. 225. An outside curve is sanded against disc rotation. Take light cuts and keep the work moving.

Fig. 226. A bevel or chamfer can be moved to the desired angle and sanded. The arbor could also be tilted for this operation.

Fig. 227. For some operations, the angle can be set on the mitre gauge for sanding. The mitre gauge also provides greater control over the work.

Fig. 228. This sanding jig allows you to sand a perfect circle. Stock is roughed out to a slightly oversized circle before sanding.

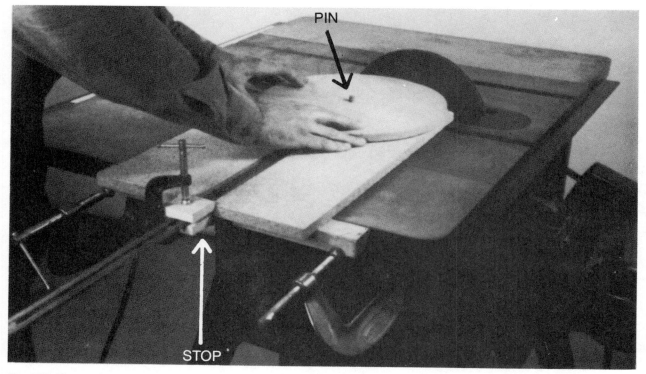

Fig. 229. The work turns around the pin in the center. The stop clamped to the pin controls the diameter of the circle.

Fig. 230. Some sanding discs are designed to sand edges. Take light cuts and keep the disc as low as possible.

6
Intermediate and Advanced Operations

As you gain experience on the table saw, you will want to try some of the intermediate and advanced operations. Practice these operations on scrap stock. Save your expensive wood until you master the operation.

Remember: New experiences can present new hazards! Review Chapter 4 before you attempt any new operation. The information in Chapter 4 will help you identify an accident-producing situation and suggest ways of avoiding it.

Cutting Rabbets and Dadoes

Rabbets are L-shaped channels along the edge. Dadoes are U-shaped channels going through a piece of stock. These may be cut with a dado head or a single blade. For 1 or 2 rabbets or dadoes, it may be faster to use a single blade. It may take longer to set up a dado head than it takes to make the cut with a single blade. For multiple cuts, the dado head is much faster.

Single Blade Rabbets and Dadoes A single-blade edge rabbet consists of 2 cuts. Set the distance from the fence to the blade for the rabbet width. Use a tooth that points away from the fence for this setting. Raise the blade to the rabbet height or slightly less. Turn on the saw and make the first cut on all pieces (Fig. 231). *Note:* The guard with the splitter cannot be used for this operation. Be sure to feed the stock with a push stick.

The second cut is now set up. With the stock on edge, adjust the fence. The piece being cut away should fall free as the cut is completed (Fig. 232). The distance between the blade and fence equals the thickness of the stock minus the rabbet. Use a tooth that points towards the fence. Set the blade height so that it meets the other kerf in the corner of the rabbet. Check the set-up, and make the cut. A solid piece will be cut away (Fig. 233).

End grain rabbets may be cut in a different way. Set the distance from the fence to the far side of the blade at the desired rabbet width. Set the blade height to the desired rabbet height. Place the edge of the work against the mitre gauge, and the end against the fence.

Turn on the saw and make the cut (Fig. 234). Now move the stock 1 saw kerf away from the fence, and make another cut (Fig. 235). Continue moving the stock (Fig. 236) until the rabbet is completed (Fig. 237). The top of the rabbet may be rough or irregular. Smooth it with a chisel or plane.

This procedure for cutting a rabbet may also be used to cut a dado. Set the fence to the near side of the blade for the first setting (Fig. 238). Use the distance from the end or edge to the top (part of dado closest to the fence) of the dado. Make this cut in all pieces (Fig. 239). Use the mitre gauge to control cross-grain cuts.

Set the fence to the far side of the blade for the second setting. Use the distance from the end or edge to the bottom (part of dado furthest from the fence) of the dado (Fig. 240). Make this cut in the piece. If the dado is a cross-grain dado, move 1 saw kerf away from the fence and make another cut (Fig. 241). Continue until you meet the first kerf (Fig. 242). For a dado with the grain, the fence must be moved 1 saw kerf towards the waste stock. Another cut is made in all the pieces. Continue moving the fence until you meet the first saw kerf (Fig. 243).

Single blade rabbets and dadoes are sometimes called lazy dadoes. This implies the operator is too lazy to set up a dado head. For a few rabbets or dadoes, the single blade method may be best. When several dadoes or rabbets must be cut, the dado head should be set up. This reduces handling and set-up time.

Fig. 231. Set the rabbet width from the fence to a tooth pointing away from the fence. Elevate the blade to rabbet height or slightly less. Guards having a splitter cannot be used for this cut.

Fig. 232. The thickness of the stock minus the rabbet determines the distance from the fence to a tooth that points towards the fence. Blade height should be set to meet the first kerf.

Fig. 233. A solid piece will be cut away when the rabbet is made. Notice how it falls free. If it were between the fence and blade, there could be a kickback.

Fig. 234. A series of saw kerfs can be used to make an end rabbet, the distance from the fence to the far side of the blade. Blade height determines rabbet height.

Fig. 235. The work is moved away from the fence for the second cut.

Fig. 236. The final kerf is cut into the work.

Fig. 237. The completed end rabbet. The slight roughness on the rabbet face can be trimmed away with a chisel.

Fig. 238. A single blade dado is similar to a single blade rabbet. Set the blade height to dado depth and adjust the fence so the blade cuts the top of the dado.

Fig. 239. Make the first cut in all pieces before changing the set-up. Control stock with the mitre gauge.

Fig. 240. Set the fence so the blade cuts the bottom of the dado. Do not change the blade height.

Fig. 241. Make the cut and move the piece away from the fence. Continue cutting until you meet the first kerf.

Fig. 242. The dado produced shows some irregularity. This can be smoothed with a chisel.

Fig. 243. When a dado is cut with the grain, the fence must be moved one saw kerf towards the waste stock. Be sure to cut all parts before moving the fence.

Cutting Rabbets with the Dado Head The best way to cut rabbets with the dado head requires the use of an auxiliary fence. The dado head is mounted and set up. The dado head should be wider than the rabbet. A ¾-inch (19-mm) or 1-inch (25-mm) auxiliary fence is then attached to the fence (Fig. 244). The dado head is dropped below the table, and the auxiliary fence is placed over the throat plate and locked in position. Mark the fence at the desired dado height (Fig. 245). Turn on the saw and raise the dado into the auxiliary fence (Fig. 246). Stop the dado at the mark on the fence. Shut off the saw and re-adjust the fence. The amount of dado head exposed should equal the rabbet width. Make a test cut on a piece of scrap.

When edge rabbets are being cut, the stock can ride along the fence (Fig. 247). Use a push stick for narrow pieces. End rabbets should be controlled with the mitre gauge (Fig. 248). If you are rabbeting sheet stock, it is best to use a carbide dado head. Steel dado heads dull rapidly.

A shaper or moulding head equipped with jointer cutters may also be used to cut rabbets. The moulding head is raised into the auxiliary fence in the same way as the dado head. The set-up and cutting procedures are the same (Fig. 249). Shaper cutters are made of high-speed steel and should be used on solid stock.

Cutting Blind Dadoes Blind dadoes are dadoes that do not go through the piece. They stop somewhere in the part. Blind dadoes are often used in cabinetwork. A blind dado joint looks like a butt joint from the front. A blind dado shows no tear-out, and a loose fit is not visible from the front. It is cut in the same way as a regular dado except it is not fed completely through.

After the dado head is set up correctly, you can locate stops or stop marks. These help indicate where to stop the dado. If the table is long enough, clamp a stop to the table or place a piece of masking tape on the table. If the dado is longer than the table, mark the end of the cut on top of the stock. Mark the end of the dado on the fence using masking tape (Fig. 250). When the lines meet, the dado is cut (Fig. 251).

Cut a blind dado as you would a regular dado. When you hit the stop or the stop marks line up, turn off the saw (Fig. 252). Let the dado head come to a complete stop before you move the stock. Lift the stock off the dado head, and check the end of the cut (Fig. 253). Be sure you have cut far enough into the stock. You may wish to square out the end of the dado with hand tools (Fig. 254). It is also possible to cut an arc on the mating piece so no hand work is needed.

Fig. 244. When rabbets are being cut with a dado head, an auxiliary fence must be attached to the fence. Attach it on the side closest to the dado head.

Fig. 245. Mark the desired height of the dado head on the auxiliary fence.

Fig. 246. The dado head is turned on and raised into the auxiliary fence. Make sure the dado head does not contact the metal fence.

Fig. 247. The stock rides along the auxiliary fence for edge rabbets. Feed the stock with a push stick.

Fig. 248. When cutting end rabbets, butt the stock against the auxiliary fence. Use the mitre gauge to control and feed the stock.

Fig. 249. A shaper head equipped with jointer cutters can also be used to cut rabbets. An auxiliary fence covers the portion of the cutters not in use.

Fig. 250. Mark the end of a blind dado on the fence and the work. Use masking tape for this purpose.

Fig. 251. Feed the stock into the dado head as you would any other piece.

Fig. 252. When the marks line up, shut off the saw. Do not release the stock until the dado head stops.

Fig. 253. The end of the cut will be curved due to the shape of the dado head.

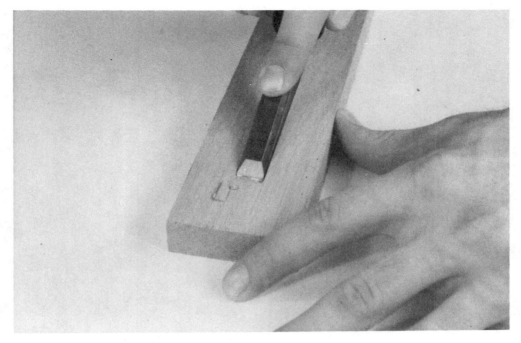

Fig. 254. The end of a blind dado can be squared with a chisel.

Cutting Lap Joints Lap joints are corner or cross joints where 1 piece laps over the other. They are commonly used on cabinet-face plates. The lap joint can be cut with a dado head. Set the height of the dado head to ½ the stock thickness. For end laps, use the stock width to set the fence (Fig. 255). The distance from the far side of the dado head to the fence should equal stock width.

Mark your pieces. One-half of the pieces will be cut on the good or exposed face (Fig. 256). The other half will be cut on the back. Use the mitre gauge to control your stock (Fig. 257). You will have to make several cuts to make the lap joint (Fig. 258). The fence will mark the end of the joint. *Note*: If your pieces tear out as they are cut, you may wish to back the cut with a scrap attached to the mitre gauge (Fig. 259). Careful layout and set-up will produce a good-fitting lap joint (Fig. 260).

Cross laps require 2 marks or stops. This is because they are not on the end of the piece. You can clamp 2 stops to the table. Each stop marks 1 end of the lap joint. Masking tape can also be used to mark the ends. Butt the work to the first stop and make a cut (Fig. 261). Use the mitre gauge to control the work (Fig. 262). Use the second stop to make another cut (Fig. 263). Both ends of

the lap are now cut (Fig. 264). If more stock remains between the 2 cuts, continue cutting until it is gone (Fig. 265). Several identical cross laps can be produced quickly with this method (Fig. 266).

Cutting a Series of Dadoes Often, a series of equally spaced dadoes is needed. Pigeon holes are a good example of this (Fig. 267). After the dado head is set up, a stop is clamped to the table, or a jig is fitted to the mitre gauge. This stop should be slightly smaller than the dado. The distance from the stop to the dado should be the desired distance between dado cuts (Fig. 268).

Make the first dado cut (or rabbet), and butt this cut to the stop. This locates the next dado (Fig. 269). Proceed with the cutting. Control your stock with the mitre gauge (Fig. 270). The fence can also locate dadoes (Fig. 271). The stop clamped to the table is used for blind dadoes (Fig. 272).

When dadoes go with the grain, the fence has to be moved for each successive cut. A piece of stock has to be laid out for this to mark and set up the cuts. Always test the set-up on a piece of scrap before cutting your parts.

Fig. 255. For end lap joints, use the stock width to set the fence.

Fig. 256. Mark your pieces. When lap joints are made, the good side of one piece and the bad side of the other are cut.

Fig. 257. The mitre gauge is used to control the stock. The stock is butted to the fence for the first cut.

Fig. 258. The piece is moved away from the fence for the second cut.

124

Fig. 259. Note how the work is backed by a piece of scrap stock. This keeps the work from tearing as the cut is made.

Fig. 260. A careful layout will produce a good-fitting lap joint.

125

Fig. 261. The stop clamped to the table marks both ends of a cross-lap joint. Butt the work to the first stop.

Fig. 262. Make the first cut. Control the stock with the mitre gauge.

Fig. 263. Butt the work to the second stop.

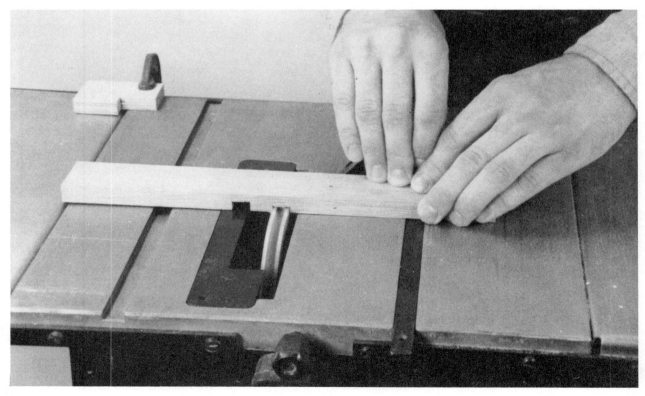

Fig. 264. Make the second cut. This cut marks the other end of the cross-lap joint.

127

Fig. 265. Make additional cuts to remove the remaining stock.

Fig. 266. Tight cross-lap joints can be produced easily with this method.

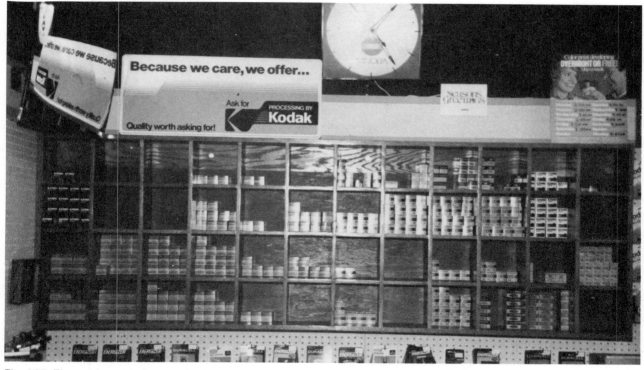

Fig. 267. These pigeon holes required several series of dado cuts. This cabinet was built in my shop.

Fig. 268. A stop attached to the mitre gauge is used to locate dadoes in a pigeon hole set-up. The distance from the stop to the dado head controls dado spacing.

Fig. 269. *The rabbet butted against the stop locates the first dado.*

Fig. 270. *The stop is under the first dado as the second one is cut. The mitre gauge controls the feed of the work.*

Fig. 271. The fence can also locate dadoes. The stop clamped to the table is used to make blind dadoes.

Fig. 272. All of the blind cuts are uniform because of the stop clamped to the table.

131

Cutting Mortises and Tenons

A mortise and tenon is a 2-part joint. The mortise is a slot or hole cut into 1 piece. The tenon is a mating tongue that fits into the mortise. The 3 most common mortise-and-tenon joints are the open, blind and haunched joints. The open mortise-and-tenon joint can be cut completely on the table saw. The blind and haunched tenons can be cut on the table saw, but the mortises must be cut elsewhere.

Using the Tenoning Jig The tenoning jig is a device used to control stock while the tenon is cut (Fig. 273). It may be shop-made or commercially manufactured. Some tenoning jigs ride on or along the fence (Fig. 275), and others ride in the mitre slot. The chief job of the tenoning jig is to hold stock in a vertical position while the cheek cut is made.

The shoulder cuts are made on the tenons first. Set the blade height to the layout line. Set the fence to the length of the tenon. Use the far side of the blade. On open mortise-and-tenon joints, this will be equal to stock width. On haunched and blind joints, it will be less than stock width. Make the shoulder cuts on both sides (faces) of all pieces (Fig. 274).

Set up the tenoning jig to make the cheek cuts. Adjust the tenoning jig so that the blade cuts a kerf that meets the shoulder cut (Fig. 275). This kerf should be in the waste portion of the cheek. Be sure the stock that is cut

away during the cheek cut is not pinched between the fence and jig. This may cause a kickback. Make all cheek cuts (Fig. 276). The tenon can now be used to lay out the open mortise.

The tenoning jig may also be used to cut the open mortise. The open mortise is a series of cuts that match the tenon. Lay out the open mortise and set up the tenoning jig. The tenoning jig should make a cheek cut in the mortise area of the piece (Fig. 277). When the piece is reversed (Fig. 278), the tenoning jig will cut the other cheek of the mortise. Re-adjust the tenoning jig to remove the rest of the mortise. Check the fit of the mating parts (Fig. 279).

A chisel may be needed to true up the bottom of the mortise or improve the fit between the mortise and tenon. Work carefully and take light cuts. Removing too much stock will ruin the fit.

A haunched mortise is cut to fit the groove made on the vertical parts (Fig. 280). The haunch is usually as long as the depth of the groove or mortise, and ½ inch (13 mm) deep. Haunches are usually cut on the tenon with the dado head (Fig. 281). Use the haunched tenon to lay out the mortise (Fig. 282). The mortise can be drilled out and squared up with a chisel. It can also be cut with a mortising machine. Mortising machines cut mortises of a nominal size, such as: ¼ inch (6 mm), ⅜ inch (10 mm), ½ inch (13 mm), ⅝ inch (16 mm) and ¾ inch (19 mm). Keep this in mind when you first lay out your tenons. Odd-sized tenons may make the mortises more difficult to cut.

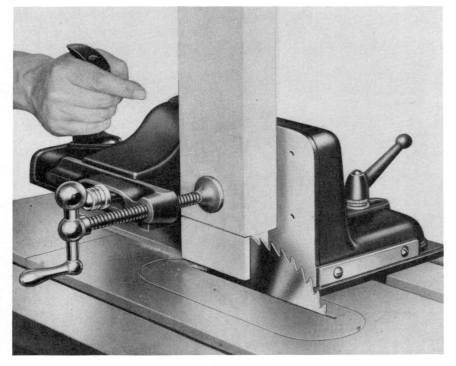

Fig. 273. The tenoning jig is a device used to control stock while the tenon is cut. This one is commercially manufactured and rides in the mitre slot.

Fig. 274. The shoulders are cut on both faces of the stock when making a through tenon.

Fig. 275. The tenoning jig makes the cheek cuts. This tenoning jig is shop-made. It rides on the fence.

Fig. 276. Make the second cheek cut on all of the parts. Be sure the kerf is in the waste portion of the stock. Use the tenon to lay out the open mortise.

Fig. 277. The first cheek in the open mortise is cut using the tenoning jig.

Fig. 278. Reversing the piece allows the second cheek cut to be made. Any stock between the cheeks should now be removed.

Fig. 279. Check the fit of your open mortise and tenon to assure accurate set-up.

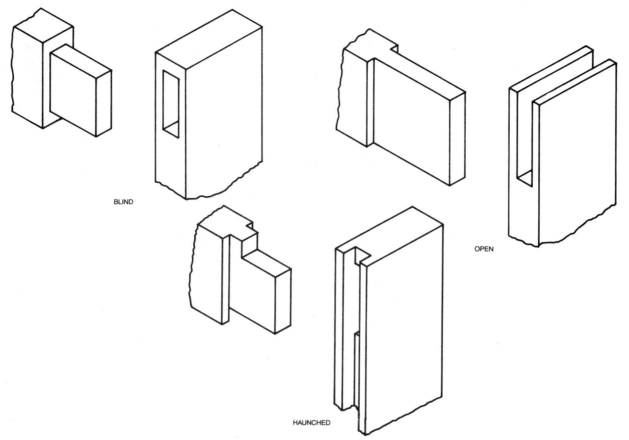

BLIND

OPEN

HAUNCHED

Fig. 280. Three types of mortises. A haunched mortise has a step (or haunch) cut into it. This allows it to fit the groove made on the vertical parts.

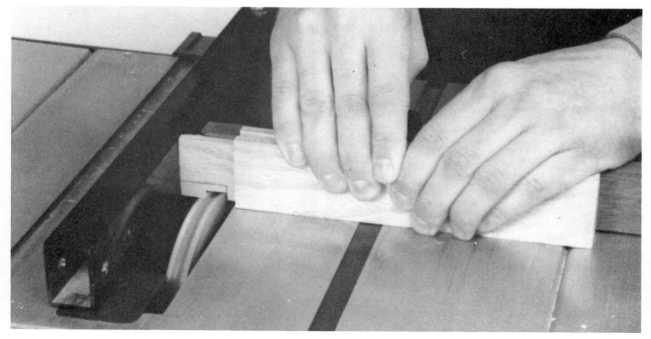

Fig. 281. The dado head is commonly used to cut out the haunched area of a tenon.

Fig. 282. The haunched tenon can be used to lay out the mortise. Note the slight angle of the haunch. It fits tight at the surface, but there is no interference beneath.

Blind mortises are also laid out with the tenon. The tenon usually has 4 shoulders. It is easiest to cut with a dado head if all shoulders are of equal depth. On thinner stock 1 inch (25 mm) or less, 2 different shoulder depths are used. Shoulder depth on the faces is usually ¼ to ⅓ of the stock thickness. Shoulder depth on the outer edge is at least ½ inch (13 mm) (Fig. 283). This keeps the joint from being fragile.

The mortises must be held at least ½ inch (13 mm) away from the end of the stock. Mortises closer to the end of the stock put too much stress on the end-grain fibres of the wood. This produces a weak joint. A blind mortise is cut in the same way as a haunched mortise.

The tenoning jig may also be used to cut lap joints. The shoulder cut for the lap joint is cut the same way as the shoulder cut for a tenon. Shoulder-cut depth for a lap joint equals ½ stock thickness. The fence is set to the width of the stock. Use a tooth that points away from the fence. Mark all pieces so you know which face must be cut away.

Set up the tenoning jig to make the cheek cut. The cheek cut is made in the waste stock, and meets the shoulder cut. The 2 cuts should form a right angle (Fig. 284). Make a few practice cuts to be sure the pieces fit together correctly. Tenoning jigs are a challenge to make. A shop-made tenoning jig can be as accurate as a manufactured jig if it is built carefully. All the parts for the tenoning jig can be made on the table saw. Small pieces of sheet stock work well for most parts because they are less likely to swell or warp.

Fig. 283. Shoulder depth on the outer edge (left) is ½ inch (12 mm). This keeps the joint from being fragile.

137

Fig. 284. The tenoning jig is used to make the cheek cut on a lap joint. The cheek cut meets the shoulder cut squarely.

Cutting Tenons with the Dado Head Tenons made with the dado head require no more handling than tenons cut using the tenoning jig. This is because the dado head makes the shoulder cut and part of the cheek cut in 1 pass. Set the tenon length from the fence to the far side of the dado head (Fig. 285). Adjust the dado height to meet the face of the tenon. Test the fence and dado height adjustments on a scrap. Make any minor adjustments needed, and test the set-up again.

On a tenon with edge shoulders, a different dado height may be needed. Cut the faces first (Fig. 286), then re-adjust the dado height for the edge shoulders (Fig. 287). Test the set-up on a scrap. Re-adjust the set-up if necessary.

Face shoulders and edge shoulders are cut in the same way. Stock is controlled with the mitre gauge. The fence limits the length of the tenon. After the first cut, the stock is moved away from the fence so another cut can be made (Fig. 288). Repeat the process until all stock is removed. Cut the opposite side of the stock in the same manner.

Dado heads cannot be used to cut mortises. Lay out and cut the mortises using the same procedures listed under the section on cutting mortises and tenons with the tenoning jig (pages 132–137).

Resawing

Resawing is the process of ripping a thick piece of stock into 2 thinner pieces. Resawn pieces are often glued together to make wider panels for cabinet sides or doors (Fig. 289). The grain of the 2 thinner pieces is often matched at the glue line to give a book effect. This is commonly known as a book match. Stock to be resawn should be true. Edges and faces should be parallel. There should be no knots or other defects.

Choose a fine-cutting rip or combination blade. The teeth should have a moderate set. This will minimize pitch accumulation and the chance of kickback.

Select a piece of stock that is thick enough to yield pieces of the desired thickness. For example, a ¾-inch (19-mm) piece of stock cannot be resawn into 2 pieces ⅜ inch (10 mm) thick. This is because the saw blade will turn ⅛ inch (3 mm) or more of the thickness into saw kerf. A ¾-inch (19-mm) piece will produce 2 pieces of ¼-inch (6-mm) stock with no trouble. This allows ¼ inch (6 mm) for a saw kerf and sanding or planing of the sawn surfaces.

Set the distance from the fence to the blade at the desired stock thickness. Allow a little extra thickness for sanding or planing the stock. Set the blade height at slightly less than ½ the stock width or no more than 1 inch (25 mm). With the face against the fence and an edge on the table, make a rip cut through the piece. Place the other edge on the table, and make another rip cut (Fig. 290). Keep the same face against the fence. On narrow stock, there will be a thin strip separating the 2 pieces. In most cases, the pieces will split apart easily (Fig. 291). They can then be sanded, planed or glued together.

On wider stock, the blade will have to be raised another inch (25 mm) or to slightly less than ½ the stock width (Fig. 292). Make another rip cut from each edge. Be sure to keep the same face against the fence. Separate these pieces when a thin strip remains (Fig. 293).

The blade is set at 1 inch (25 mm) for each cut to reduce the stress on the blade and minimize the chance of kickbacks. The stock hardness and the horsepower of the saw may allow a slightly higher (or lower) setting. Experience will tell you the correct setting for your saw.

When resawing some pieces, you may wish to make cuts with both faces touching the fence (Fig. 294). This will make the saw kerf wider, and assure that the resawn pieces are the same thickness. It will be easier to glue up panels when the resawn pieces are the same thickness.

Fig. 285. Tenon length is the distance from the far side of the dado head to the fence.

Fig. 286. Both faces are cut before changing the set-up to cut edges.

Fig. 287. Edge shoulders are cut after the height of the dado head is readjusted (if necessary).

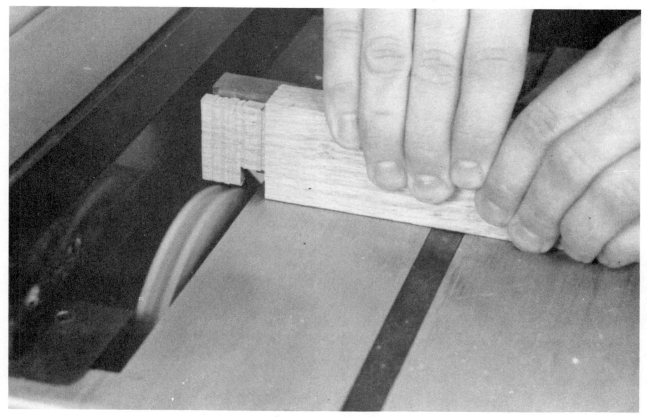

Fig. 288. The second edge shoulder is being cut. Stock is moved away from the fence for consecutive cuts.

140

Fig. 289. Resawn pieces are often glued together to make wider panels for cabinet sides or doors. Can you see the book-match line down the center of the panel?

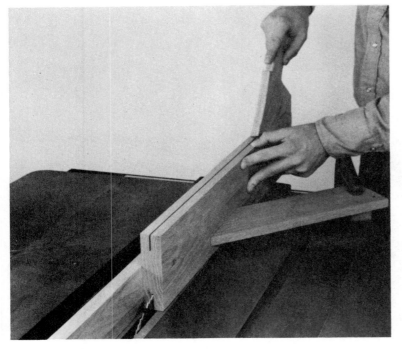

Fig. 290. The resaw cuts are about 1 inch (25 mm) deep. Keep the same face of the stock against the fence for both cuts.

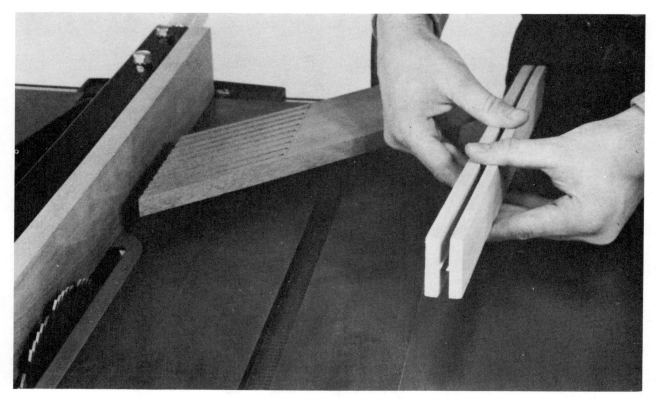

Fig. 291. The thin strip separates or splits easily. The split surfaces can be sanded or planed.

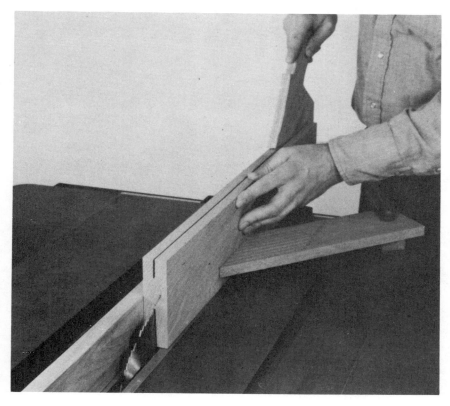

Fig. 292. On wider stock, a second cut is necessary.

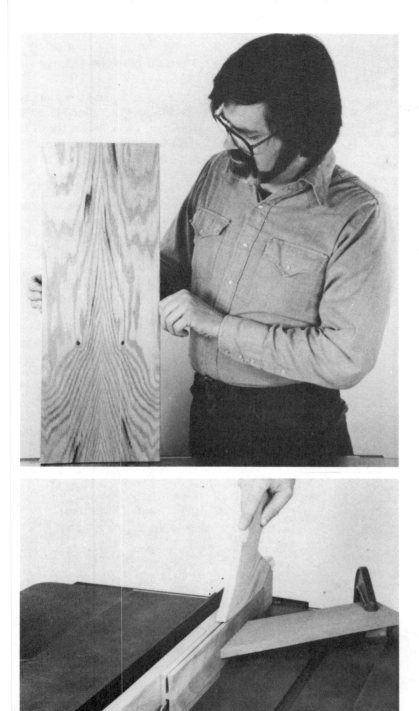

Fig. 293. The wider stock in Fig. 292 was book-matched and glued into this panel. The knot was inside the stock.

Fig. 294. The kerf on this resawn stock is wider than the blade. This is because it was resawn with both outside faces against the fence. Both pieces will be exactly the same thickness.

143

Cutting Keys and Keyways

Keys are reinforcing members added to mitre joints. Mitre joints are end-grain joints. They are the weakest type of wood joint. When a key is added to the mitre joint, it becomes stronger. This is because the key is glued face-to-face in the 2 parts of the mitre joint. Face-grain joints are the strongest type of wood joint.

A keyway is cut into the mitre joint after it has been assembled and the glue has cured. The keyway or key-cutting jig is similar to the tenoning jig (Fig. 295). It has a V-shaped cradle instead of a vertical stop (Fig. 296). The V-shaped cradle holds the mitre joint while the keyway is cut.

Adjust the key-cutting jig to the desired position over the blade or dado head. A blade is used for thin keys, and a dado head is used for thicker keys. Set the height of the blade or dado head to the desired key depth. Place the mitre joint in the cradle (Fig. 297), and feed it into the blade. For a frame, this process has to be repeated for each corner.

Rip some stock to fit the keyways. The stock is going to be glued into place, so allow some space for the glue. A key that is too thick for the keyway could break the joint during installation. Make a trial fit of the keys (Fig. 298). Mark them and cut them slightly long. Apply glue to the key and keyway. Insert the key and allow the glue to cure (Fig. 299). It is difficult to clamp the keys in place. If they do move around, secure them with a piece of masking tape. Sand the key flush with the stock when the glue has cured (Fig. 300).

Keys can also be cut the entire length of the mitre joint. A universal jig is also used to cut the dado along the face of the mitre joint (Fig. 301). Keep the exposed face of all parts facing the same direction when you make this cut.

Fig. 295. This key-cutting jig rides on the fence. The V-shaped cradle holds the stock while the key is cut.

Fig. 296. This key-cutting jig rides in the mitre slot. A test piece is in the cradle. The test piece assures that the set-up is correct before the work is cut.

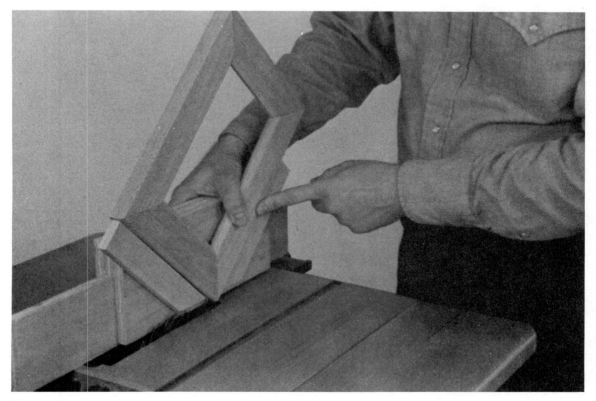

Fig. 297. The jig is fed into the blade at a moderate speed. Remember, the joint has little strength at this point.

Fig. 298. Make a trial fit of the keys. Be sure they fit correctly. Allow some space for glue.

Fig. 299. Glue the keys in place and allow them to cure. Use masking tape to hold them if necessary.

Fig. 300. After the glue cures, sand the keys flush with the frame.

Fig. 301. Keys can also be cut the entire length of the mitre. A commercial jig is being used for this purpose. This joint is sometimes called a spline mitre joint.

Cutting Coves

A cove is a curved recess cut into a piece of stock. Most simple cove cuts are made with the moulding head (Fig. 302). Some coves, however, do not follow the arc of a machined cutter. These coves must be cut using a saw blade and an inclined fence. The blade and inclined fence method may also be used for simple coves, but they are usually cut with the moulding head. Many objects require this method of cutting coves. Restoration work (Fig. 303) often requires cove cuts to reproduce some type of moulding. The brush shelf (Fig. 304) has a coved base.

This keeps hairpins, combs and brushes from being easily knocked off the shelf. Many picture frames with graceful coves are also cut with a saw blade and inclined fence.

Begin by laying out the cove. Determine the arc of the cove and its relative location in the piece of stock. This layout can be photocopied and then glued to the ends of your stock (Fig. 305). Patterns may also be made to trace the profile on your work (Fig. 306).

Remove most of the stock in the cove area with straight cuts (Fig. 307). Adjust the fence and blade height for each cut, or use a dado head if several parts are to be made (Fig. 308).

Fig. 302. Most standard coves are cut with a shaper head. Large coves cannot be cut with the shaper head.

Fig. 303. (Left) This partial cove was cut with a saw blade and an inclined fence. (Right) After a few more operations, this stock became the base moulding used in my restored kitchen.

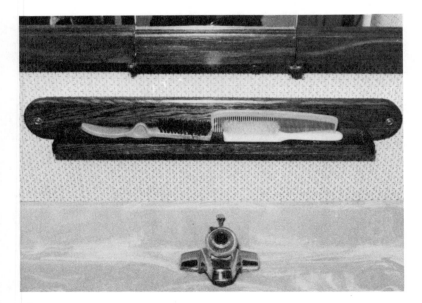

Fig. 304. This brush shelf has a coved base. The plans for this project appear in Chapter 8 (pages 289–292).

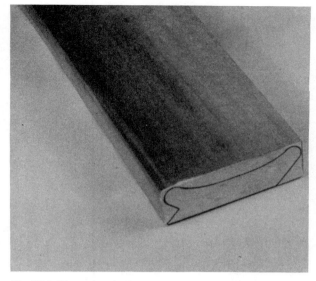

Fig. 305. The cove design has been glued to the end of the set-up piece. This makes set-up much easier.

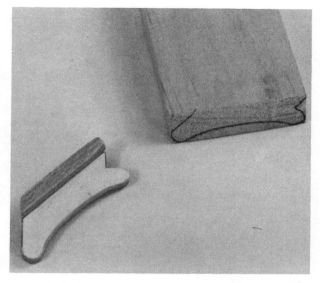

Fig. 306. Patterns can also be made to trace the profile on both ends of the work. Both ends of the piece may now be used for layout.

Fig. 307. Straight cuts can be used to remove most of the stock in a cove. Adjust the fence and blade height for each cut.

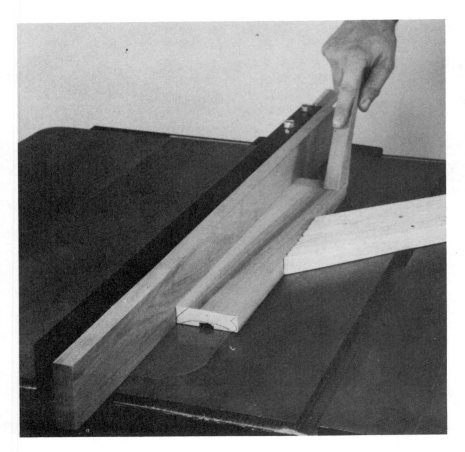

Fig. 308. A dado head may also be used to remove the stock in a cove.

Select the appropriate blade for cove cutting, and install it. For thin, wide coves, a 10-inch (25.4-cm) diameter or larger works well. For more circular-shaped coves, an 8-inch (20.3-cm) diameter works well. Make sure the blade you select has fine teeth. This will reduce the amount of sanding required. Adjust the blade height to the deepest portion of the cove (Fig. 309). Set the parallel guide to the cove width (Fig. 310), and place the parallel guide over the blade. Turn the guide so that 1 edge touches each side of the blade (Fig. 311).

The parallel guide is now resting at an angle to the blade. This angle is the angle at which the fence must be adjusted for cove cutting. Copy this angle with a sliding T-bevel (Fig. 312). Select a stiff, true piece of stock to use as your auxiliary fence. Set the fence to the angle of the sliding T-bevel. Make sure the fence is between the front of the saw and the blade (Fig. 313). This allows the thrust of the blade to force the work against the fence.

Adjust the fence with reference to the stock being cut. The edge of the cove should just touch a tooth that points towards the fence (Fig. 314). Clamp the fence securely in place. Make sure the clamps do not block the control side of the fence. *Note*: For partial coves (Fig. 315), the fence actually covers a portion of the blade. The fence is adjusted with the blade beneath the table. The blade is then

raised while it is running. It makes a cut in the wooden fence.

Lower the blade. About ⅛ inch (3 mm) of the blade should be above the table for the first cut. Light cuts produce the best results. Clamp 2 featherboards to the table (Fig. 316). These will hold the stock against the fence. Mark the fence side of your stock. Do this on the bottom of each piece. Marking the stock should keep you from reversing pieces. This is very important if the cove is not centered.

Turn on the saw and feed pieces across the blade. Keep them held firmly against the inclined fence. Push sticks keep hands clear of the blade and improve control of the stock (Fig. 317). *Note*: If you encounter resistance as you feed your stock across the blade, the blade may be too high. Lower the blade and try again.

After all the parts have been cut, raise the blade ¹⁄₁₆–⅛ inch (1.5–3 mm). Make the second cut and repeat the process. Remember, as the blade is raised more teeth come in contact with the blade. This means the blade has to work harder and is more likely to kick back. As your cove cut gets deeper, take lighter cuts—no more than ¹⁄₁₆ inch (1.5 mm).

As you near the desired shape, take light cuts. This will reduce the amount of sanding needed. Feed the stock slowly on the final pass to make it smoother. Sometimes 2 passes at the final setting make the cove smoother. The cove must be sanded after machining (Fig. 318). Begin with 60-grit or 80-grit abrasives and work up. A dowel or a piece of stock cut to the shape of your cove can be used as a sanding block (Fig. 319).

As you work with coves, you may wish to make a parallel guide (Fig. 320). The guide is 5½ inches (14.0 cm) wide and 29½ inches (75.0 cm) long. Accurate layout and drilling are all that are necessary to complete the project. Use "T" nuts to hold the pieces together. The "T" nuts allow you to lock the parallel guide at the desired setting. More information is provided in Chapter 8 (Figs. 488–490).

If you frequently cut the same cove, you may want to make a layout guide (Fig. 321). This will make cove set-up faster. Remember to use the same blade and fence with the layout guide. You may want to list this information on the guide.

If you wish to experiment with the cove-cutting process, try using a moulding head with a cove cutter installed. It can also be used with an inclined fence. If you experiment with this process, remember the following points:

1. Remove most of the stock in the cove area with straight cuts.

2. Set up the inclined fence carefully. It is more difficult to set up the fence using the moulding head.

3. Take light cuts! Heavy cuts can cause kickbacks, and may damage your work.

Fig. 309. The first step in the cove set-up is to adjust the blade height to full cove depth.

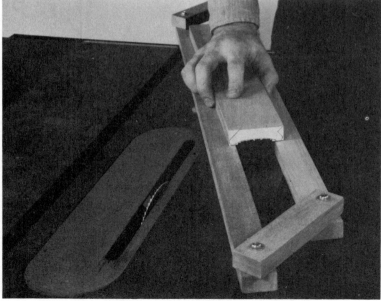

Fig. 310. The parallel guide is set to the cove width next.

Fig. 311. The parallel guide is turned so that one edge touches each side of the blade.

Fig. 312. A sliding T-bevel is used to copy the angle established by the parallel guide

Fig. 313. Use the sliding T-bevel to set the fence at the correct angle.

Fig. 314. The fence should be adjusted to the correct place on the cove with the blade adjusted to full cove depth. The fence should be between the blade and the operator.

Fig. 315. When a partial cove is cut, the fence actually covers part of the blade.

Fig. 316. Two featherboards may be used to hold the work against the fence. Push sticks should be used to feed stock across the blade.

Fig. 317. (Left) A second fence may be used instead of featherboards to hold stock in place. (Right) Light cuts should be taken. There is a great deal of side thrust on the blade when a cove cut is made.

Fig. 318. Note the saw marks in the cove. A coarser blade would leave much larger saw marks. These marks have to be sanded.

155

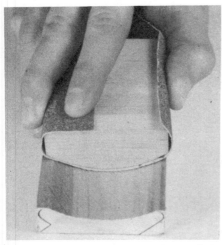

Fig. 319. A sanding block can be made to follow the contour of the cove.

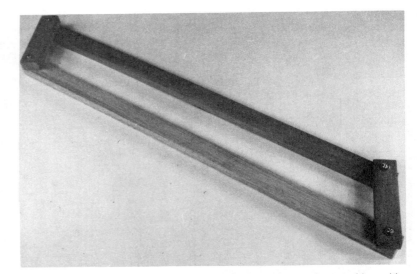

Fig. 320. A parallel guide is a handy accessory to have when working with coves. A drawing and details for construction appear in Chapter 8 (Figs. 488 and 489).

Fig. 321. This layout guide has the correct fence angle cut on one edge. This accessory is desirable if the same cove is made frequently.

Cutting Finger Joints

Finger joints, or box joints, are corner joints made up of mating fingers (Fig. 322). The corner slips together to form a strong joint. Each finger exposes extra edge grain, which increases the amount of gluing surface. Finger joints are cut with a jig. Usually, the jig is attached to the mitre gauge, but some are designed to be attached to the fence. Fingers are usually no wider than the stock thickness. Fingers cut in ½-inch (13-mm) stock would be ½ inch (13 mm) wide or less. Narrower fingers look nicer, but take longer to cut.

After you decide on a finger width, set up the saw to cut that width. Use a dado head or a single saw blade. When using a single saw blade, use a combination or rip blade. These blades usually leave the end of the finger cut flat. Adjust the blade height to stock thickness or slightly more. By cutting fingers slightly deeper than stock thickness, a small amount of stock can be sanded off the fingers after assembly. This assures flush joints.

Select a true piece of stock about 4 inches (10.2 cm) wide and 8–12 inches (20.3–30.5 cm) long. Cut a dado through the edge of the piece near 1 end (Fig. 323). Measure the kerf or dado width. Mark off a space that size right next to the kerf. Insert and glue a piece of stock into the kerf (Fig. 324). The piece of stock should be equal to the kerf size and about 1 inch (25 mm) long. This piece of stock (the spacer) controls spacing between the fingers. Attach the finger jig to the mitre gauge (Fig. 325). There should be a space equal to the finger size between the kerf and spacer.

Lay out pieces. Set them on edge in the way they will fit together. Mark the pieces and determine which pieces start with a finger and which pieces start with a cutout. One way of keeping order is to start the long pieces with a cutout. Mark the pieces accordingly (Fig. 326). Cut the pieces that begin with a finger first.

Place the stock against the jig with the edge next to the spacer (the piece of stock in the right kerf) (Fig. 327). Push the piece of stock across the blade. Hold the stock firmly against the jig as the cut is made. Place the cutout area over the spacer and make another cut (Fig. 328). Continue cutting until all fingers have been cut (Fig. 329).

Pieces beginning with a cutout are now cut. Start the cut by placing a finger between the spacer and the left kerf. Use a piece of stock that has already been cut. The first finger goes between the kerfs and the first cutout goes over the spacer (Fig. 330). Butt the stock to be cut against the finger and the jig. Hold it firmly and make the first cutout.

After all of the cutouts have been made, remove the piece of stock with a finger over the spacer. Make the rest of the cutouts, using the spacer as a stop (Fig. 331). After all cuts have been made (Fig. 332), test the fit between the parts (Fig. 333). If the fingers are too big, the parts will not fit together. This indicates that the space between the kerfs is too great. Too little space between the kerfs makes the fingers too small. This produces a sloppy fit. Adjust spacing or blade size to produce a satisfactory fit. Remember, glue must be added between each finger, so a little clearance is desirable.

Other factors that can affect the fit of finger joints include:
1. Slop in the mitre slot or jig that affects the spacing of the cuts.
2. A blade that is not perpendicular to the table or mitre gauge.
3. Slippage between the jig and the mitre gauge.
4. Failure to hold parts securely while they are being cut.

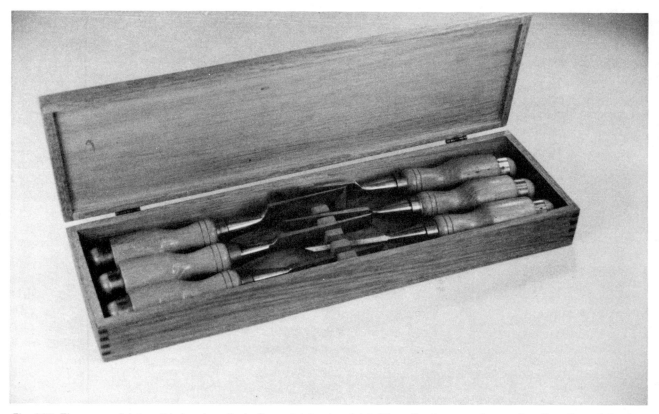

Fig. 322. The corner joint on this box is called a finger joint or box joint. It is quite strong and very attractive. Complete plans for this box appear in Chapter 8 (pages 255–263).

Fig. 323. A through dado is cut on the edge of the piece used as a finger-cutting jig. This dado is equal to the size of the desired fingers.

Fig. 324. A piece of stock is glued in the dado or kerf. It acts as a spacer when the fingers are cut.

Fig. 325. The finger jig is now attached to the mitre gauge. There should be space equal to the finger size between the kerf and spacer.

Fig. 326. Mark the pieces so that 2 begin with cuts and 2 begin with fingers. These pieces have been marked with "C"s and "F"s to keep order.

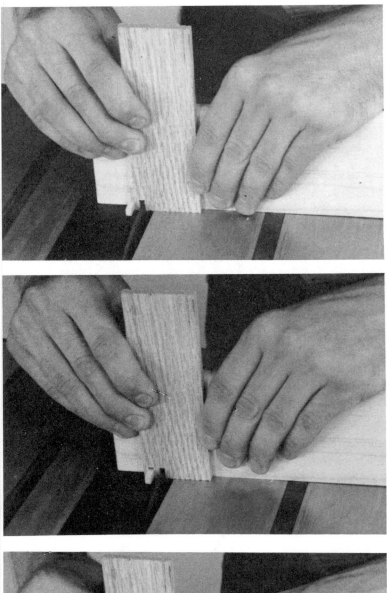

Fig. 327. Cut the pieces starting with fingers first. Butt the piece to the spacer and make the cut.

Fig. 328. The first kerf goes over the spacer as the second cut is made.

Fig. 329. Continue moving the stock until all the fingers have been cut.

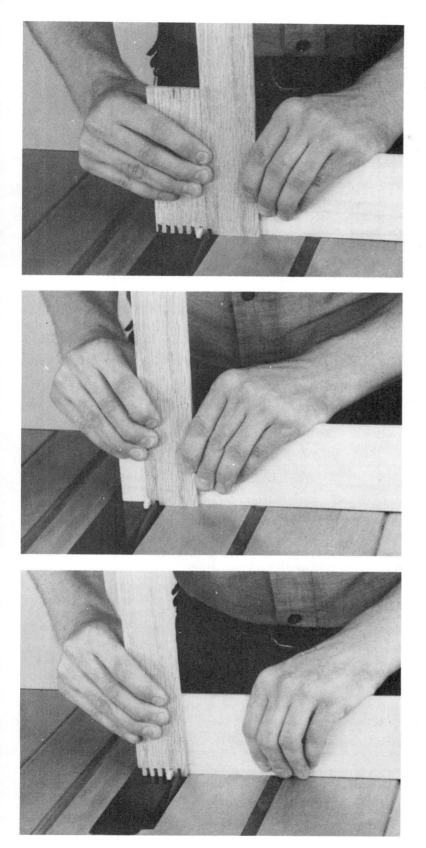

Fig. 330. Place the first finger of a piece between the spacer and kerf to cut pieces beginning with a cutout. Make the cutout on all pieces first.

Fig. 331. Continue making the cuts using the spacer for control.

Fig. 332. Cut both ends of all pieces before changing the set-up. Work slowly and carefully.

161

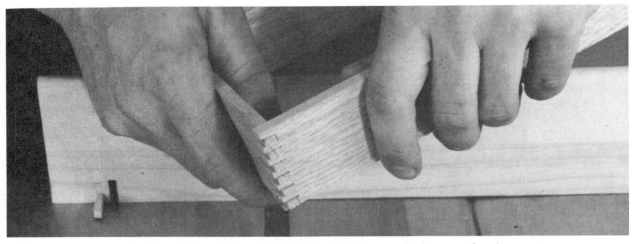

Fig. 333. Test fit shows that careful set-up is worthwhile. There is just enough clearance for glue.

Cutting Edge Joints

Edge joints are often just glued together without any reinforcement. For certain edge joints, a spline or tongue-and-groove reinforcement improves the joint. Splines are commonly used when banding the edges of plywood with solid stock. Tongue-and-groove joints are used to line up pieces that are not perfectly true. Gluing and clamping pieces with a tongue-and-groove joint usually makes the glued panel much truer.

Tongue-and-Groove Joint   Tongue-and-groove joints are best cut with the moulding or shaper head. Install the groove cutters in the shaper head and mount it on the table saw. Adjust the fence so that the center of the groove cutter is aligned with the center of the work (Fig. 334). Be sure the auxiliary fence is attached to the fence before making any adjustments. In most woods, the groove can be made with 1 cut (Fig. 335). Very hard wood may require 2 cuts to shape the groove.

Set up a featherboard to help you control the stock. Make a trial cut and any minor adjustments before you begin. Cut the groove on 1 edge of all pieces. *Note*: If you are making a panel, the first piece should not have a groove, and the last piece should not have a tongue.

After all grooves have been cut, remove the shaper head. Remove the groove cutters and replace them with the tongue cutters. Mount the shaper head and re-adjust the fence (Fig. 336). Tongues may require 2 successive cuts (Fig. 337). This is because twice as much stock is removed . Make a trial cut to determine correct depth of cut. Make sure the tongue lines up with the groove before cutting any parts (Fig. 338).

Work slowly and carefully when shaping tongue-and-groove joints. Guide the stock with featherboards and push sticks. Avoid defective pieces or pieces with loose knots. Straight-grained pieces shape easily; pieces with slanted grain may kick back. Lighter cuts minimize the chance of kickback.

A tongue-and-groove joint may also be cut with a dado head. The groove is cut first. Then, 2 rabbets are cut to make the tongue. More cuts may be needed when using the dado head, and the surfaces of the tongues and grooves will not be as smooth.

Glue Joint   A glue joint is a form of edge joint similar to a tongue-and-groove joint. It is cut with a shaper head. The center of the cutter is lined up with the center of the work (Fig. 339). All parts are cut with this set-up. This is because the cutter is a mirror image of itself from the centerline.

Feed stock slowly across the cutter head (Fig. 340). Use a featherboard to hold the stock against the fence. Check your set-up in scrap stock before you cut your work (Fig. 341).

Spline Joint   Spline joints use a thin piece of stock as a tongue. It fits into a groove cut on both pieces. Splines line up the 2 parts and provide increased gluing surface. Splines can be cut with a dado head or a single blade. The groove should be centered in the piece and no wider than ⅓ of the stock thickness. The groove must be slightly larger than the spline. This is to allow for glue.

Cut a spline joint the same way you would cut grooves (Fig. 342). The spline should be slightly deeper than it is wide. Remember to keep all exposed faces pointing towards (or away from) the fence when cutting the grooves (Fig. 343). Any error is doubled when all parts are not cut uniformly (Fig. 344). This will make it difficult to align the pieces when fitting them together (Fig. 345).

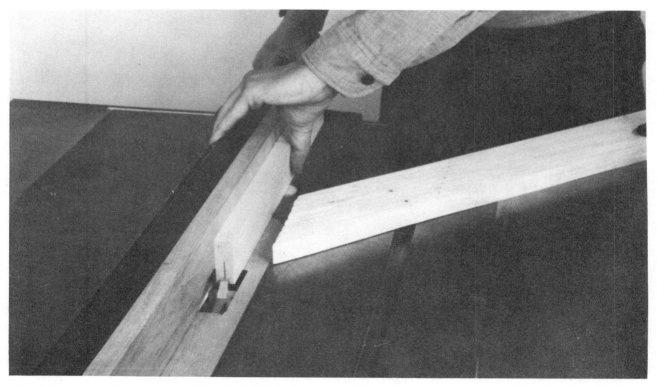

Fig. 334. When cutting a groove, adjust the fence so the center of the cutter lines up with the center of the work.

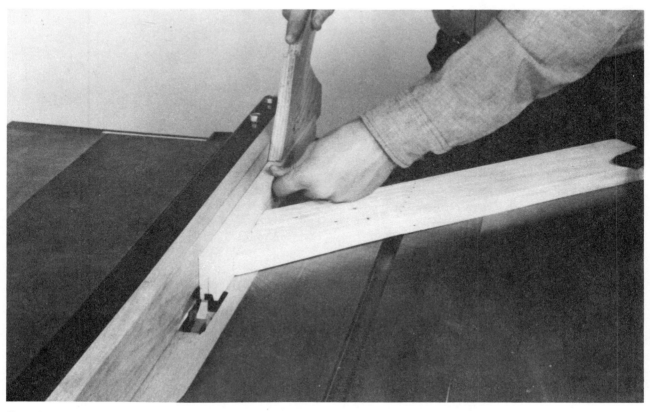

Fig. 335. A groove can usually be cut in 1 cut. Very hard wood may require 2 cuts.

Fig. 336. The tongue cutters are mounted and the center of the work is lined up with the center of the tongue.

Fig. 337. Tongues usually require 2 successive cuts. This is because twice as much stock is removed.

164

Fig. 338. Make sure the tongue and groove line up before cutting your parts. Practice stock should be the same thickness as the work.

Fig. 339. Line the center of the glue-joint cutter up with the center of the work.

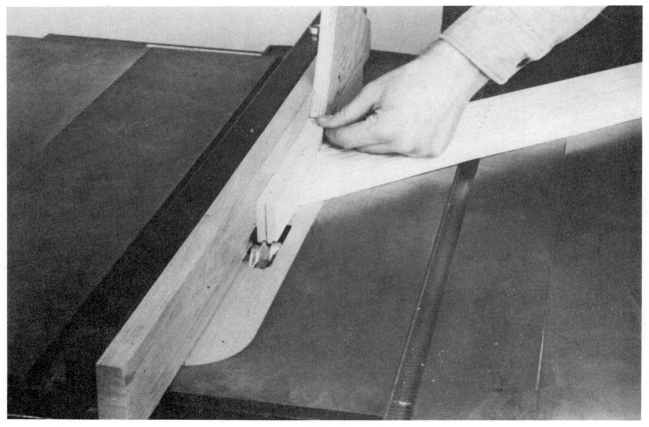

Fig. 340. Feed stock slowly across the cutter head. All parts are cut on this set-up.

Fig. 341. Test your set-up in scrap stock before you cut your work.

Fig. 342. Spline cuts are cut the same way as a groove. A spline cut is slightly deeper than it is wide.

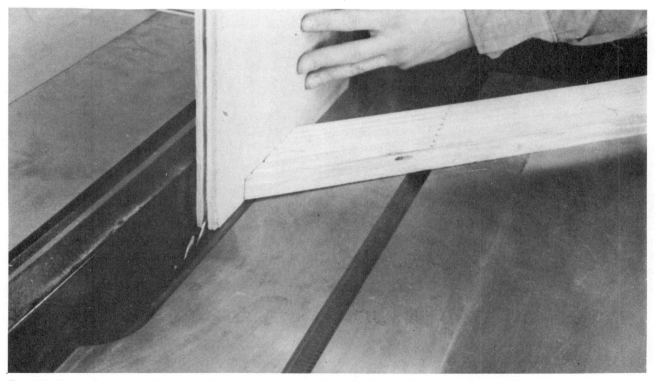

Fig. 343. Keep all exposed faces pointing towards (or away) from the fence. The error is doubled if parts do not all point the same way.

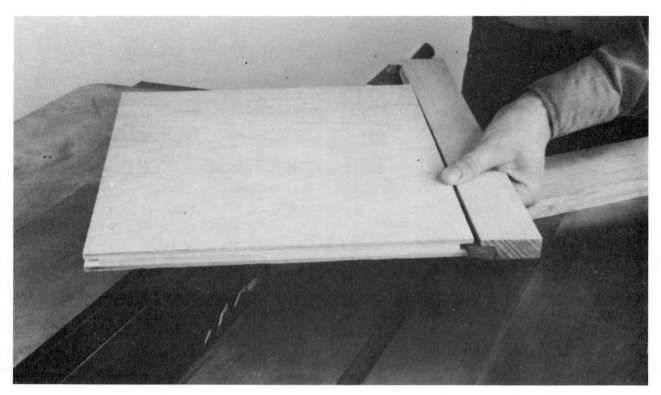

Fig. 344. The exposed side of this spline joint lines up perfectly. Plywood has been used for a spline.

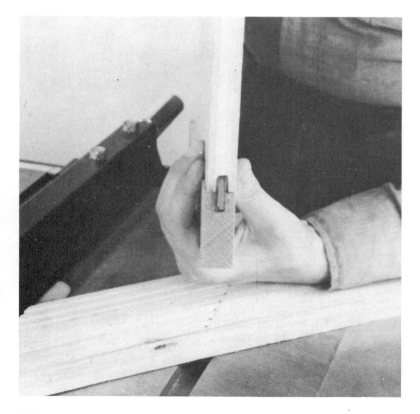

Fig. 345. The plywood and solid stock are not the same thickness, but the exposed side lines up.

Kerfing Stock for Bending

Cutting kerfs in the back of a piece of solid stock allows it to be bent easily. The apron for a round table is 1 application of kerf bending. The depth of the kerfs is about ¾ to ⅞ of the stock thickness. Shallow kerfs make the curve or arc appear to have flats opposite the kerfs.

Kerf spacing is important. The kerfs must be uniformly spaced to produce a smooth arc. To determine spacing, use a scrap about 5 inches (12.7 cm) longer than the radius of the bend. Cut a kerf about 3 inches (76 mm) from the end of the piece. Mark a line parallel to the kerf. The distance from the line to the kerf should equal the radius of the bend. Clamp the layout board with the kerf up to a true surface. Clamp it on the short side of the kerf.

Raise the long side of the board until the kerf closes. Measure the distance from the surface to the bottom of the board at the radius line. This distance equals the kerf spacing (Fig. 346).

These kerf cuts can be laid out on the stock or a spacing jig can be attached to the mitre gauge. Make a jig similar to the finger-cutting jig to space the cuts. The jig will assure uniform spacing.

The pieces can now be bent to shape (Fig. 347). Usually, glue is applied to all of the kerfs so the piece will hold the bend (Fig. 348). Some woodworkers glue a veneer to the kerf side of the bent piece to hide the kerfs (Fig. 349). Clamp the stock to a form until the glue cures (Fig. 350). *Note*: When kerfs are cut at an angle, the stock can be bent into a spiral.

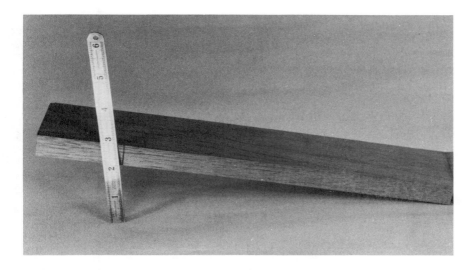

Fig. 346. In this example, the spacing between kerfs is 2 inches (51 mm).

Fig. 347. In this scrap set-up, the bend appears smooth. Note the flats that form on the face of the work. They are sometimes removed by sanding. The kerf width and kerf depth can affect spacing. They will also affect the flats, and how obvious they are.

169

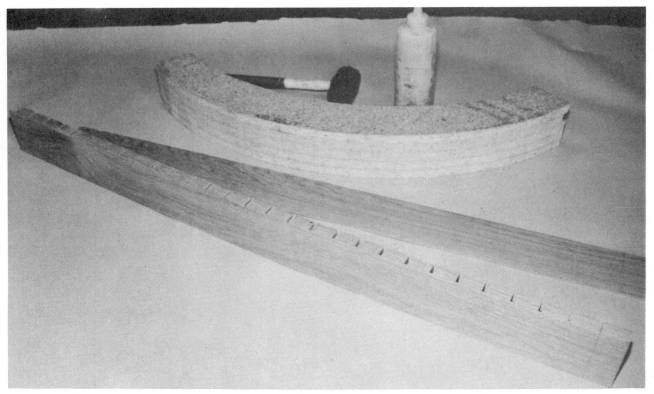

Fig. 348. This oak has been prepared for kerf bending. A layer of veneer will go on the inside to hide the kerfs and add strength.

Fig. 349. Glue is spread carefully on the veneer and the kerf side of the bent piece.

170

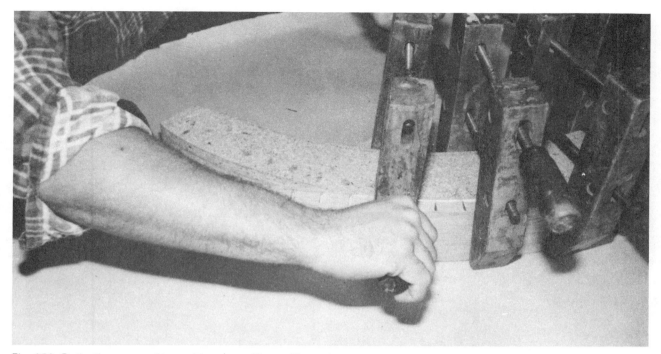

Fig. 350. Both pieces are clamped to a form. They will remain clamped until the glue cures.

Jig and Pattern Cutting

Jig and pattern cutting are commonly employed when cutting wedges, tapers and polygons. The jigs and patterns are designed for special purposes. Each of the jigs and patterns is discussed separately.

Pattern Cutting   For some shapes such as pentagons, hexagons and octagons, pattern cutting works well. The pattern can be the same size or smaller than the desired part. It is attached to the back of the workpiece with screws or nails (Fig. 351). The pattern is controlled by a guide that is attached to the auxiliary fence (Fig. 352). The workpiece slides under the guide and is cut to pattern shape by the blade.

The distance from the face of the guide to the blade must be subtracted from each side of the pattern. Lay out the pattern carefully and cut it precisely. Use a dense hardwood, plywood or particle board for pattern stock.

The pattern must be anchored securely to the workpiece. Nails or screws should be used for this purpose. On thin stock, double-faced tape may be used. Usually, the pattern is attached to the back of the work so that the nail or screw holes are not visible.

Feed stock slowly into the blade, with one side of the pattern in full contact with the guide (Fig. 353). Avoid twisting the pattern; this could cause a kickback. Make sure that pieces trimmed from the workpiece do not get caught between the fence and the blade. This could also cause a kickback. Make the workpiece size as close as possible to the desired size, as this minimizes the amount of cutting needed and the scrap size or waste. Remove scraps frequently. Avoid pattern-cutting stock greater than ¾ inch (19 mm) thick.

Cutting Wedges   Wedge cutting is done with a jig (Fig. 354). The jig is made for a specific wedge size. Wedge-cutting jigs ride along the fence. The jig is made of sheet stock or solid stock. A wedge-shaped notch is cut out along the blade side of the jig. The narrow end of the wedge is cut first. Fasten a piece of clear plastic or thin plywood over the notch. This will prevent the wedge from being thrown out of the jig as the cut is completed.

Keep the base of the jig wide enough so that your hands are always clear of the blade. A shop-made handle or the handle from a hand plane can be mounted on the jig. This will make it easier to use and control.

Place the jig on the table and move the fence into position. The stock is placed in the jig and fed into the blade (Fig. 355). After the first wedge is cut, turn the workpiece over. The wide side of the workpiece will now face the wide end of the notch. Push it into the jig and make another cut. Turning the work over between cuts allows more wedges to be cut from the workpiece. It also keeps the grain running straight in all of the wedges (Fig. 356). Long, thin wedges can be used as an inexpensive clamping device (Fig. 357).

171

Fig. 351. Patterns are usually attached to the back of the work with screws or nails.

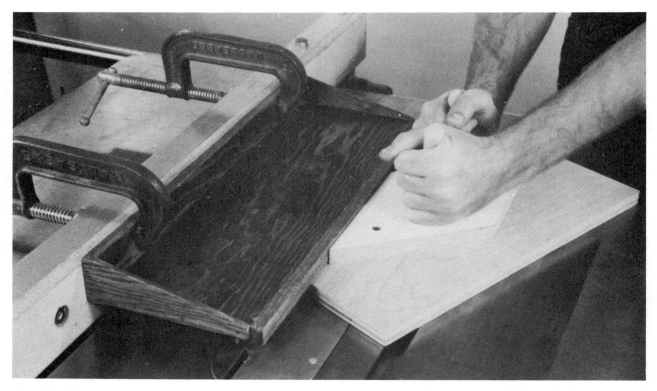

Fig. 352. The pattern is controlled by a guide that is attached to the fence. The accuracy of the work depends on the accuracy of the pattern and guide.

Fig. 353. Feed the stock slowly into the blade. Keep the pattern in contact with the guide. Avoid twisting the pattern.

Fig. 354. This jig is designed to cut small wedges. The notch holds the wedge as it is cut.

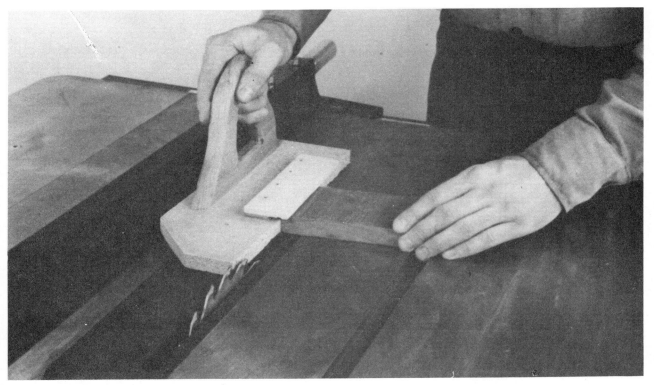

Fig. 355. Stock is fed into the blade while it is in contact with the jig. The strip of wood over the jig keeps the wedge from being forced upwards.

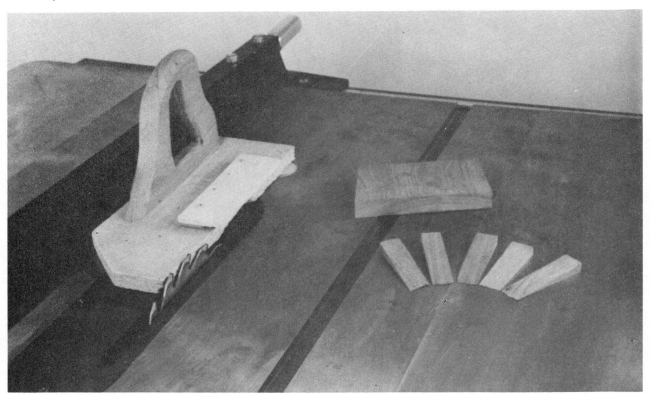

Fig. 356. The wedges have straight grain if the work is flipped over after each cut.

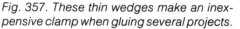

Fig. 357. These thin wedges make an inexpensive clamp when gluing several projects.

Cutting Tapers Tapers are inclined surfaces along the edge of a board. A jig is used to cut a taper. Some jigs are single purpose, and others are adjustable. A taper is measured or laid out by the amount of incline in a foot (30.5 cm). A taper of ⅜ inch (10 mm) per foot (30.5 cm) would equal ¾-inch (19-mm) incline on a board 2 feet (61.0 cm) long.

A single-purpose jig can be made from a piece of sheet stock (plywood or particle board). Select a piece 1–2 inches (25–51 mm) longer than the stock that will be used. Square up the piece you will be using. Lay out 2 steps on the edge of the piece. One step is equal to the taper per foot. The other step is equal to twice the taper per foot.

On a piece 18 inches (45.7 cm) long, with a taper of ½ inch per foot (12 mm in 300 mm), the first step would be ¾ inch (19 mm). The second step would be 1½ inch (38 mm). The single-purpose jig will be capable of cutting a single- or double-edge taper.

To make this jig, cut away the stock along the layout line using the rip fence. Finish up the cuts with a hand saw or band saw. The jig is now ready to cut tapers.

Adjustable taper jigs can be purchased or built in the shop (Fig. 358). Shop-built jigs are made from solid stock 3 inches (76 mm) wide and 24 inches (61.0 cm) long. Two pieces are needed. Cut a dado at 1 end of each part for the

hinge (Fig. 359). Join the parts with a butt hinge (Fig. 360). A cleat is fastened to the opposite end of 1 piece (Fig. 361). With the hinge pointing away from you and the cleat on your left, fasten an adjusting mechanism at the back of the jig. This mechanism can be part of a lid support (Fig. 362).

Screw the stationary end to the top of the right wing of the jig. A hanger bolt is installed in the left wing of the jig. The sliding part of the lid support is placed over the hanger bolt. A washer and a wing nut provide the clamping force that holds the jig at the desired setting.

Measure back from the hinge end of the jig exactly 1 foot (30.5 cm). Scribe a line across both wings at this point (Fig. 363). The distance between the wings at this point is the taper per foot. Any taper per foot adjustment is made at this point. The taper jig is now ready for use.

Either taper jig rides along the fence (Fig. 364). The starting point of the taper is lined up with the blade. The fence is adjusted so that the jig is touching the fence while it holds the work in position. The fence is locked in place, and the taper may be cut (Fig. 365).

When both sides of the work are to be tapered, the second edge is cut using the second step of the single-purpose jig (Fig. 366). The adjustable jig must be opened to twice the taper per foot. Make this adjustment at the 1-foot line scribed on the jig.

175

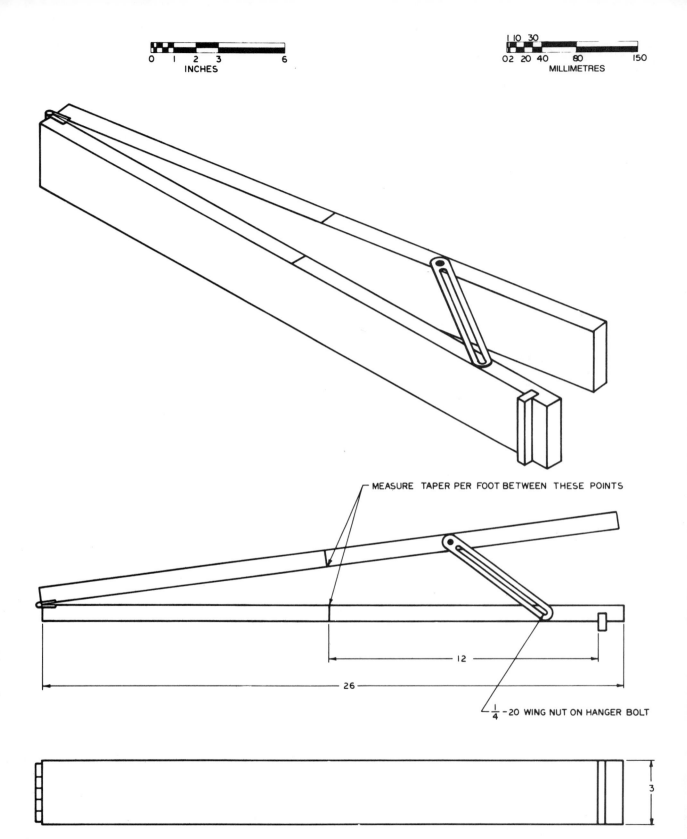

INCHES

MILLIMETRES

MEASURE TAPER PER FOOT BETWEEN THESE POINTS

12

26

$\frac{1}{4}$ -20 WING NUT ON HANGER BOLT

3

Fig. 358. These drawings show how to make a taper jig for your shop.

Fig. 359. Make a small dado at the ends of both parts of the taper jig. Smooth the bottom with a chisel.

Fig. 360. Locate and install a butt hinge in the dado.

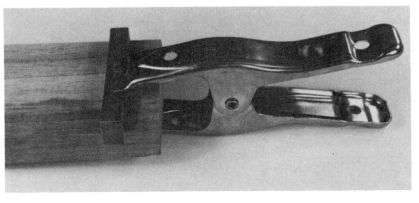

Fig. 361. Fasten a cleat in the opposite end of 1 piece. Cut a small dado and glue it in.

177

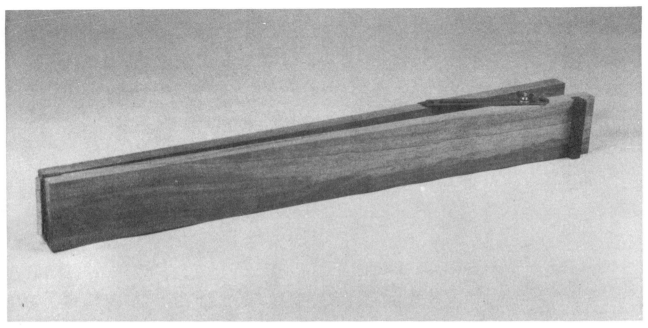

Fig. 362. The mechanism on this tapering jig is a lid support. A hanger bolt and wing nut lock the moving end of the lid support.

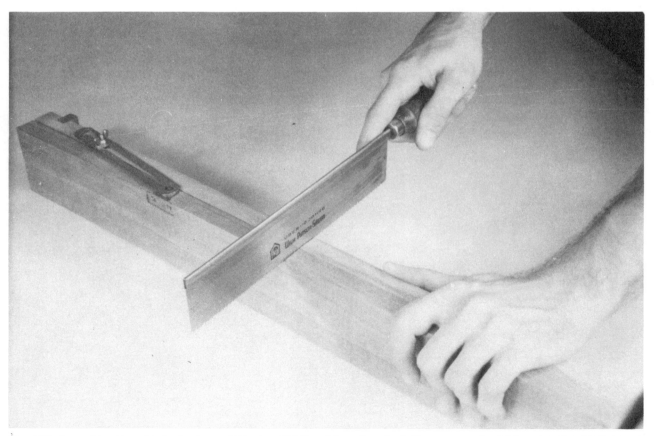

Fig. 363. A small kerf is cut in both pieces 12 inches (30.5 cm) from the cleat. Measurements at this point give the taper per foot.

Fig. 364. This commercial taper jig is being used to make a simple taper cut.

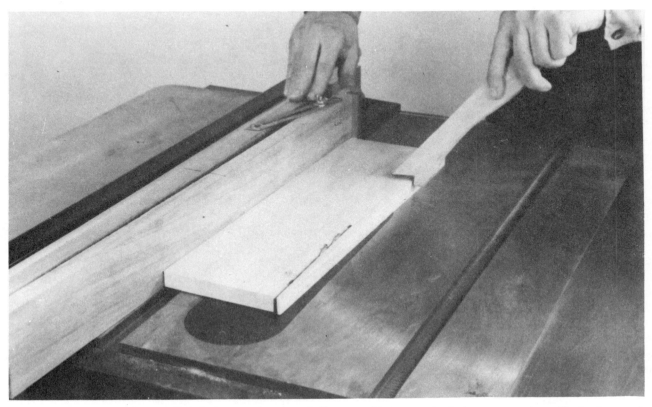

Fig. 365. This shop-made taper jig is being used to cut a similar taper. Make sure the jig is set correctly and locked securely before you begin.

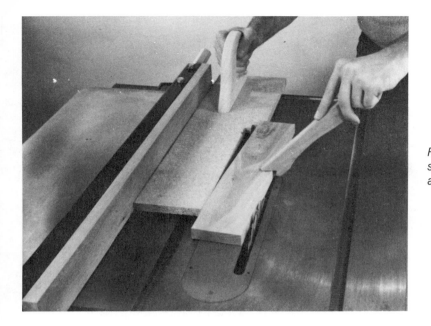

Fig. 366. This taper jig is next used to cut a second taper on the work. Note the comfortable handle on the jig.

Cutting Circles Circles can be cut on the table saw with a special sawing fixture (Fig. 367). This fixture has a center pin on which the work pivots, and a clamp to hold the piece while the cut is made. There are 2 positions for the clamp. The outer position is used until the piece becomes an octagon, then the clamp is shifted to the inner position.

The procedure is simple; first place the work over the pin. A blind hole is drilled in the back of the work. This hole fits over the pin (Fig. 368). The piece is clamped in place, and the 4 corners are cut off (Fig. 369). The clamp is now moved to the inner position, and cutting continues (Fig. 370). By turning the work a few degrees between cuts, it will become a circle. The tangent cuts make a smooth edge. Use a sanding disc to make it smoother.

All circle-cutting fixtures must be custom-made for the work being done. The distance from the center of the pin to the blade determines the radius of the work you cut. The clamping device must be mounted in relation to that radius.

Cutting Irregular Parts on the Table Saw Parts with an irregular shape cannot be guided or controlled easily with the fence or mitre gauge. Parts of this type must be controlled with a fixture designed for the part. Cutting a diamond (Fig. 371) would be difficult without the fixture. The steep angle of the sides would make control on the mitre gauge difficult. The clamping mechanisms are located to hold the part in all 4 cuts. The part is turned over for the third and fourth cuts (Fig. 372).

Whatever the shape of the work, it can be held against a similar fixture for cutting. Consider the shape of the part when you make the fixture. Locate the clamping devices where they will do the most good. Remember, irregularly shaped parts *must* be held securely while they are cut.

Cutting Plastic Laminates In small shops, plastic laminate sheets are cut on the table saw. A fine-cutting carbide blade works best. Since the laminate is very thin, an auxiliary fence is often clamped to the fence. This keeps the laminate from sliding under the fence.

Plastic laminates are very hard. This causes them to resist cutting. They climb over the saw blade. A featherboard can eliminate this problem. It holds the laminate in place (Fig. 373) while the cut is made.

When long sheets of plastic laminates are being cut, the counter-blank can be used to support the laminate while it is cut. Lay the counter-blank on 2 saw horses in front of the saw. The laminate can rest on the counter-blank while the cut is made. This process eliminates unrolling the laminate as it is fed into the saw. This approach also minimizes any chance of breakage.

Sometimes laminated counters are cut on the saw. Again, a fine-cutting carbide blade works best. When a counter-blank is laminated on both sides, the bottom laminate tends to chip or tear out when it is cut.

For cabinetmakers who cut laminated blanks frequently, a scoring table saw is desirable. It is designed to eliminate tear-out. The scoring table saw has 2 circular saw blades. The smaller blade at the front of the table scores the bottom laminate. The larger blade then cuts through the piece. Both blades cut in the same plane. This means that the larger blade exits through the kerf made with the scoring blade. Tear-out is eliminated with the scoring saw.

Fig. 367. This sawing fixture is used to cut circles on the table saw.

Fig. 368. The blind hole in the work fits over the pin on the fixture. The wing nut exerts the force needed for clamping.

Fig. 369. The first step is to cut off the 4 corners. The stock is clamped securely while the cut is made.

Fig. 370. The circle begins to appear as more cuts are made. The clamping device was moved closer to the work for these cuts.

182

Fig. 371. This diamond would be difficult to cut without a fixture. Steep angles on the work require a fixture like this.

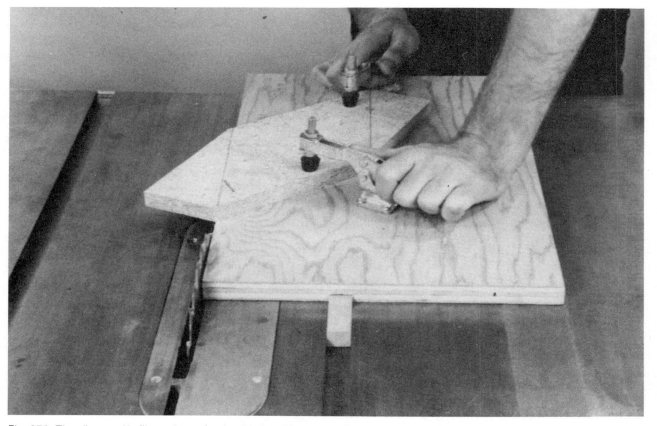

Fig. 372. The diamond is flipped over for the third and fourth cut. Placement of these industrial clamps is determined by the shape of the work.

183

Fig. 373. The auxiliary fence keeps the plastic laminate from creeping under the fence. The featherboard holds the laminate down and acts as a guard.

Making Cabinet Doors

Most cabinet doors consist of a frame around some type of panel. The panel may be glass, cane, solid stock or plywood. The joinery and the panel differ from the door style.

Frame and panel doors can be flush, ⅜-inch (10-mm) rabbet or overlay (Fig. 374). Flush doors sit in the door frame. Rabbeted doors have a ⅜-inch (10-mm) rabbet on all edges. The door sits inside the door frame. The door is actually larger than the opening. Overlay doors are also larger than the door frame. They simply cover the opening.

Flush doors are the most difficult to fit. This is because the door frame and the door must both be square for a nice fit. When the door and door frame are out of square, hand fitting and planing are required.

Rabbeted doors are easier to fit. The door is cut ½ inch (13 mm) longer and wider than the opening. A ⅜-inch (10-mm) rabbet is cut on all edges. The rabbeted length and width of the door is reduced ¾ inch (19 mm). This allows ¼ inch (6 mm) in width and length for adjusting the door in the frame.

Overlay doors are the easiest to fit. They are cut ¾–1 inch (19–25 mm) wider and longer than the opening.

They are located over the opening and hinged. Hand work is rarely required on overlay doors.

Cope Joints Cope joints are 2-part joints (Fig. 375). They are cut with the moulding head. The panel edge of the vertical pieces (stiles) and horizontal pieces (rails) is shaped with a panel door cutter (Fig. 376). This cutter grooves the edge of the stock and leaves a decorative radius in front of the groove (Fig. 377).

The groove accommodates the panel. The radius gives the exposed side of the door a decorative shape. The door rails have to be shaped with the rail end cutter. The rail ends are held vertically for shaping. A tenoning jig is used to guide the part. The complementary shape of the edge is cut on the ends of the rails (Fig. 378). The panel is then fitted to the frame, and the door is assembled.

When shaping the door edges, be sure the pieces are marked so the best sides become the door front. Set up the shaper in the manner discussed in Chapter 5 (pages 98–105). When edge shaping, feed the stock with push sticks. Use a featherboard to hold the stock securely to the fence. Use the tenoning jig to shape the rail ends. Be sure to back the pieces with scrap. This will eliminate tear-out on the rails.

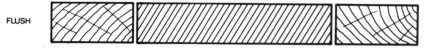

FLUSH

LIP

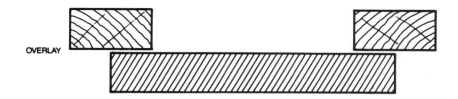

OVERLAY

Fig. 374. These are the common types of doors used on cabinets.

Fig. 375. Cope joints are 2-part joints for door corners.

Fig. 376. The panel door cutter shapes the inside edge of the rails and stiles.

Fig. 377. The panel door cutter shaped the stile on the right. The rail end was shaped with the rail end cutter.

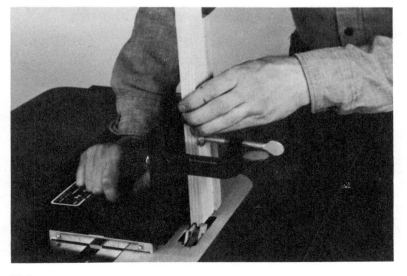

Fig. 378. The rail end cutter cuts the mating shape on both ends of the rails.

Lap Joints   Lap joints work well for doors. The stiles are completely exposed. The rails go behind the stiles and are not completely exposed. Lap joints appear to be blind mortise-and-tenon joints when the door edge is rabbeted. This is because the rabbet hides the lap joint. The easiest way to make a lap joint door is to glue up the frame and then rout a rabbet for the door panel. The rabbet is routed from the back of the door (Fig. 379). The panel is then slipped in from the back. Moulding can be made to hold the stock in place.

This door works quite well for glass panels. The glass can be held securely with moulding. The moulding also allows the panel to be changed easily in the event of breakage.

Lap joints can be cut with the tenoning jig or the dado head. The process is discussed on pages 122–128. Be sure to mark the stock before you cut the lap joints. Remember, the stile is completely visible. Lap joints are cut on the back of the stile. Part of the rail is hidden by the stile. The lap is cut on the front of the rail.

Open mortise-and-tenon joints can also be cut with the tenoning jig. These door frames are also glued up, and then routed for a panel. The stiles of these frames are completely visible, and part of the rails is hidden. The technique for cutting open mortise-and-tenon joints is discussed on pages 132–138. Mark your stock carefully before cutting the joints.

Raised Panels   Many doors use plain hardwood or plywood panels. These panels are usually ¼ inch (6 mm) thick. Raised panels are ½–¾ inch (13–19 mm) thick. They have edges that taper to ¼ inch (6 mm) and appear to be raised in the center. Raised panels are more decorative than plain panels (Fig. 380). The raised panel is first cut to the desired width and length. The typical panel is ½ inch (13 mm) thick. This thickness makes the panel even with the front of a ¾-inch (19-mm) door frame when assembled.

Fig. 379. A rabbet is routed on the back of the lap joint frame. A wood or glass panel can be held in the rabbet with moulding. Square out the corners with a chisel.

Begin by kerfing the face of the panel. Set the distance from the fence to the blade at about 1½ inch (38 mm). Raise the blade to cut a kerf ⅛ inch (3 mm) deep. Make a cut along both ends and edges (Fig. 381). There will be 4 kerfs that cross in the corners (Fig. 382).

Set the distance from the fence to the blade at slightly more than ¼ inch (6 mm). Raise the blade and tilt it so that it cuts up to the kerf. The tilt angle will be about 6°. Clamp a straightedge to the back of the panel before making any cuts. The straightedge rides along the fence and keeps the piece from pinching (Fig. 383). It also keeps the piece from dropping down through the throat plate. Make all 4 cuts with the help of a straightedge. To minimize sanding of the inclined surfaces, a fine-cutting blade should be used. Sand the surfaces completely before installing the panel in a door.

Raised panels can be used in almost any type of door frame. Coped joints and haunched mortise-and-tenon joints are the highest-quality frames for raised panels. Lap joints, open mortise-and-tenon joints and mitre joints also make a nice frame for raised panels.

When using solid panels in a door frame, be sure to allow for expansion and contraction. Make the grooves in the rails and stiles about ⅛ inch (3 mm) deeper than the panel width and length. This allows for panel movement in the frame.

Raised panels are sometimes used as lids. The decorative shape of the panel makes it appealing as a box top (Fig. 384). Cut the panel slightly larger than the box. Trim it after it is glued to the box. Box tops may be thicker or thinner than the raised panel used in a door. Adjust your cutting plan accordingly.

Mitre Joints   Doors using mitre joints give the door panel a wrapped look. The frame wraps around the panel (Fig. 385). All frame parts are grooved and shaped before the mitre joints are cut (Fig. 386). The mitering jig or 2 mitre gauges can be used to cut the mitres. It is a good idea to key the mitre joints after the door is assembled. This increases the strength of the door.

Mitre-trim doors look like mitred frame doors but require less work to make. The trim is purchased in random lengths (Fig. 387). It is mitred and glued and/or nailed around a ¾-inch (19-mm) panel (Fig. 388). The rabbet butts against the panel and leaves a ⅜-inch × ⅜-inch (10-mm × 10-mm) offset. This offset is the ⅜-inch (10-mm) lip that is common on lipped doors. After the trim is installed, the door is ready for hinges. Similar trim can be made using the shaper head on the table saw.

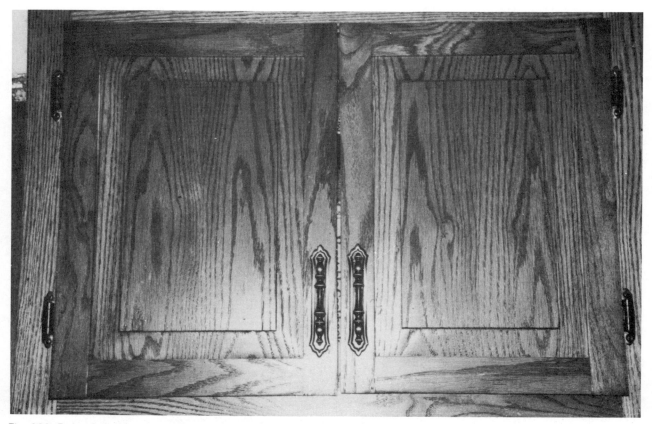

Fig. 380. Raised panels are much more decorative than plain panels.

188

Fig. 381. Make a kerf cut along all 4 edges of the panel on the exposed side.

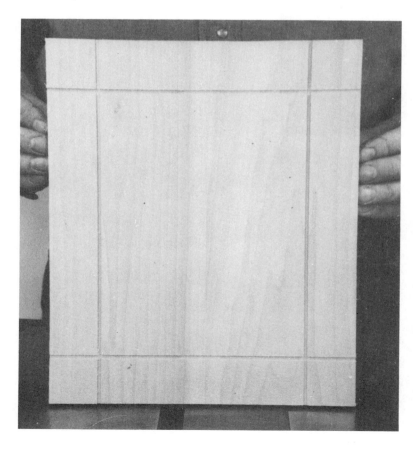

Fig. 382. The 4 kerfs cross in the corners. These kerfs form the shoulders of the raised panel.

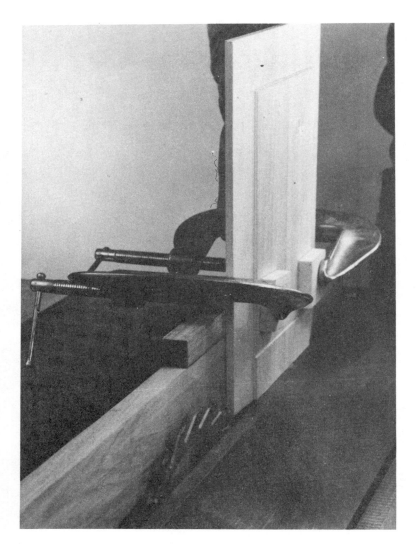

Fig. 383. A straightedge is clamped to the panel when the bevel cuts are made. If the panel is warped slightly, the straightedge pulls it into a true plane.

Fig. 384. Raised panels are sometimes used as box tops. This one will be trimmed to size after the glue dries.

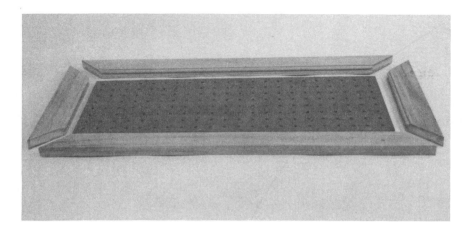

Fig. 385. The mitres give the center panel a wrapped look.

Fig. 386. This stock was shaped before the mitres were cut. Mitres on large doors and doors with glass panels require reinforcement.

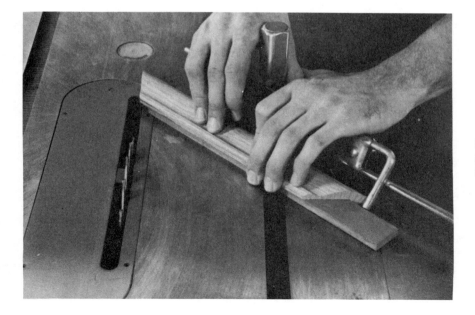

Fig. 387. Mitre trim is purchased in random lengths. It is mitred and attached to sheet stock.

191

Fig. 388. This door front has mitre trim attached to it. It is ready for hinges and fitting.

Shaping Door Edges   Most lip doors have a rabbet cut on all 4 edges. This rabbet is usually ⅜ inch × ⅜ inch (10 mm × 10 mm). The rabbet can be cut with a single blade, a dado head or a moulding head. The straight or jointing shaper cutters are used in the moulding head. Follow the procedures outlined on pages 109–131 for cutting or shaping rabbets.

Some door frames have a decorative shape cut on the exposed edge. These shapes can be made with various shaper cutters. Round-over cutters and cabinet-door lip cutters can be mounted in the moulding head for shaping the edges.

The cabinet-door lip cutter cuts a rabbet on the back of the door and a radius on the front of the door edge in 1 cut. Be sure to review shaping procedures before making this cut. Remember, harder woods will require 2 or more light cuts to shape a door edge; there is a great deal of material being removed.

Cutting Drawer Parts and Joints on the Table Saw

Cutting drawer joints and drawer parts on the table saw are common operations. Drawers, like cabinet doors, can be flush, lip or overlay. The joinery differs with the type of drawer, but the drawer sides and back are all made about the same way.

Making Drawer Parts   Most drawer parts are made from ½-inch (13-mm) stock. Drawer parts usually have a groove cut near the edge to hold the drawer bottom in place. The drawer bottom is usually ¼ inch (6 mm) thick, but may vary according to the drawer size and purpose.

The groove is at least ¼ inch (6 mm) from the edge (Fig. 389). This minimizes the chance of splitting or breakage. With some types of drawer guides, the drawer bottom must be higher to accommodate the drawer guide. The drawer guides should be selected before any drawer parts are cut.

Grooves can be cut with the dado head, moulding head or a saw blade. The dado head allows easy adjustment to slightly more than ¼ inch (6 mm). The increased size makes it easy to drop the drawer bottom in position. Always check the groove size with a piece of the stock used for drawer bottoms (Fig. 390). Too large a groove causes excess drawer rattle when it is opened or closed.

After the groove is cut, the top may be "radiused." This makes the drawer sides less likely to catch on clothing or other articles. Some pieces are radiused from end to end. Others are radiused to within 1 inch (25 mm) of the end or ends (Fig. 391). This is common with flush drawers. The square end helps guide the drawers into position and makes the joint between the side and front look neater.

To "radius" drawer sides, set up a round-over cutter in the shaper head. Use a stop block (Fig. 392) to prevent a kickback. Position the stop block so the drawer side extends about 1 inch (25 mm) beyond the cutter. With the face of the drawer side against the fence, slowly lower it onto the moulding head (Fig. 393).

Feed the piece across the cutters with a push stick (Fig. 394). Now, with the edge against the fence and the end against the stop block, slowly lower the drawer side onto the moulding head (Fig. 395). Feed the work with a push stick (Fig. 396). The finished drawer side will resemble the one in Fig. 397. Remember, if you have already cut the groove for the drawer bottom, you will have to make right- and left-hand sides.

192

Fig. 389. Use a dado head or a single blade to cut the groove for the drawer bottom. The depth of the groove should be about one-half the drawer thickness.

Fig. 390. Check groove size with the stock being used for drawer bottoms. A loose fit means the bottom may rattle. A tight fit can make drawer assembly difficult.

Fig. 391. High-quality drawers usually have square ends and a radius in the center of their length. This radius can be cut with the shaper head.

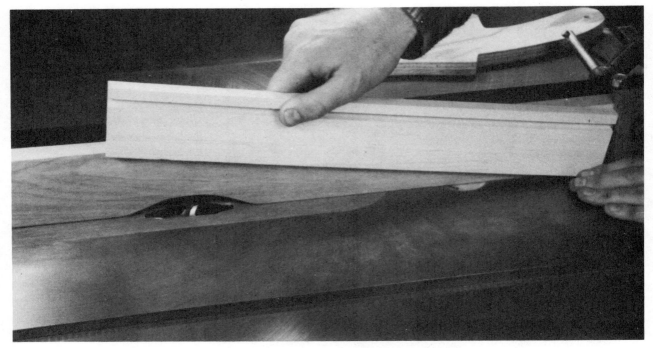

Fig. 392. The round-over cutter and a stop block are used to "radius" drawer sides.

Fig. 393. Lower the drawer side slowly onto the moulding head. The back of the drawer should be butted to the stop block. The face of the drawer should be against the fence.

Fig. 394. Feed the work across the cutters with a push stick.

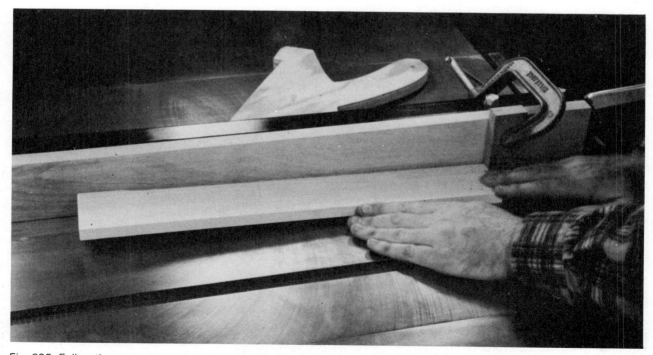

Fig. 395. Follow the same procedure for the second radius. This time, the drawer edge is against the fence.

195

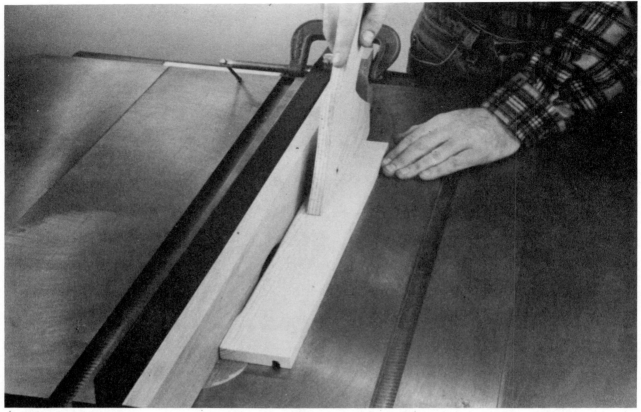

Fig. 396. Use a push stick to feed the work. Feed the stock slowly and uniformly to reduce the chance of tear-out.

Fig. 397. Here is the finished drawer side: square at the front and "radiused" to the back.

196

Overlay Drawers Overlay drawers usually have 2 drawer fronts. The decorative front is larger than the opening. It is screwed to the false front. The false front is part of the drawer assembly (Fig. 398).

The joints on an overlay drawer can be as simple as butt joints. Butt joints are glued and nailed together. A rabbet dado joint on the drawer front and a dado joint on the back make a stronger drawer (Fig. 399). Drawers made with these joints are easier to glue and assemble.

The dadoes at the back of the drawer are wide enough to accommodate the drawer back (Fig. 400). The depth is ½ the thickness of the side. Make sure you mark the sides right and left. The sides are not the same. They are mirror images of each other.

The dadoes at the front of the drawer sides are narrow (Fig. 401). They should be about ⅓ of the drawer-side thickness. A saw kerf is often wide enough. The depth of these dadoes is equal to those at the back of the drawer. When cutting this dado, the distance from the fence to the far side of the blade should equal the thickness of the false front.

Drawer backs need no dado work. They are ready to install. The false front must have a tongue cut on each end. This tongue fits the dado on the drawer side. An auxiliary fence is attached to the fence. The dado head is adjusted to cut the tongue (Fig. 402). Some of the dado head will be under the auxiliary fence.

Mark the pieces before you cut the tongue. The groove for the drawer bottom should be up when the tongues are cut. Test the fit of the drawer joints (Fig. 403). Make any needed adjustments. After the drawer is assembled, the exposed front can be attached. Screws are usually driven through the false front into the exposed front.

Fig. 398. Overlay drawers usually have 2 fronts: a decorative front and a false front. The decorative front is usually screwed to the false front.

Fig. 399. A rabbet dado joint is used between the drawer side and false front.

Fig. 400. Cut the dadoes at the back of the drawer sides large enough for the drawer back.

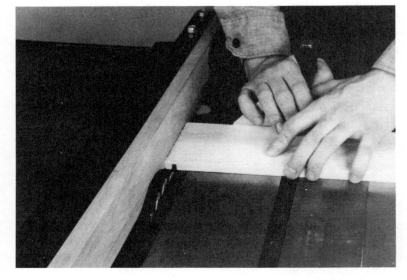

Fig. 401. The narrow dadoes at the front of the drawer sides can be cut with a saw blade.

Fig. 402. The dado head cuts the rabbet, which produces a tongue on the drawer front.

Lip Drawers   Lip drawers often have a rabbet joint at the front and a dado joint at the back. The drawer front is usually ¾ inch (19 mm). The rabbet is ⅜ inch × ⅜ inch (10 mm × 10 mm) on the top and bottom. The sides have a wider rabbet. It is ⅜ inch (10 mm) plus the drawer-side thickness.

The rabbets may be cut many different ways. The sides are glued and nailed to the rabbet joint. The drawer front must also have a groove cut for the drawer bottom. Use a drawer side to determine where the groove should be cut.

Flush Drawers   Flush drawers can be joined with many different types of drawer joints. The rabbet joint is probably the simplest joint. Rabbets are cut on both ends of the drawer front. These rabbets are slightly wider than the drawer sides to allow some clearance for fitting. The depth of the rabbets should be at least ½ the thickness of the drawer front. The sides are dadoed so the back can be joined to them.

A drawer corner is similar to a rabbet joint except the drawer front has a tongue that goes into the side for added strength. A dado is cut on both ends of the drawer front (Fig. 404). The dado is about ¼ inch (6 mm) wide (on a ¾-inch [19-mm]-thick drawer front). The depth is slightly greater than the thickness of the drawer side. The dado may be centered in the stock or off-centered so that the tongue on the drawer back is slightly smaller than the 1 on the front.

A mating ¼-inch (6-mm) dado is then cut in the drawer sides (Fig. 405). This dado should be about ¼ inch (6 mm) from the end. Remember, the right and left sides are not the same. Mark your pieces carefully before you make any cuts. The side should now fit the tongue and dado on the drawer front (Fig. 406). The tongue will now have to be trimmed so the side can be butted against the drawer front (Figs. 407–409).

A lock corner is another variation of the drawer corner.

The lock corner has a tongue on the drawer front and a tongue on the drawer side. This joint must be slid together. The back slides into dadoes in the sides. The back is not grooved. It rests on the drawer bottom. The sides and front are grooved to support the drawer bottom.

With the exception of 1 dado, drawer fronts with a drawer corner joint or a lock joint look alike. They are cut in the same way. The first dado cut on the ends of the drawer front is closer to the back (Fig. 410). The second dado cut trims the tongue and puts a dado in the front (Fig. 411).

The drawer side is then cut to fit the front. A tongue is cut on the front of the side (Fig. 412), then a dado is cut on the inner side (Fig. 413). The pieces should slide together without force. If the pieces must be forced together, the glue will make it impossible to put the parts together (Fig. 414).

Flush drawers using metal side guides can be joined with through dovetails. The drawer front is dadoed to accommodate the sides. Determine where the drawer sides should be placed. Mark the center line and cut a ¼-inch (6-mm) dado ½ inch (13 mm) deep. (Fig. 415). Lay out the dovetail over the dado. Use a saw blade to cut the dovetailed sides (Fig. 416). The bottom of the dovetail dado should be ½ inch (13 mm) wide (Fig. 417).

Cut a kerf 1/16 inch (1.5 mm) deep on each face of the ½-inch (13-mm)-thick drawer side (Fig. 418). The distance from the fence to the far side of the blade should be ½ inch (13 mm). Tilt the blade so that the sides of the dovetail can be cut.

Use a tenoning jig or straightedge to hold the pieces while the angular cuts are made on both faces (Fig. 419). Check the fit of the mating parts. They should slide together easily (Fig. 420).

The drawer back should be fitted to a dado. The drawer back will rest on the drawer bottom. It could not be installed if it were grooved.

Fig. 404. A dado is cut on both ends of the drawer front. A tenoning jig could also be used to control the work.

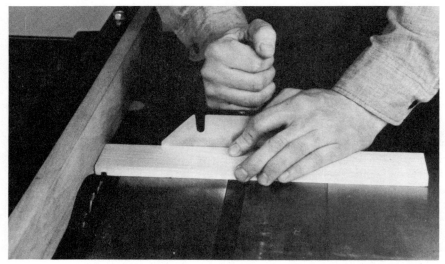

Fig. 405. A mating dado is cut into the front of the drawer sides.

Fig. 406. The dado and tongue should fit correctly. Mark the tongue length with the drawer side.

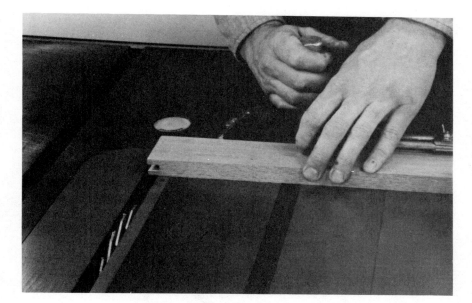

Fig. 407. Saw the tongue to correct length. A stop rod can be used to control the work.

Fig. 408. The drawer corner joint fits correctly. Careful layout makes the work rewarding.

Fig. 409. This bird's-eye maple drawer has drawer corner joints. Note the dado on the drawer side. This is for a drawer guide.

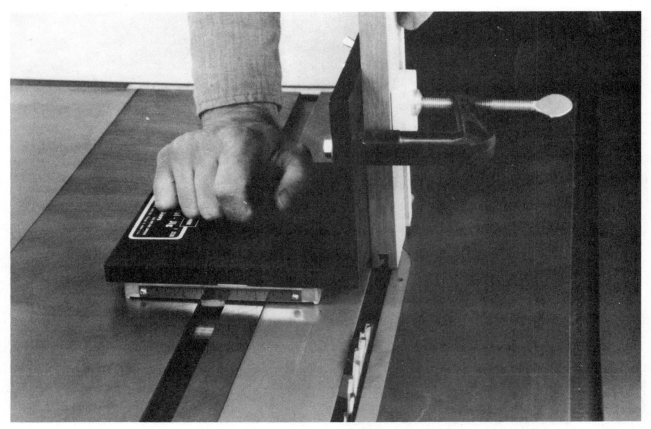

Fig. 410. The dado cut on the ends is closer to the back. A tenoning jig is being used to hold the work.

Fig. 411. The second dado cut trims the tongue as it makes the dado. A stop rod can be used to locate the cut.

Fig. 412. A tongue is cut on the front of the drawer side. The stop rod is used to locate the tongue, but the fence could also be used.

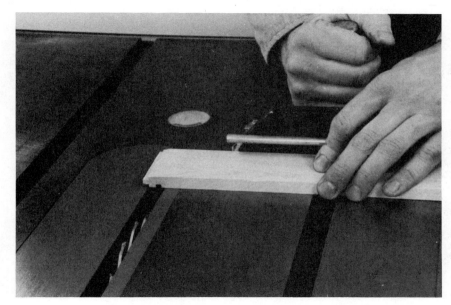

Fig. 413. A dado is cut on the inside of the drawer side. This dado matches the tongue on the drawer front.

Fig. 414. Check the fit; the pieces should slide together easily. A tight fit will be impossible to assemble when the glue is applied.

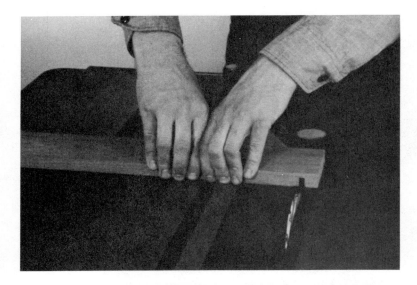

Fig. 415. A straight dado is cut in the drawer front first when making a dovetail dado joint.

Fig. 416. The blade is tilted to the desired angle to cut the angled sides in the dovetail dado joint.

Fig. 417. The angled sides are cut on the dovetail dado. The widest part of the dado should be ½ inch (13 mm). The narrowest part should be ¼ inch (6 mm). Overall dado depth is ½ inch (13 mm).

Fig. 418. Both sides of the drawer fronts are kerfed. This kerf becomes the shoulder of the dovetail.

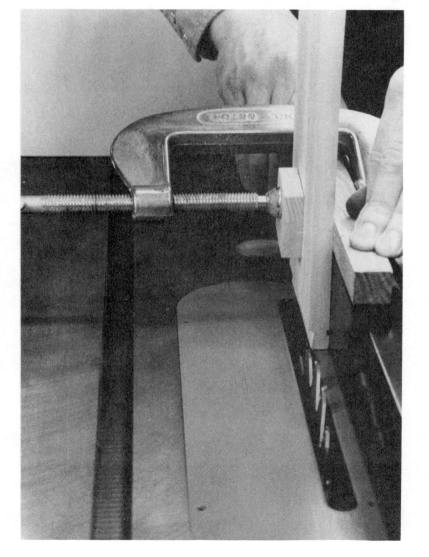

Fig. 419. A straightedge clamped to the work controls the cut. A tenoning jig could also be used to control the cut. Angular cuts are made on both sides.

Fig. 420. Check the fit between the parts. The dovetail dado should slide together easily.

Part III:
Table Saw Guidelines

7

Useful Information About Table Saws

The more you use your table saw, the greater your desire becomes to do a better, safer, more accurate job. This chapter is devoted to topics that will help you improve the job you do.

General Maintenance of Your Table Saw

Maintenance of your table saw is important. A saw that is out of adjustment makes the job more difficult and usually yields poor results. The most common maintenance area on a table saw is the blade. Keep the blade sharp and free of pitch. Review Chapter 3 for blade maintenance procedures.

Keep the table clean and protected. A light coat of paste wax reduces friction between the table and the work (Fig. 421). On cast-iron tables, the wax will also inhibit corrosion.

Clean the table saw frequently. Keep chips and sawdust from accumulating under the motor and elevating and tilting mechanisms (Fig. 422). When sawdust gets packed around the motor or control mechanisms, problems can result. The motor can overheat or the chips and sawdust can become packed in the control mechanisms. This will make them difficult to operate, and can cause the failure of gears or their teeth. Changing gears on a table saw is time-consuming and unnecessary. The parts

are usually quite expensive. Often their cost equals the down payment on a new table saw.

Lubricate the saw according to the manufacturer's specifications. These specifications are normally found in the owner's manual. Do not over lubricate. Too much oil on the control mechanisms can cause chips to be impacted between gear teeth. Some paste waxes and silicone spray lubricants will work as a substitute for oil. They do not attract sawdust like the oil does.

When lubricating the control mechanisms, check them for sawdust accumulation. Use a pitch remover and a wire brush to remove any accumulated sawdust.

A visual inspection of the saw during lubrication can identify potential problems. Look at the cord and electrical supply lines. Be sure they are not cut or frayed. Check the castings and stand for loose nuts and bolts. They increase saw noise and vibration, and can cause increased wear between 2 loose parts.

Surface rust can be removed from an iron table with auto rubbing compound and a wool bonnet (Fig. 423). Work slowly and carefully; use the rubbing compound liberally. After the table is clean, apply a coat of paste wax. If the saw is to be stored for any length of time, lightly oil any surface that may rust before storing. The oil can be removed later with mineral spirits or other solvents. The oil is much easier to remove than rust.

Fig. 421. Paste wax reduces friction on the table and inhibits corrosion.

Fig. 422. Clean the motor housing and the control mechanisms frequently. Chips can become packed around the motor or control mechanisms and cause problems.

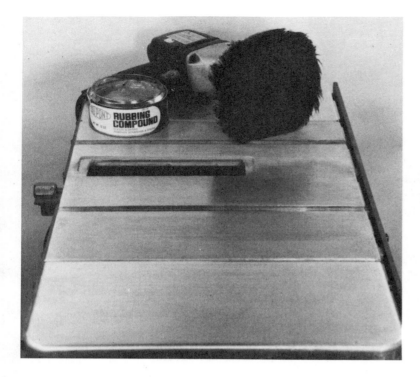

Fig. 423. Auto-rubbing compound and a wool bonnet can restore an oxidized table.

Improving Table Saw Accuracy

One of the most common accuracy problems is the relationship between the blade and the table. Many times, the blade is not parallel to the mitre slots in the table. This causes heeling; that is, the blade is not parallel to the saw cut.

Heeling is hard on the blade. It sometimes causes excess vibration in the blade. To check for heeling, disconnect the saw and raise the blade to full height. Measure the distance from a selected tooth to the mitre slot. Do this at the front of the table, and record the distance (Fig. 424). Now, roll the blade to the back of the table. Using the same tooth, measure the distance to the mitre slot (Fig. 425). Record this number and compare your findings. If the distance is not the same at the front and back, the saw must be adjusted.

On some table saws, the table must be turned to eliminate the heeling problem. Loosen the bolts at the 4 corners and turn the table. On other table saws, you must turn the trunnion (tilting and elevating mechanism that is bolted to the bottom of the table). Check the owner's manual before making any adjustments.

After the table is lined up, square the mitre gauge to the blade and adjust the fence. The fence is locked in position next to the mitre slot. If it is parallel to the mitre slot, no adjustment is needed. Most fences have a bolt or 2 on top. These bolts are loosened and the fence is adjusted (Fig. 426). Some are adjusted with the fence

locked in position, and others are not. Consult the owner's manual for details.

The blade itself may also affect table saw accuracy. A blade that vibrates while cutting makes an uneven cut. If heel has been corrected, vibration may be caused by a warped blade, a dull blade or a blade with too thin a rim.

Check for warp with a pencil. Disconnect the saw and place the point of a pencil against the blade (Fig. 427). Slowly turn the blade while watching the pencil point. If the blade moves the pencil or a gap appears between the blade and pencil, the blade is warped. Try it again with a true blade. If the condition still exists, the arbor washers are worn or the arbor is not running true. Consult with a machinist or machinery repairman if you believe the arbor is not running true.

A thin blade will sometimes vibrate excessively. You can minimize this problem with blade collars. The collars give the blade increased rigidity.

Looseness or slop between the mitre slot and mitre gauge can affect crosscut accuracy. It is possible to tighten the fit between the gauge and slot. This is done by offsetting the metal tongue to make it larger. A ball-peen hammer is used to tap the tongue until the fit is tighter. This must be done slowly or the tongue will be too large for the slot.

If the mitre gauge is worn, a new mitre gauge may improve the fit. Holding the mitre gauge firmly against 1 side of the slot will increase accuracy when the fit is loose. Hold the gauge and stock firmly. Keep the tongue engaged with 1 side of the slot, and feed the work into the blade at a uniform speed. For most work, this cut will be accurate enough.

An improperly set splitter can affect ripping and crosscutting accuracy. The splitter is supposed to go through the kerf to keep the parts separated (split) (Fig. 428). This reduces the strain on the blade. If the splitter is not aligned with the blade, it may push the work away from a straight line (Fig. 429).

Changing blades or adding blade collars will affect the alignment between the blade and splitter. Check the alignment whenever blade changes are made.

Table extensions or a throat plate that is too high or low can also affect cutting accuracy. Check them with a straightedge to be sure they are aligned correctly. Some stamped throat plates and extensions are not true. Adjust their high point even with the table height (Fig. 430).

Fig. 424. Check for "heeling" by first measuring the distance from the mitre slot to the blade. Do this at the front of the table with the blade at full height. Make sure the power is disconnected.

Fig. 425. Use the same tooth to measure the distance at the back of the table. A difference between the 2 measurements means the saw must be adjusted.

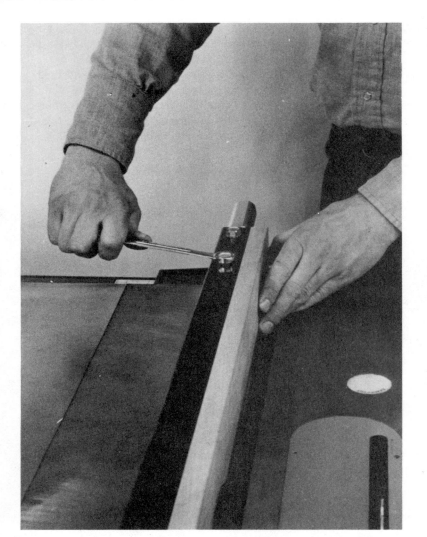

Fig. 426. The fence is adjusted parallel to the mitre slot. The bolts on the fence lock it to the desired setting.

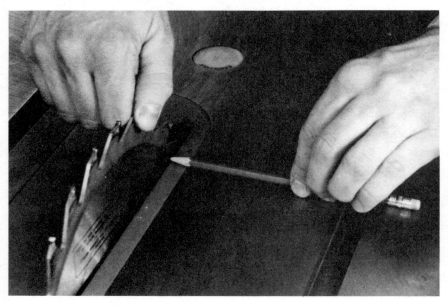

Fig. 427. A pencil may be used to check for a warped blade. Rotate the blade slowly. Make sure the power is disconnected.

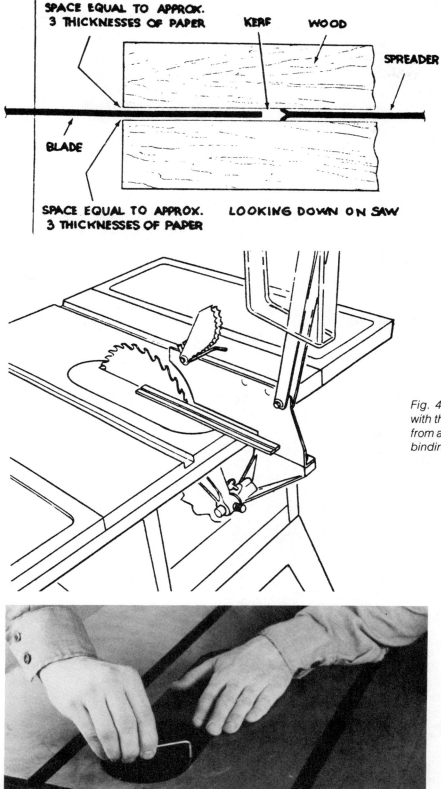

SPACE EQUAL TO APPROX. 3 THICKNESSES OF PAPER

KERF   WOOD

SPREADER

BLADE

SPACE EQUAL TO APPROX. 3 THICKNESSES OF PAPER   LOOKING DOWN ON SAW

Fig. 428. The splitter, or spreader, keeps the kerf open while cut is made. This reduces the strain on the blade.

Fig. 429. Make sure the splitter is aligned with the blade, or it may push the work away from a straight line. It could also cause blade binding.

Fig. 430. A high or low throat plate can sometimes affect accuracy. Check it to be sure it is even with the table.

213

Layout Techniques at the Saw

Many errors in measurement are caused by an incorrect layout or set-up at the saw. For example, when a rabbet is cut, the fence is set to the thickness of the piece that fits in the rabbet. First, the thickness of the piece is measured, and then the fence is set to this measurement. A ruler is used twice. This means there are 2 opportunities to make a measurement error.

A better approach would be to set the fence using a piece of stock (Fig. 431). The stock thickness is placed over the blade and against the fence. The fence can be moved into exact position without the use of a ruler. Two chances for making an error have been eliminated.

Cutting lap joints or other joints where the blade must cut to the center of the piece provides several chances for measurement error. Use 2 scraps of the correct thickness to set the blade height. No measurement is needed.

Set the blade slightly below the center of the pieces and make a cut on the end of both pieces. Flip 1 piece over and push the cut ends together. The interference between the 2 ends is exactly twice the distance that the blade must be elevated.

Raise the blade slightly and check the pieces. Continue this process until the blade is adjusted (Figs. 432–434). It is important that the blade be elevated only during the process. Lowering the blade may cause creep. The slope or lash in the gears will allow the elevating mechanism to slowly drop from its adjusted height. As you practice this method of setting blade height, you will find it to be easier and more accurate than any measuring method.

Some table saws have a plastic circle set in the table. This circle is used to mark the blade's path. A line scribed on this circle can be matched to the layout line on your work. This will assure an accurate cut and will be very helpful when the guard blocks your vision. The scribed line may be not accurate when the blade is changed or saw collars are added. Additional marks will have to be scribed.

To scribe marks on any saw, clamp a scrap to the mitre gauge. Cut a kerf into, but not through, the scrap. Move the mitre gauge towards the front of the table and scribe both sides of the kerf (Fig. 435). Use a scratch awl for a permanent line, and a pencil for a temporary line.

Fig. 431. Using a piece of stock to set the fence assures an accurate setting.

Fig. 432. The space between these 2 blocks means the dado head is too high.

Fig. 433. The interference between these 2 blocks means the dado head is too low.

Fig. 434. The blocks fit together correctly. The dado head is set correctly.

215

Fig. 435. A scratch awl can be used to mark the table for the path of the saw blade. Changing blades or adding blade stabilizers will affect the accuracy of these marks.

Minimizing Tear-Out Problems

Grain tear-out is an annoying problem at the table saw. Tear-out may occur at the back, top or bottom of the piece. If the wrong blade or a dull blade is used, tear-out is sure to occur. A rip blade will usually cause tear-out when crosscutting. Dull blades pound through the wood and cause tear-out. Feeding too fast can also cause tear-out. Moderate feeding speed will reduce tear-out.

One of the best methods of eliminating tear-out through the back of your work is by placing a piece of stock behind it. The tear-out occurs in the stock behind the workpiece. Attach a true piece of stock to the mitre gauge. Stock butted firmly to this piece will not tear out through the back.

Tear-out through the top and bottom can be controlled by taping or scoring the stock. Tape applied over the area to be cut holds the wood fibres in place. The blade cuts through the tape, and the tape holds the fibres down on both sides of the kerf (Fig. 436).

Scoring the layout line with a utility knife will cause the wood fibres to break evenly at the line (Fig. 437). A sharp utility knife must be used. The wood should be scored to a depth of 1/16 inch (1.5 mm) or greater. Scribe both faces and edges to completely control tear-out.

How Safe Is a Guard?

It is very difficult to cut yourself when the guard is in place. The guard covers the blade and minimizes the chance of contact with it. The splitter and anti-kickback pawls protect the operator from a kickback. The guard is a valuable, safe accessory for any table saw.

A guard is not perfect, however. Some intermediate and most advanced operations cannot be done with the guard in place. On the table saws in some shops, the operations are usually intermediate or advanced. In this case, the guard quickly disappears and gathers dust. If the guard is removed for an advanced operation, it is rarely replaced for simple operations.

In many shops, you will find that the table saw is never operated with a guard. Operators often feel the guard is an added hazard. Three common complaints about guards are that they limit the operator's vision, are kickback hazards and that they make it difficult to do accurate work.

For extremely accurate work, the guard makes it difficult to cut along a layout line or trim a "hair" off the piece. Also, if a cutoff gets pinched between the blade and guard, it can kick back. This is a common problem with most guards. One other problem is that the removal and replacement of the guard throws it out of alignment. The splitter then pulls the piece off a straight line cut.

Some newer types of guards can be added to an older table saw (Fig. 438). These guards can be used for most intermediate and advanced operations (Figs. 439–441). They have been criticized by some because they do not have a splitter for ripping operations. However, I have found this type of guard to be a very safe device. It is used most of the time in my introductory class. I have never had an injury occur when this guard was mounted on the saw.

It is good practice to use the guard whenever possible. When the guard cannot be used, a cautious attitude is your best defense against an accident. This attitude is displayed when you do the following when using the table saw: Limit the exposure of the blade; quit working at the first sign of fatigue; and never work while under the influence of drugs or medication. Other procedures are covered in Chapter 4. Review the chapter occasionally; make it part of your work philosophy. Approach every job with that philosophy, and your risks will be minimized.

Fig. 436. Taping the work with masking tape will prevent grain tear-out. The tape holds the fibres in place while the blade cuts through it.

Fig. 437. Scoring the faces and edges of the work with a utility knife will also prevent tear-out. Be sure the cut goes into the wood about 1/16 inch (1 mm).

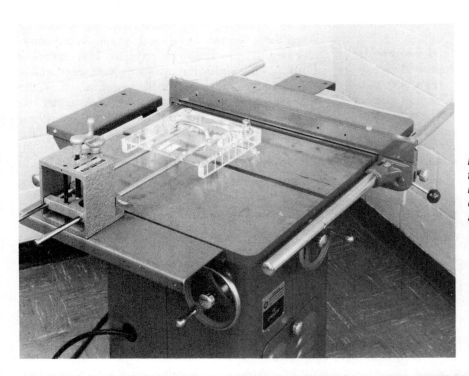

Fig. 438. This guard can be added to most table saws. The guard does not have a splitter, but it is the most effective guard for advanced operations.

Fig. 439. The mitring jig is being used with the guard. The operator cannot contact the blade with this set-up.

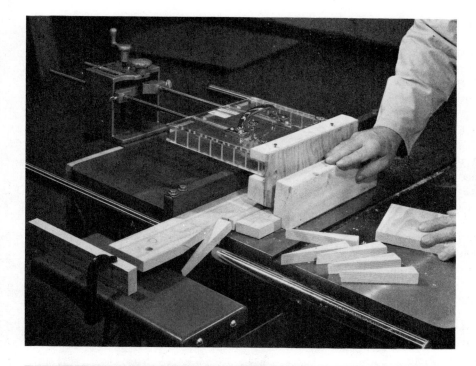

Fig. 440. This wedge-cutting set-up also guards against contact with the blade.

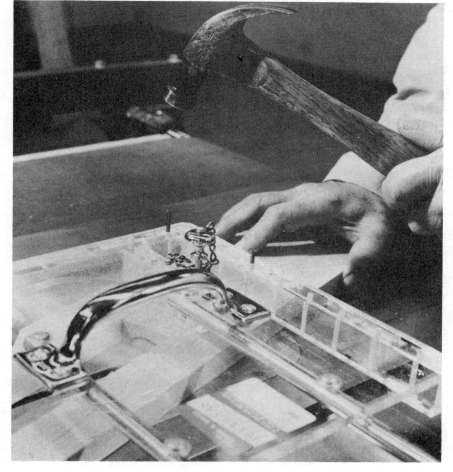

Fig. 441. The guard is being used to cut coves. The auxiliary fences are nailed to the guard.

Bringing the Table Saw to the Job

Ever since my uncle Irven mounted his table saw to the base of an old wheelbarrow, I have realized the importance of portability. Rolling casters (Fig. 442) may be more convenient than a wheelbarrow, but both are mobile.

The small table saw featured in Figs. 443 and 444 breaks down into 2 parts: the base (Fig. 443) and the saw (Fig. 444). The wooden base protects the mounting bolts and stores the cord (Fig. 445). These bolts (Fig. 446) secure the saw to the base. The guard is then attached (Fig. 447), and the saw is ready to be levelled and used.

This small saw can be carried easily to the job. It also fits nicely in the back seat of an intermediate-sized car. For long rips on the job, an extension is attached to the fence (Fig. 448). This allows support when no help is available on the job (Fig. 449).

Larger saws are sometimes needed on the job. The one in Fig. 450 was brought up by elevator to the third floor of a bank. A shop was set up to remodel the entire floor.

When working on the job, be sure the electrical supply is compatible with your saw. I burned up a motor using a circuit that was fused too high for the motor. The fuse attached to the motor (Fig. 451) protects me from another expensive error.

Fig. 443. This small base is easily moved to the job

Fig. 442. Rolling casters make the table saw more portable.

Fig. 444. This small saw is easily moved by 1 person. It can be attached to the base at the work site.

220

Fig. 445. The wooden base holds the cord inside the saw and protects the bolts from damage.

Fig. 446. These bolts are used to secure the saw to the base.

Fig. 447. The guard is attached after the saw is set up.

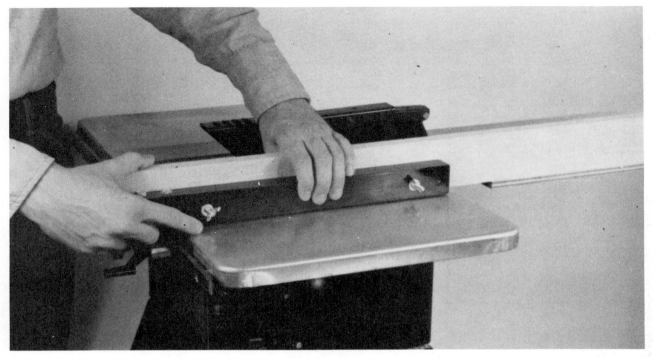

Fig. 448. This extension can be attached to the fence for long rips.

Fig. 449. This extension supports the stock when no helper is available.

Fig. 450. This table saw was transported to the third floor of a bank for a remodelling job. The office space became our workshop for the entire job.

Fig. 451. The fuse attached to the motor protects it from burning up when connected to a high-amperage circuit.

223

Buying a Table Saw

Buying a table saw is similar to buying a car. When buying a new car, you know what options you want and how much you are willing or able to pay. When you buy a used car, your choice is limited to what is available. You may not get exactly what you want, but you save money.

The same is true of a table saw. A new saw can be equipped to suit your needs. Everything is under warranty, and no one has abused the tool. A used table saw, however, is like a used car. You must take the previous owner's word about the condition of the saw and how it was used. There is no warranty, and most repairs will be made by the owner.

A New Saw   When you decide to buy a new table saw, the saw should fit your needs. Some of the following questions will help you determine what type of table saw fits your needs:

1.   What type of stock will I be cutting? What is the thickest, widest and longest piece I will cut?
2.   How large a table and blade will be needed to handle the stock I will be cutting?
3.   Is the shop space large enough to accommodate the table saw? A clear space 8 feet (2.4 m) wide by 16 feet (4.9 m) long is desirable. Smaller areas can be used, but stock size will be limited.
4.   What type of electrical service is available? What voltage, amperage and phase? For home use, a 110-volt circuit of 20 amps is needed. A 220-volt circuit of 10 amps will also work. A single phase is used exclusively in the home. A 3-phase system is available for industrial use. It is used at voltages of 220 and above.
5.   Under what budget constraints am I working? What price range is desirable? Could options be added later to keep the initial price lower?
6.   Should the table of the saw be cast iron, cast aluminum, stamped steel or a composition material? Generally, cast iron minimizes vibration best, but in a damp basement cast aluminum may be better because it does not rust. Many of the composition materials resist rust and work as well as cast iron or aluminum.
7.   Should the table saw be motorized or motor driven? Generally, motorized saws will not cut as deeply as motor-driven saws with the same blade diameter. This is because the motor limits the blade elevation. Motorized saws are usually louder than motor-driven saws. Motor-driven saws usually have less vibration than motorized saws, but the mass (weight) of the elevating mechanisms can also affect this (Figs. 452 and 453). More mass usually means less vibration. More than 1 belt (Fig. 454) also means more power and less chance of slippage.

8.   What accessories are standard, and what other accessories will I need? Most table saws come with a guard (Figs. 455 and 456) a fence, mitre gauge and throat plate. A sliding table may be standard on some table saws (Fig. 457).

Accessories like a moulding head, dado head, extra throat plates and additional mitre gauges will raise the initial cost of the saw. It is nice to have an extra mitre gauge. The convenience of 2 mitre gauges is worth the slight cost increase. One mitre gauge can be left at 90°, while the other can be set at any desired angle. The 2 may be used as a team when cutting mitres.
9.   What horsepower is needed to power the table saw adequately? This will depend on the stock you will be cutting and the blade diameter used on the saw. The discussion in Chapter 1 (page 16) will help you determine needed horsepower.
10.   How does the fence lock to the table? Some work easier and are more accurate than others. How about the mitre gauge; is it a tight fit? Mitre slop also means accuracy problems. Constant adjustment of a table saw is aggravating. You cannot use the saw if you are adjusting it.

The planning sheet (Fig. 458) will help you put your needs on paper. You can fill in motor and saw specifications. The saw weight is included here because some woodworkers feel that the weight of the saw can be an indicator of quality. This tends to favor cast iron, but this should not be the only consideration.

At the bottom of the planning sheet you can list table saws that meet your specifications. The list price can be noted and any general comments, such as accessories included, or how the fence locks to the table.

After you determine which table saw(s) will meet your needs, ask some experts for their opinion of the saw. People who use the saw will be able to tell you about adjustment problems, ways to repair the saw and general operation techniques, Cabinetmakers, carpenters and woodworking teachers are usually willing to share their knowledge of woodworking equipment. This knowledge will help you make a wiser purchase.

The list price is a guideline of price. Not all sales agents hold that price, so it pays to shop. Also consider shipping charges and sales tax when comparing prices. Sales tax varies in cities and states. A 30-mile ride could mean 2 percent less sales tax.

Picking up the table saw at the factory or a distribution center can also reduce the actual cost of the table saw. Be ready to bargain; table saw suppliers know an informed buyer. They may be willing to compromise to make the sale.

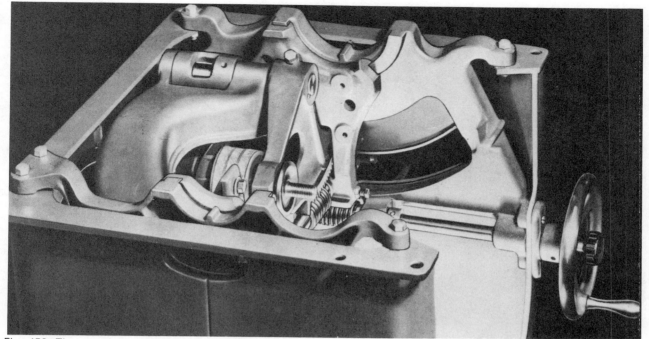

Fig. 452. The massive castings in the elevating mechanism dampen vibration and resist wear. This is considered an industrial-grade table saw.

Fig. 453. The castings are fewer and lighter in this table saw. This is considered a contractor-grade table saw.

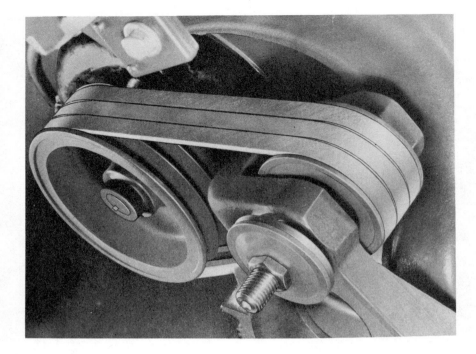

Fig. 454. The 3 belts driving the arbor mean more power and less chance of slippage. These belts must all be replaced at the same time to be sure they are the same length.

Fig. 455. The guard on this saw is not attached to the splitter. It can be used with many advanced operations.

226

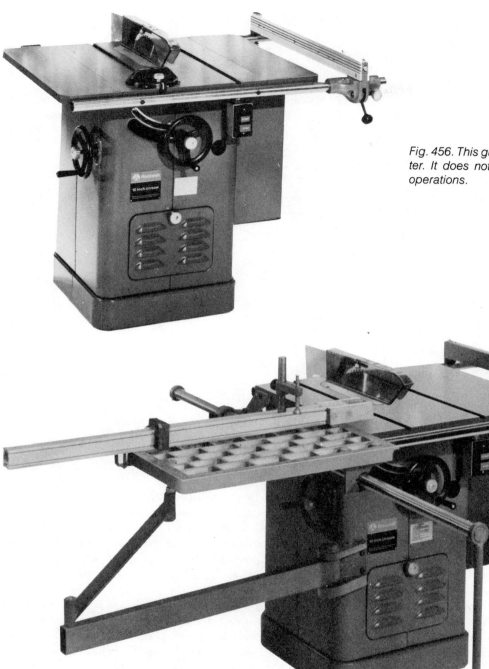

Fig. 456. This guard is attached to the splitter. It does not work well with advanced operations.

Fig. 457. This table saw is set up with a sliding table as standard equipment. This table could be added to the saw at a later date. This would keep the initial cost of the saw lower.

Desired Motor

_____Volts   _____Amps   _____Horsepower

_____Phase   _____24-volt Switch

_____T.E.F.C. (Totally Enclosed Fan-Cooled, Dust Proof)

_____Motorized   _____Motor Driven

Desired Saw

_____Blade Diameter   _____Sliding Table

_____Table Width   _____Table Length

_____Enclosed Base   _____Open Base

_____Tilting Table   _____Tilting Arbor

_____Weight   _____Table (Cast Iron, Cast
                                                Aluminum, etc.)

Desired Options (List)

_____   _____

_____   _____

Brand	List Price	Comments
1.		
2.		
3.		
4.		

Fig. 458. This planning sheet will help you determine your table saw needs on paper.

A Used Saw   The cost of a new saw may be beyond your means. In this case, a used table saw may be more appealing. Though the planning sheet will still help you focus in on your needs, the used table saw evaluation sheet (Fig. 459) can help you determine the value of any table saw you consider buying. It will help you compare 2 or more used table saws when shopping.

The brand and age of the saw are important indicators of value. Some table saws have higher resale value because of the manufacturer's reputation. The fact that parts are still available for the table saw is important too. It is very costly and sometimes impossible to have parts custom-made for a used table saw. The part could cost more than the saw is worth.

Electrical information is also important. A 3-phase motor would have to be replaced to operate the saw where only 1 phase of electricity is available. Be sure you can use the saw before you buy it.

Listing accessories helps determine value. A saw that has extra blades, a dado head and a moulding head is worth more than a basic table saw. Features or options like a sliding table or a tenoning jig can also add to the value of the saw. Be sure to list all options, features and accessories offered for sale with the table saw.

Comparing today's list price with the seller's asking price helps determine the value. If the saw is 10 years old and the price difference is small, the value may be questionable. Consider this information carefully before you buy.

The general condition of the saw is usually obvious. Check the table condition and look for rust, cracks in the castings and any signs of repair. If the saw is 5 to 10 years old and the owner still has the manual, the saw has probably been well-maintained. The manual should show some signs of wear. Pencil marks circling replacement parts or oily thumb prints indicate the manual was used on the job. If the table saw needs repair, estimate the cost of that repair. Make sure the seller's price reflects the repair, and that replacement parts are available.

When buying a used table saw, decide on a fair price before making the seller an offer. Some woodworkers refuse to pay more than 60 percent of retail price for any woodworking tools regardless of age or condition. Their rationale is that you can buy so much more with the extra

40 percent that the used tool is not worth the gamble. The 60 percent rule does not fit all sales, but it is another guideline.

When you shop for a used table saw, there are many places to look. Suppliers of new table saws often take used saws as trade-ins. These saws are usually reconditioned and sold. Sometimes a warranty is included. Used saws from a supply house are usually more expensive and in better repair.

The want ads in newspapers and tabloids often have table saws for sale. Price and quality will vary with each ad. You must inspect and compare the merchandise to determine value.

It is also possible to advertise for a table saw in the "Wanted to Buy" section of the want ads. A person who wishes to sell a table saw will find it easier to call you than place an ad. This gives you a better bargaining position because the seller does not have other buyers coming to inspect the saw. The seller has only 1 offer—yours!

The auction advertisements often have table saws. An estate auction or a woodworking shop auction might have a table saw that fits your needs. Be careful when buying at an auction. Sometimes the excitement of the auction will cause the bidding to reach a price close to that of a new saw. Decide on your top bid before the auction begins, and stick with it. Auction-bought tools are not always a bargain.

Table Saws in the Future

Three trends are likely in table saws manufactured in the future. First, better, safer guards will be developed. This will make operation of the saw safer and easier.

Second, fences will be improved so that they are more accurate, safer and easier to adjust. Some prototypes of fences described are already on the market.

Third, electronic controls will be incorporated into the design of new table saws. An electronically controlled saw (Fig. 460) is being marketed by a major manufacturer. This saw features programmable blade height adjustment within $\frac{5}{1000}$ of an inch and blade tilt within $\frac{1}{10}$ of a degree (Fig. 461). The programmable feature allows the saw to be set up again exactly the same way as the original set-up. This means duplicate parts are easy to reproduce.

Used Table Saw Evaluation Sheet

Name of Seller
     Address
     Phone
Table Saw Brand _____
Model Number _____Year Manufactured _____
Company Still Makes Saw   Yes   No
Repair Parts Available   Yes   No
Owner's Manual Included   Yes   No
_____Volts   _____Amps   _____Phase
_____Table Width X   _____Table Length
Options, Features, Accessories Included (List and Estimate Value)

_____
_____
_____
_____

Today's List Price of Same or Similar Saw _____
Asking Price of the Seller _____
         Difference _____
General Condition of Saw (List descriptions of condition and cost of repair if damaged)

_____
_____
_____

Fig. 459. With the used table saw evaluation sheet, you can determine the value of a used table saw.

Fig. 460. This table saw has electronic controls for blade height and blade tilt.

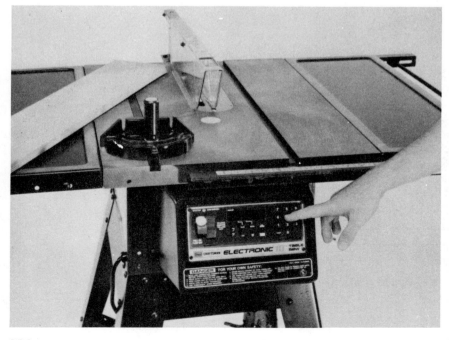

Fig. 461. The electronic controls will adjust blade height within $5/1000$ of an inch and blade tilt to $1/10$ of a degree.

Part IV: Projects

Fig. 462. Bathroom storage cabinet.

Fig. 464. Hall chest.

Fig. 465. Wall clock.

Fig. 463. Nightstand.

Fig. 466. Storage trunk.

8

How to Build
Table Saw Accessories
and Items for Your Home

The projects in this chapter can be divided into 2 groups. The first group is jigs or accessories. These are devices you can make for your table saw. The second group consists of projects for general use. These projects make nice gifts or accessories for your home or shop. They have been designed to help you hone your table saw and woodworking skills.

This project chapter is last for good reason. You must digest the information in the first 7 chapters before you begin building projects. If you begin a project without a full understanding of table saw operation, you could waste material or incur an injury. Plan projects carefully and review unfamiliar operations before you begin.

Tips for Building Projects

When you start a project, consider the following tips. These tips will help you do a better job with fewer mistakes.

1. *Study the plans carefully.* Check the dimensions or the scale on the plan to be sure all parts will be cut correctly. Make allowances for joints or trimming on all parts. Remember: Some jigs are dimensioned for a particular saw. These dimensions may have to be changed to fit your saw.

2. *Develop auxiliary sketches when needed.* When plans are modified or an assembly is complex, develop an auxiliary sketch that you can take to the table saw. Sketches of picture frame profiles can be glued to the stock. This makes the table saw set-up much quicker and more accurate.

3. *Develop a bill of materials.* A bill of materials is a list of all parts needed to build the project. The list includes the part's dimensions (thickness, width and length). The bill of materials helps in stock selection and table saw set-up.

4. *Write a plan of procedure.* The plan of procedure is a list of steps one should follow to build a project. The list is an orderly series of events. For example, the drawer opening would be made before the drawer front was cut to exact size. It is not considered good practice to make the drawer and then build the opening.

5. *Think before making any cuts.* Plan your cutting to reduce the chance of error. When cutting parts, cut the longest parts first. Any parts cut too short can then be used for shorter parts on the bill of materials.

Before making a cut in your work, test the set-up in a scrap. Be sure it is correct before you begin. Mark complex cuts: Drawers and cabinets have a right and left side. The sides are not the same! They are mirror images of each other. Cut them carefully.

When several operations are being performed on a number of parts, mark the control edge. The control edge is the edge on the parts that always rides along the fence or against the mitre gauge. These marks will minimize the chance of reversing the parts after a few operations have been performed. The mark is important on parts such as moulding, picture frame parts and cabinet sides.

6. *Check the fit of all parts before assembly.* Fit the parts together dry before gluing. Tight fits can cause problems when glue is applied. Both parts will swell, and the parts may not fit together. It is much easier to trim parts and make minor adjustments when there is no glue on the parts.

7. *Plan ahead for finishing.* Sand all internal surfaces before assembling a box or cabinet. These surfaces may be difficult or impossible to sand after assembly. It may also be easier to stain and finish these surfaces before assembly.

Watch for glue smears on the wood. They can make your stain and finish appear blemished. Scrape or sand away these smears before applying stain or finish.

Table Saw Devices

Basic Design of Table Saw Jigs

Most jigs designed to be used on a table saw are controlled by the mitre slot (Fig. 467) or the fence (Fig. 468). Jigs used in the mitre slot are often adjustable. They move towards and away from the blade on a track. Jigs that are controlled by the fence are usually not adjustable. All adjustments are made by moving the fence towards or away from the fence.

The jig pictured in Fig. 468 is easy to construct. A piece of plywood is attached to the fence, and jigs are built to ride on the plywood. A piece of plywood the same thickness as the piece attached to the fence separates the 2 sides of the jig. This makes a perfect fit. Sometimes a piece of paper is added to the center strip to make movement of the jig easier.

The jig pictured in Fig. 467 appears to be painted white. It actually has a plastic coating bonded to it. This coating resists wear and slides easily. When making a jig, select stock carefully. Most sheet stock resists warping, swelling and wear. Sheet stock is a good material for jig construction.

Make the cleats that ride in the mitre slot out of dense, hard wood. This will keep the cleat from wearing and getting sloppy. Use quarter-sawn stock for cleats when-ever possible. A quarter-sawn cleat will have annular rings running parallel to the saw blade. Quarter-sawn cleats will not swell across the mitre slot. This means the jig will still operate well even with a moisture change.

Always consider safety when designing a jig for the table saw. Many times the table saw owner builds the jig carelessly because it is regarded as a means to an end rather than an end itself. A well-made jig will be an accurate tool that can be used for many different operations. A poorly made jig may be dangerous, yield poor results and be used only once.

A safe jig is planned carefully. The mitre jig in Fig. 469 has a hook on the mitre slot cleat. This hook prevents the operator from sawing through the jig. This is easily done when doing repetitive cuts. The piece of wood behind the mitre fences acts as a guard (Fig. 470). When the blade cuts through the work, it is housed inside the wooden guard. This keeps the blade from cutting the operator's thumb, which is also a common mishap when repetitive cuts are being made.

This jig could be made safer if a piece of clear plastic covered the blade's path on the front side of the jig. This would minimize contact with the blade without impairing vision.

Any jig you build can probably be improved or made safer, but careful planning will help you begin with a safe, accurate jig. Follow the basic safety rules in Chapter 4 when operating any jig on the table saw.

Fig. 467. This jig is guided and controlled by the mitre slot. A cleat on the jig fits snugly in the mitre slot.

234

Fig. 468. This jig is guided and controlled by the fence. Moving the fence moves the position of the jig.

Fig. 469. The hook on this jig prevents the operator from sawing through the jig, which is a common error when making repetitive cuts.

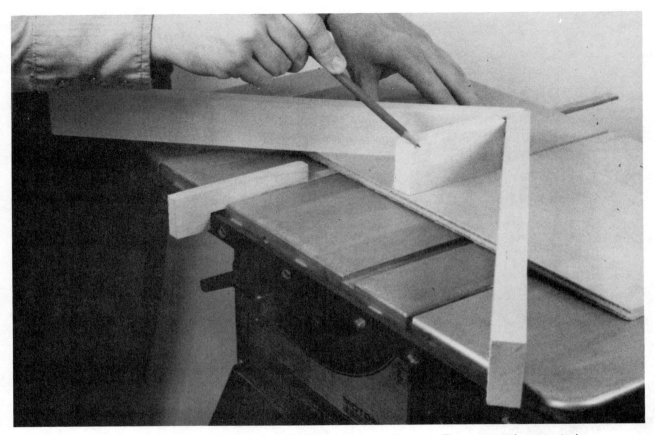

Fig. 470. This block of wood acts as a guard when the jig cuts through the work. The operator is protected.

Building Basic Jigs and Accessories

Many jigs and accessories were presented in the first 7 chapters. You may wish to make some of them for your table saw.

In Chapter 2 (pages 33 and 34), some shooting boards were presented. These allow greater control of stock when crosscutting. A small one can be made to be used as an extra mitre gauge (Fig. 471), or a large one can be made to be used for crosscutting large parts (Fig. 472).

Make sure the cleats are installed accurately and screwed down securely (Fig. 473). The size of the shooting board will depend on the size of your table saw. Make sure the (fence) control surface is higher than the blade.

A mitring jig (Figs. 469 and 470) is quite similar to a shooting board. Cut the board the same size as the table of your saw. Attach cleats and cut a kerf to the center of the board. Lay out 1 mitre from the kerf and attach a fence. Use a framing square to lay out the other mitre. Place 1 leg of the square against the 45° fence. The other leg determines placement of the other fence. Add a hook and a blade guard and test the jig.

If the framing square is not 90°, the jig will be off. Check the square before using it. A piece of tape on the fence can compensate for minor errors.

Wooden extensions for your mitre gauge may also be made. Glue a strip of abrasive to them to reduce slipping between the work and mitre gauge. Prepare for complex operations by making some auxiliary throat plates (Fig. 474). Trace them on sheet stock and cut them to fit. See Figs. 44–49 for more details on making and fitting auxiliary throat plates.

For advanced table saw operations, a few featherboards (Fig. 475) would be helpful. A featherboard holds stock down or against the fence. This allows greater control of the work and reduces the chance of a kickback. See Figs. 54–63 for details on laying out and cutting a featherboard.

Be sure to make some push sticks for your table saw. Use the templates in Figs. 65–68. Drill a hole in them so they can be hung on the table saw. Make some hooks that can be mounted on the table saw (Fig. 476). These hooks assure that a push stick will be where it is needed at all times.

236

Fig. 471. This small shooting board can be used as a substitute mitre gauge. This is very handy when the mitre gauge is set up for a cut.

Fig. 472. This shooting board is ideal for crosscutting large parts. Be sure the control surfaces are taller than the highest blade setting.

Fig. 473. The cleats on a shooting board should be installed accurately and screwed down securely.

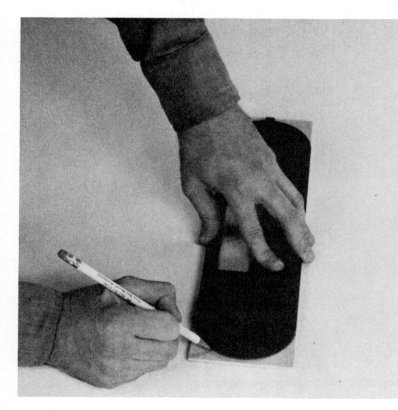

Fig. 474. Prepare for advance set-ups by making additional throat plates. See Chapter ∠ (pages 25–27) for more details.

Fig. 475. A featherboard is a nice accessory for complex set-ups. The featherboard makes it easier to control stock. See Chapter 2 (pages 28–30) for more details on making a featherboard.

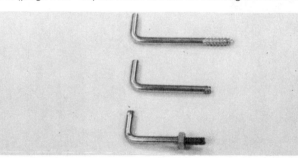

Fig. 476. Hooks like these can be used to hang push sticks on the table saw. Cut the wood threads off the hook, and cut machine threads with a die to replace them. Anchor them to the table with 2 nuts, or thread the table and use 1 nut.

For long rips, you may wish to make a dead man (Fig. 477) or a fence extension (Fig. 478). The dead man is a simple roller used in a portable sawhorse. The roller in Fig. 477 is a piece of closet rod. It is available at most lumberyards. Study Fig. 479 and modify it to suit your needs or sawhorse. It can be assembled with glue and nails or screws.

The fence extension attaches to the fence and extends the fence and table. The piece attached to the bottom of the fence extension supports the work during long rips. Study Fig. 480 and modify it to fit your table saw. Use screws and glue to assemble the 2 pieces. Remove any glue that squeezes out of the joint.

For cutting irregular pieces, you may want to make an auxiliary fence for pattern sawing (Fig. 481). The size of this auxiliary fence will be determined by the size of the part you are cutting. Use a dense, hard wood for the edge on which the pattern rides.

A jig for cutting irregular parts can also be made easily. Install a cleat onto the plywood base. The distance from the cleat to the end of the base should exceed the distance from the mitre slot to the blade. The base is then sawn to size (Fig, 482). Use the same blade for this operation as the one you intend to use when cutting parts. Anything clamped on that edge will be cut to true size (Fig. 483). Before making the cut, be sure the blade is set at the desired angle.

The circle-cutting jig (Fig. 484) is similar to the jig used to cut irregular parts. The size of the jig is determined by the diameter of the circle being cut. The jig is about 4 inches (10.2 cm) larger than the diameter of the circle. Attach the clamping device (Fig. 485) in the correct location for the circle diameter being cut. More information can be found in Chapter 6 (pages 180–182).

For pieces with inclined edges, a wedge-cutting jig (Fig. 486) or a taper-cutting jig (Fig. 487) can be built. The size of the wedge determines the layout of the wedge-cutting jig. A detailed look at the tapering jig appears in Chapter 6 (pages 175–180).

The parallels used for laying out a cove (Fig. 488) can also be made in the shop. Study Fig. 489, then rip your stock to 1¼ inch (32 mm). Cut your parts to length and lay out the holes. Drill the ¼-inch (6-mm) holes through all parts. Counterbore the bottom holes to accommodate "T" nuts (Fig. 490). Assemble the parts and test for accuracy.

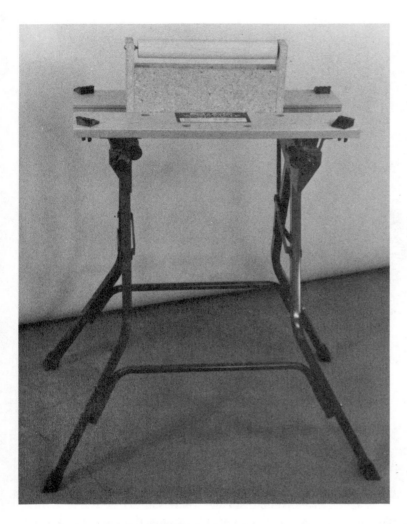

Fig. 477. This dead man is a handy device for long rips. The roller is held in place with nuts and bolts.

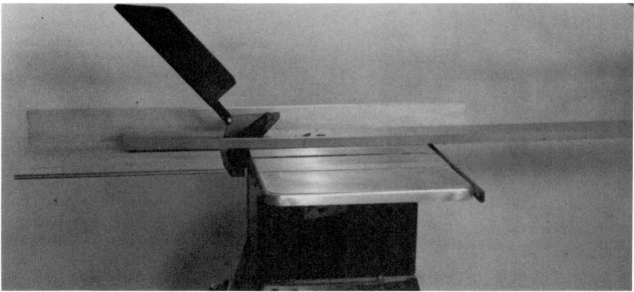

Fig. 478. This fence extension extends the fence and table for long rips. Use a true piece of stock for the fence.

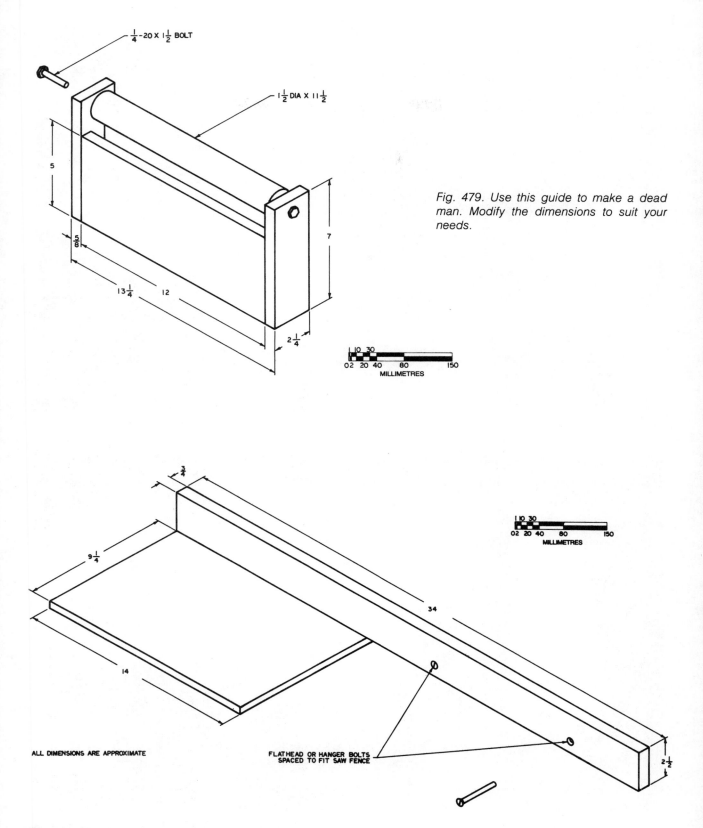

$\frac{1}{4}$-20 X 1$\frac{1}{2}$ BOLT

1$\frac{1}{2}$ DIA X 11$\frac{1}{2}$

5

$\frac{5}{8}$

13$\frac{1}{4}$

12

7

2$\frac{1}{4}$

MILLIMETRES

Fig. 479. Use this guide to make a dead man. Modify the dimensions to suit your needs.

$\frac{3}{4}$

9$\frac{1}{4}$

34

14

MILLIMETRES

ALL DIMENSIONS ARE APPROXIMATE

FLATHEAD OR HANGER BOLTS
SPACED TO FIT SAW FENCE

2$\frac{1}{2}$

Fig. 480. Use this guide to make a fence extension. Modify the dimensions to suit your needs.

241

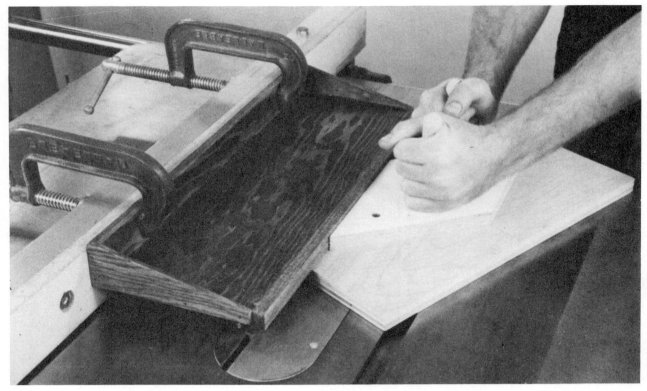

Fig. 481. This auxiliary fence is handy for pattern sawing. Use a dense, hard wood for the edge on which the pattern rides.

Fig. 482. The base of the irregular cutting jig is cut to size after the cleat is installed. Use the same blade for cutting parts as you use to cut the base.

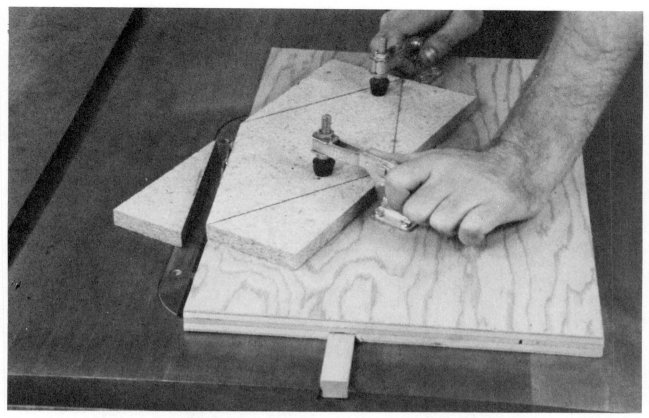

Fig. 483. Any object clamped along the edge of the irregular cutting jig will be cut on that line.

Fig. 484. This circle-cutting jig is a project that can be made for your table saw.

Fig. 485. This clamping device is used to hold stock to the circle-cutting jig. It can also be used on other shop-made jigs.

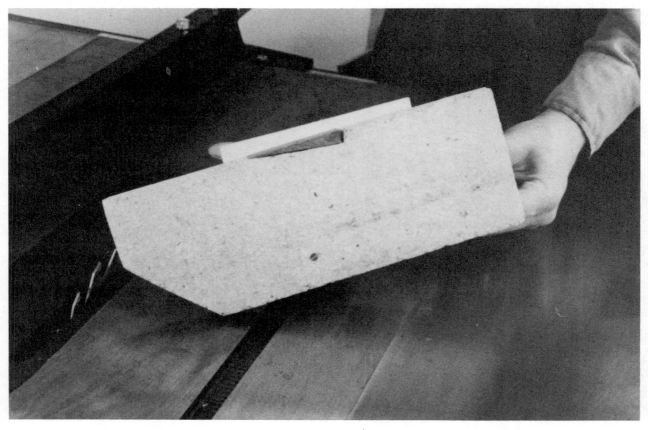

Fig. 486. This wedge-cutting jig is a project you may wish to make for your table saw.

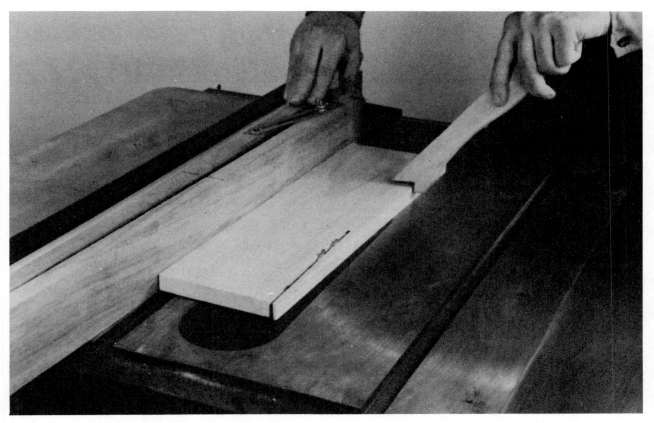

Fig. 487. This tapering jig is a handy jig for your table saw. See Fig. 358 for a detailed drawing.

Fig. 488. These parallels are helpful when laying out a cove. See Fig. 489 for a guide to building parallels.

245

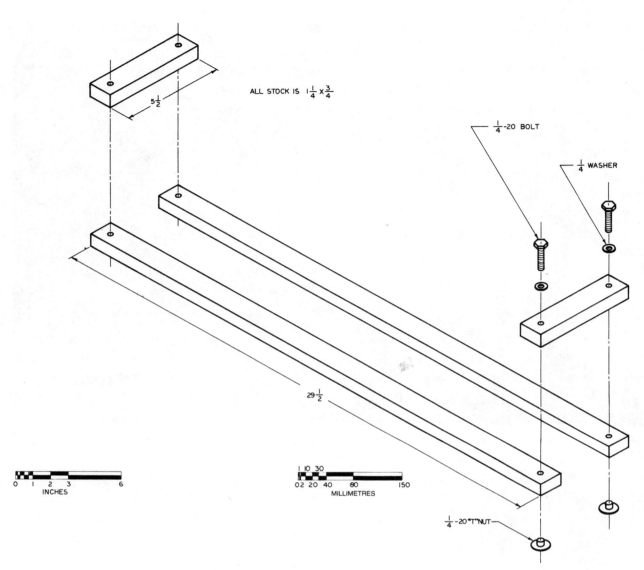

ALL STOCK IS $1\frac{1}{4}$ X $\frac{3}{4}$

$5\frac{1}{2}$

$\frac{1}{4}$-20 BOLT

$\frac{1}{4}$ WASHER

$29\frac{1}{2}$

INCHES

MILLIMETRES

$\frac{1}{4}$-20 "T" NUT

Fig. 489. Use this guide to build the cove-cutting parallels.

Fig. 490. Counterbore the bottom holes to accommodate the "T" nuts.

Building a Universal Jig

The universal jig (Fig. 491) is actually several jigs in one. It has several work faces that can be attached to it. Each work face does a different job, such as tenoning, cutting feathers or cutting splines. These work faces can also be made for specialty operations and attached to the sub-face of the jig. Only 1 jig is made. A new work face is made for different operations.

The subbase of the universal jig rides in the mitre slot. A lock knob (Fig. 492) controls movement of the base on the subbase. The base is actually 2 pieces connected to form a right angle. The work faces are attached to the vertical part of the base. They are held in position with flathead machine screws and "T" nuts.

Begin this project by studying Fig. 493. Study this assembly drawing until you can name the parts and understand how they work.

Study the subbase drawing (Fig. 494) and develop a bill of materials. Cut the base to size, and cut the dado for the cleat that rides in the mitre slot. The distance from the cleat to the edge of the subbase should be slightly less than the distance from the blade to the mitre slot. Glue the cleat in position (Fig. 495).

Study the base drawings (Fig. 496), and develop a bill of materials. Cut the bottom of the base to size. Cut a dado in the bottom of that part and a matching dado in the top of the subbase. This dado must be perpendicular to the cleat dadoed into the bottom of the subbase.

Glue a cleat in the dado cut in the subbase. Remove any excess glue. Test the fit between the bottom of the base and the subbase. The parts should slide smoothly, but should not be loose. Install the flathead bolt through the subbase. Cut a matching hole in the bottom of the base and test the movement. See Figs. 494 and 496 for placement of the bolt.

Assemble the rest of the base. The sub-face is attached to the bottom of the base. Make sure these parts are perpendicular to each other. Attach the triangular braces to anchor the base assembly parts. Use glue and screws for assembly. Remove any excess glue before it cures.

Cut a notch in the sub-face to accommodate the cleat on the subbase. Do this with hand tools. The base and subbase should slide smoothly on each other.

Study the drawing for the work faces (Figs. 497 and 498) and develop a bill of materials. Cut the actual faces first. Cut some extra faces for specialty work you may do later.

Lay out the screw pattern for anchoring the work face to the sub-face on a template. Mark all the work faces and sub-face. Drill the holes. Install "T" nuts in the sub-face and countersink the holes in the work faces. Test the fit. Make any needed adjustments. Attach the appropriate cleats to the work faces. See Figs. 497 and 498 for details.

Study the drawing for the lock knob (Fig. 499) and develop a bill of materials. Begin by laying out circles on a scrap of plywood (Fig. 500). Drill a small hole through the center of the circles. Dado through the center of these circles (Fig. 501). Make the dado ½ the depth of the stock. The dado width should be large enough for the handle.

Glue a piece of stock 1 inch (25 mm) long in the dado (Fig. 502). Cut out the circle and drill a hole through it (Fig. 503). The hole should accommodate a "T" nut. Use the small hole drilled earlier as a pilot hole. Install the "T" nut (Fig. 504) and glue the handle in place (Fig. 505).

Test the universal jig for ease of movement. Remember to make extra work faces for specialty work. You may also wish to make a few extra lock knobs. These can be used on other jigs you make.

Fig. 491. This universal jig is several jigs in one. It is controlled by a cleat that rides in the mitre slot.

Fig. 492. The lock knob controls movement of the base on the subbase.

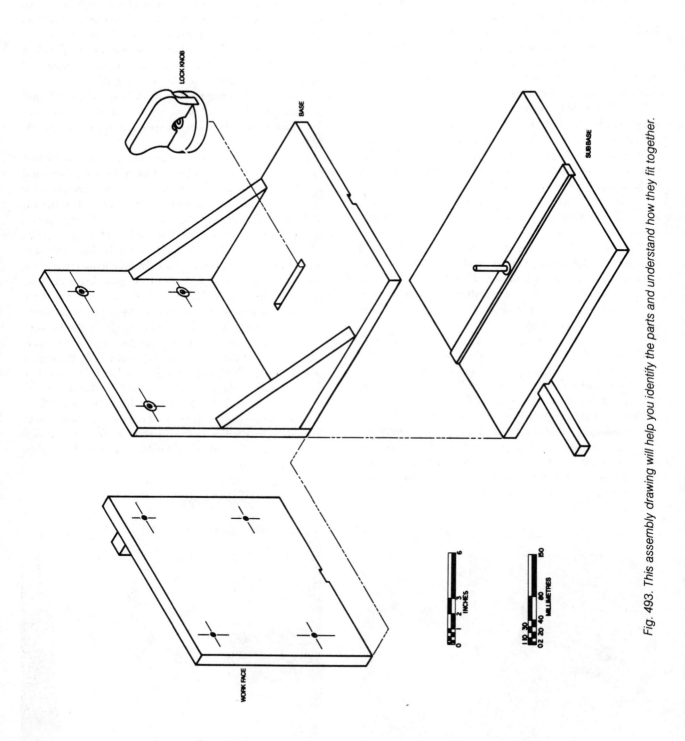

LOCK KNOB

BASE

SUB BASE

WORK FACE

INCHES

MILLIMETRES

Fig. 493. This assembly drawing will help you identify the parts and understand how they fit together.

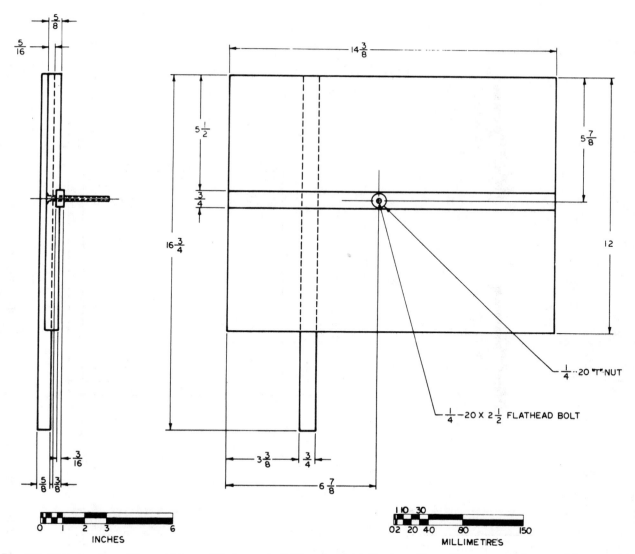

Fig. 494. This drawing of the subbase will help you build it accurately. Cleat position will vary according to table saw make and model.

Fig. 495. Glue and clamp the cleat in position. Remove excess glue before it cures.

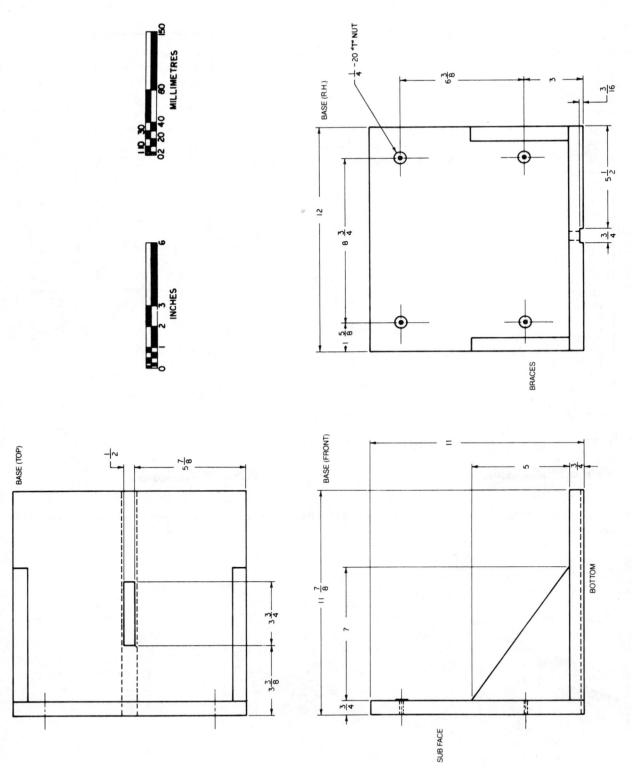

Fig. 496. Study this drawing of the base before cutting or assembling the parts.

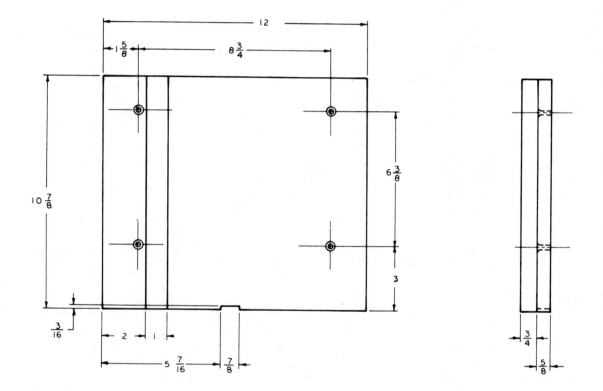

Fig. 497. This tenoning work face attaches to the sub-face on the base. Attach the cleat after fitting.

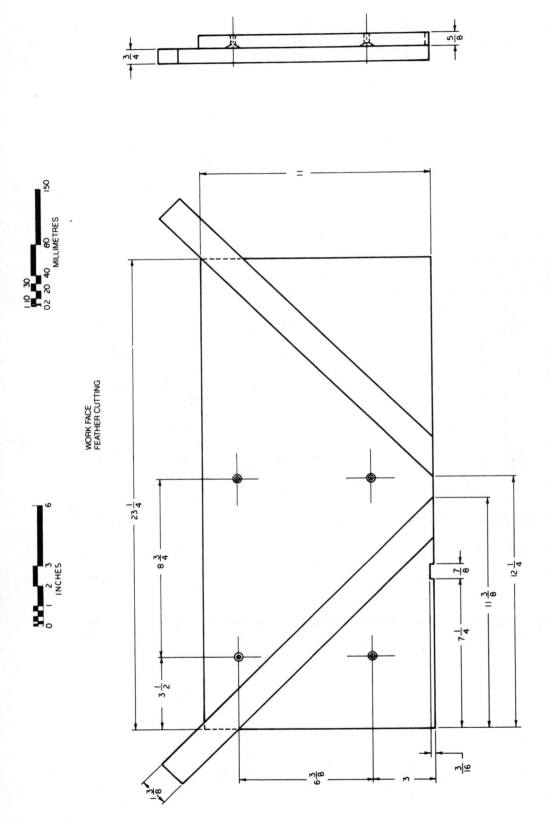

WORK FACE
FEATHER CUTTING

MILLIMETRES

INCHES

Fig. 498. This feather-cutting work face attaches to the sub-face on the base. Attach the cleats after fitting.

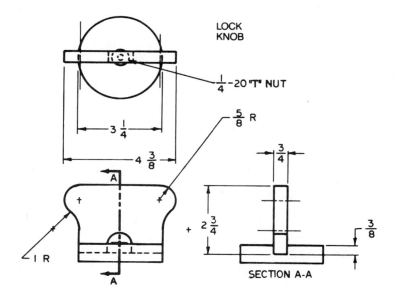

LOCK
KNOB

$\frac{1}{4}$-20 "T" NUT

$\frac{5}{8}$ R

$3\frac{1}{4}$

$4\frac{3}{8}$

A

$\frac{3}{4}$

$2\frac{3}{4}$

$\frac{3}{8}$

I R

A

SECTION A-A

0   I   2   3   6
INCHES

IO 30
02 20 40   80   I50
MILLIMETRES

Fig. 499. Study this drawing and Figs. 500–505 before making the lock knob.

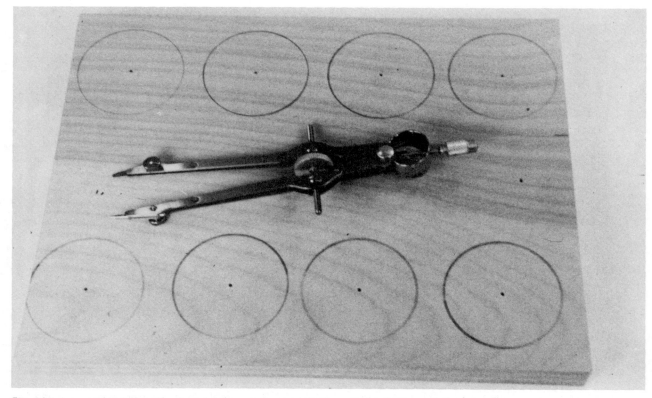

Fig. 500. Lay out circles for the lock knobs on plywood. Drill a small hole through the center.

253

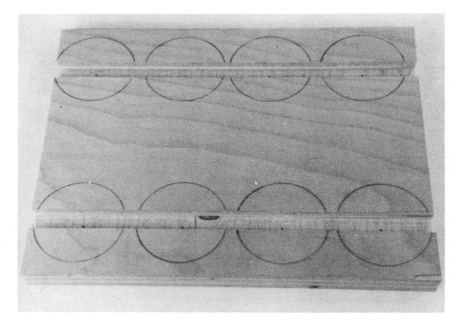

Fig. 501. Cut a dado through the circles. The handle fits in this dado.

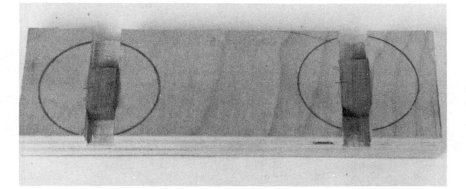

Fig. 502. A piece of stock is glued in the dado to hold the "T" nut.

Fig. 503. Drill a hole through the circle to accommodate the "T" nut. Use the small hole drilled earlier as a pilot hole.

Fig. 504. Drive the "T" nut into position with a hammer. Be sure it is centered and anchored securely.

254

Building a Chisel Case and Sharpening Stone Box

The chisel case (Fig. 506) is a challenging project to build. It allows you to experiment with finger joints, raised panels (Fig. 507) and resawing. The project is small, so any errors are inexpensive.

The sharpening stone box (Fig. 508) has no raised panel on top, yet it can be just as challenging. Begin by studying the drawings for the chisel case (Fig. 509). Notice that the box is actually made 2 fingers larger than the desired size. When the box is cut open, 2 fingers are removed. This keeps the rhythm of the fingers constant on the case corners. Note the rhythm of the corner of this box (Fig. 510). If only 1 finger were removed, the corner would have 2 dark fingers (end grain) next to each other.

In some cases it may not be desirable to remove 2 fingers from a box. Another approach is to use a "V" cutter to shape all 4 faces where the kerf is to be made (Fig. 511). A fine-tooth blade can cut through the center of the "V" cut (Fig. 512). The same cutting procedure for opening the box is used (Fig. 513). The remaining portion of the "V" cut accents the separation line and minimizes the clash of 2 fingers or 2 cuts.

Review the procedures for resawing (pages 138–143), cutting raised panels and cutting finger joints (pages 156–161) in Chapter 6. Be sure you understand the procedures before you begin. Develop a bill of materials for your case or box. Make some detailed drawings for the sharpening stone box if you decide to build it.

If you make a sharpening stone box, the length and width of your parts depend on the size of the stone. The length of your parts will equal the length (or width) of your stone plus 2 times the thickness of your stock. The width of your parts will equal the thickness of the stone plus 2 fingers. This is the exact size. You may want to make the parts longer or wider for trimming purposes (Fig. 514).

For the chisel case or other finger-joint boxes using hinges, select the hardware first (Fig. 515). Sometimes the hardware available for small boxes is limited. It is best to select it first. Not finding the correct hardware for something you have already built is disappointing.

Make the jig with the correct-sized spacer. Select a saw blade that cuts a kerf with a flat bottom if possible. Attach the jig to the mitre gauge (Fig. 516) and make a test cut (Fig. 517). Make adjustments according to the procedures outlined in Chapter 6.

Test the fit of the parts first. Glue them together carefully. Make sure the box or case is square. The stone box is now ready for the top and bottom. Cut them slightly oversize and glue them in position (Fig. 518). You may have to sand the top and bottom of the box to assure a smooth surface. Check the surface before gluing the top and bottom in position.

Make the raised panel lid for the chisel case and sand it smooth. Glue and clamp it in position (Fig. 519). The lid may be slightly oversize for sanding purposes. Sand the case or box completely before cutting it open.

Use a fine-tooth blade to cut the case or box open (Fig. 520). Set the blade height just under the stock thickness. Cut a kerf on all 4 faces. This kerf is on the edge of a finger. Make 4 more kerfs at the edge of a cut. Raise the blade height to just over stock thickness. Saw through the long faces again (Fig. 521).

The kerf placement on the sharpening stone box (Fig. 522) and the chisel case (Fig. 523) will be different. Both boxes are held together by the stock remaining in the kerfs on the short faces. Use a dovetail saw or a back saw to separate the top and bottom (Fig. 524).

Attach hardware and make the slotted rack to hold the chisels. Use your own chisels as models for this part. Apply the finish of your choice to complete the sharpening stone box and chisel case.

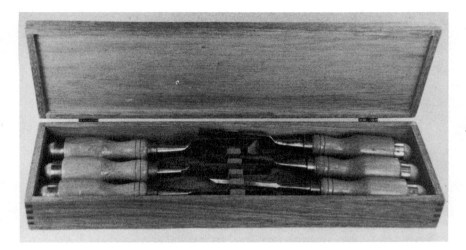

Fig. 506. This chisel case has finger joints.

Fig. 507. The raised panel lid on the chisel case adds to its appearance.

Fig. 508. This sharpening-stone box also has finger joints.

256

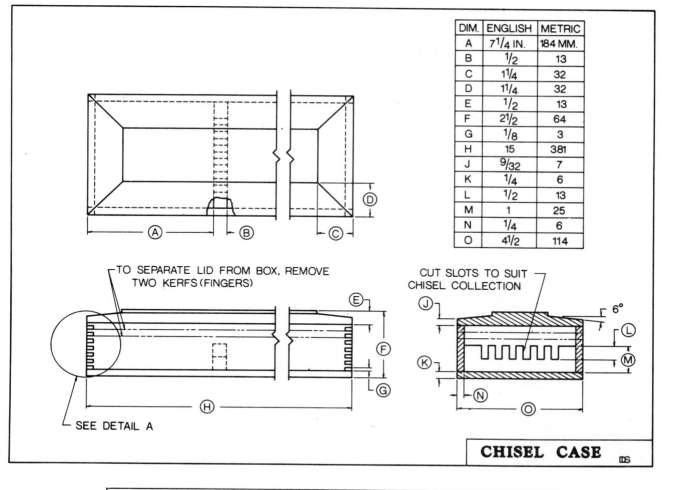

DIM.	ENGLISH	METRIC
A	7¼ IN.	184 MM.
B	½	13
C	1¼	32
D	1¼	32
E	½	13
F	2½	64
G	⅛	3
H	15	381
J	9/32	7
K	¼	6
L	½	13
M	1	25
N	¼	6
O	4½	114

TO SEPARATE LID FROM BOX, REMOVE
TWO KERFS (FINGERS)

CUT SLOTS TO SUIT
CHISEL COLLECTION

SEE DETAIL A

CHISEL CASE

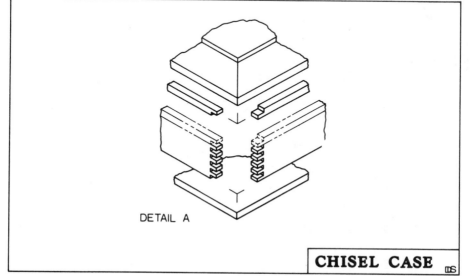

DETAIL A

CHISEL CASE

Fig. 509. Study these drawings carefully before beginning the chisel case or sharpening-stone box.

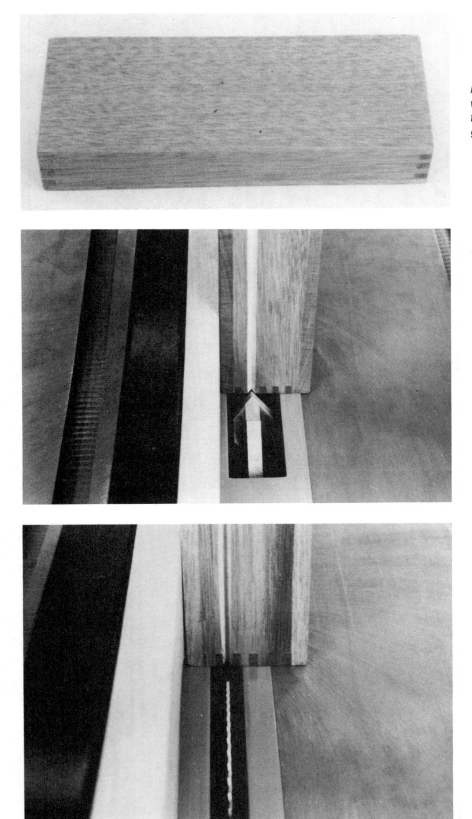

Fig. 510. Two fingers were removed when this box was cut open. Note tthe uninterrupted rhythm of the fingers because of this.

Fig. 511. A "V" cutter can be used to mark the separation line of a box. Only 1 cut is made on this box.

Fig. 512. A fine-tooth blade cuts a kerf down the center of the "V" cut.

Fig. 513. This box is opened with a dovetail saw or backsaw. Note how the kerfs go through the stock on the long faces.

Fig. 514. These fingers extend beyond the end of the box for trimming and sanding. Make an allowance on your bill of materials if you plan to do this.

Fig. 515. Select hardware that is correct for your project. It is wise to buy the hardware first.

Fig. 516. Attach the finger-cutting jig to the mitre gauge. See Chapter 6 (pages 157–161) for additional set-up details.

Fig. 517. Make a test cut and adjust the jig accordingly. Use the same species for the test cut as you plan to use for the project. The fit varies according to the hardness of the species.

Fig. 518. The top and bottom are cut oversize and glued to the box. The entire box can then be sanded smooth.

Fig. 519. The raised panel is also slightly oversize. It will be sanded after the glue cures.

Fig. 520. A fine-tooth blade is used to cut the box open. The first kerf is set at the edge of a finger.

Fig. 521. Four more kerfs are made at the edge of a cut or slot. The blade is then raised to cut through the long faces.

Fig. 522. Kerf placement is almost centered on the sharpening-stone box. The stock remaining in the kerfs of the short faces hold the box together.

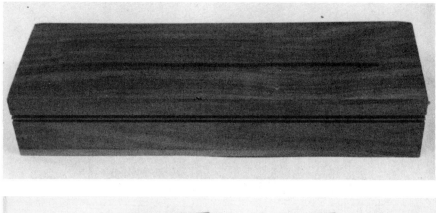

Fig. 523. Kerf placement is closer to the lid in the chisel case.

Fig. 524. The box is separated with a dovetail saw. Use the kerfs as a guide for the saw.

Building a Tool Case

Building a tool case (Fig. 525) is similar to building the chisel case and sharpening stone box. The chief difference is that a dado head is used to cut the slots between the fingers. The parts are also larger and thicker. More support is needed behind the parts when the slots are cut. A special finger-cutting jig was made to make the tool case (Fig. 526). This jig is controlled by the fence, so minor adjustments can be made by moving the fence.

This jig is easy to make. Study the assembly drawing (Fig. 527) to see how the parts fit together. The slide attaches to the fence. It guides the finger jig. The backing board is attached to the finger jig. The backing board can be changed for fingers of different widths and lengths.

Begin by making the slide (Fig. 528). The slide attaches to the fence. Make the mating part of the finger jig (Fig. 529) next. Assemble the finger jig and test operation on the slide. The cabinet glide or thumbtack on the finger jig reduces friction. Be sure it is in place before testing the operation.

Make 2 or 3 backing boards (Fig. 530). Keep them on hand for other finger cuts. Attach a backing board to the finger jig. Lock the fence at the right edge of the table (Fig. 526). This will help you determine where the slot will be cut and where the stop pin should be placed. Cut a kerf and install the stop pin. Make it smaller than the slots you plan to cut.

Fig. 525. This tool case has finger joints that must be cut with a dado head. Larger projects mean greater challenges. Large pieces are apt to warp; this can make cutting fingers or assembling the box more difficult.

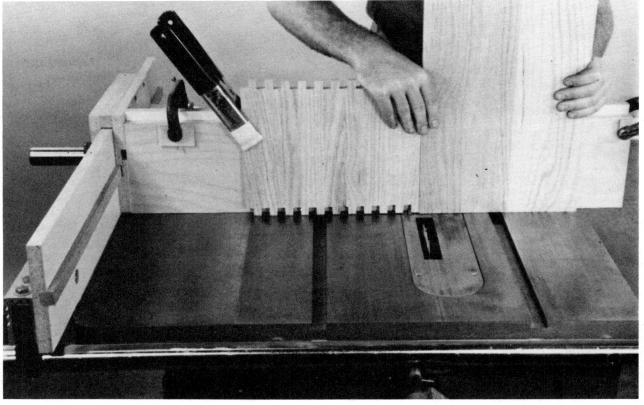

Fig. 526. The jig used to cut large fingers is controlled by the fence. Minor adjustment of finger size can be made by moving the fence.

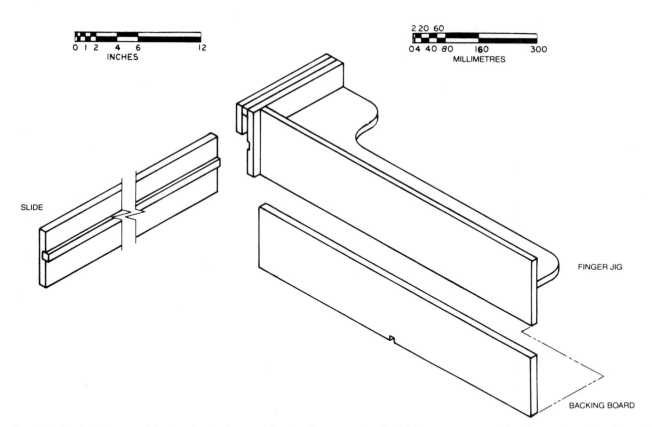

SLIDE

FINGER JIG

BACKING BOARD

Fig. 527. Study this assembly drawing before making the finger-cutting jig. Make sure you can identify each part and how it fits in the assembly.

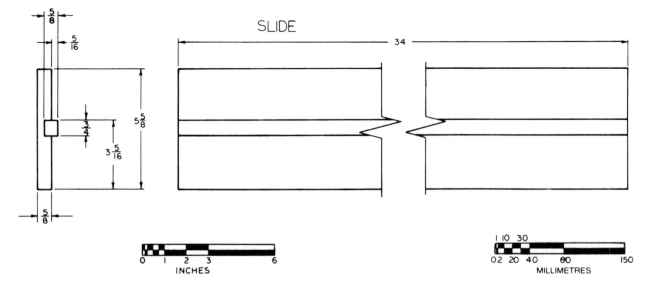

SLIDE

Fig. 528. Study the detail drawing of the slide. Lay out your stock carefully.

265

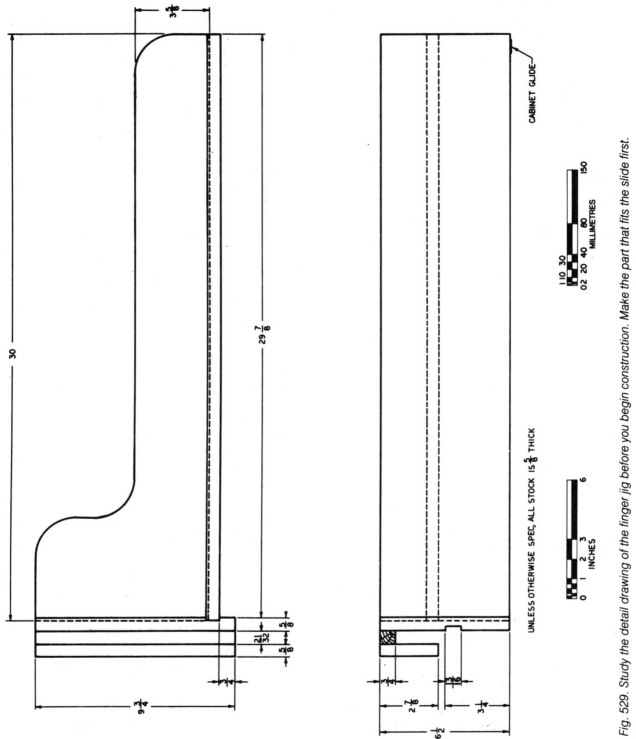

UNLESS OTHERWISE SPEC, ALL STOCK IS $\frac{5}{8}$ THICK

CABINET GLIDE

Fig. 529. Study the detail drawing of the finger jig before you begin construction. Make the part that fits the slide first.

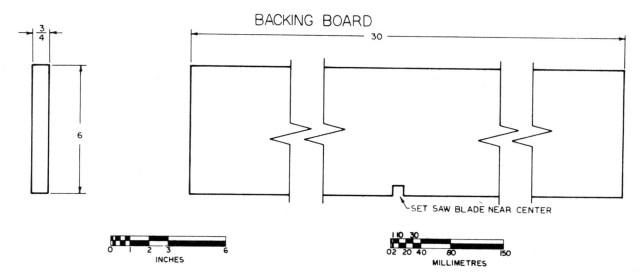

Fig. 530. Make extra backing boards from this drawing. Keep them stored for other finger-joint projects.

Install the desired-size dado head and make a trial cut. Adjust the fence until the fit between the fingers is correct. Allow some clearance for glue. A tight fit will become tighter when glue is applied.

Begin your tool case by studying Fig. 531. You can scale the drawing to make a case of the same size or you can measure the tool you wish to house and develop a bill of materials. Make the parts wide enough to inset the top and bottom, or the case may not hold the intended tool. The tool-case size in the drawing will house a 2-horse-power Milwaukee router.

Cut the parts that begin with a finger first (Fig. 532). Cut the parts that begin with a slot next (Fig. 533). Use 1 of the parts that has a full finger as a guide. Test the fit of the fingers in a dry assembly (Fig. 534). Determine where the dadoes for the top and bottom must be cut. Lay them out and cut them with a router. *Note:* Both ends of the dado are blind; this operation should not be attempted on the table saw.

The top can be made as a raised panel if desired. This adds to the appearance of the case. Sand the top and bottom (both sides) and the inside of the 4 sides before assembly. Use a slow-setting glue to assemble the tool case. I used hide glue. This allowed plenty of time to shift the pieces into place. Do not glue the top and bottom into the dado. They should be free to expand and contract in the dado. Use plenty of clamps and strongbacks (Fig. 535) to hold the parts together. Keep the clamps in place until the glue cures. Hide glue cures in about 12 to 16 hours.

Sand the case after the glue cures. It can now be cut open. Since the fingers are so large, a saw cut is all that is needed. Two fingers are not removed; this was the procedure on the chisel case and stone box. Make a "V" cut at the desired opening line (Fig. 536). Take light cuts to avoid tear-out. Cut the box open with a fine-tooth blade (Fig. 537). Do not cut completely through the box. Separate the top and bottom with a dovetail saw or backsaw.

To lock the box together, I drove brass machine screws into all the corners (Fig. 538). Make the hole small enough so that the screw cuts threads in the wood. Cut the head of the screw off with a hacksaw (Fig. 539) and file the screw smooth (Fig. 540). These screws add strength and beauty to the box. If desired, a dowel could be used instead of a brass machine screw.

Fit the handle and hinges in position. Apply the desired stain and finish.

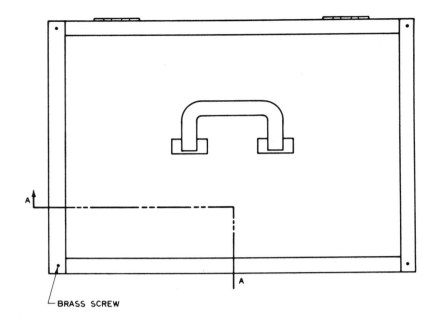

BRASS SCREW

LATCH, HANDLE AND HINGES TO SUIT

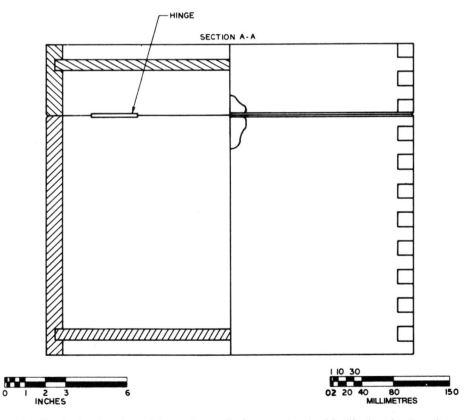

HINGE

SECTION A-A

0 1 2 3 6
INCHES

1 10 30
02 20 40 80 150
MILLIMETRES

Fig. 531. Study the drawing of the tool case before you begin. Modify the size to suit your tools.

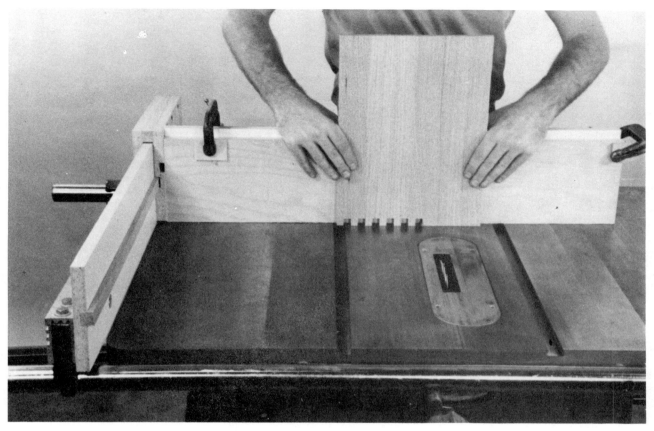

Fig. 532. Cut the parts of a tool case that begin with a finger.

Fig. 533. Use a full finger to locate the first slot on the mating sides. Hold stock securely while making this cut.

Fig. 534. Test the fit of the fingers without glue. Lay out the dadoes for the top and bottom from this assembly.

Fig. 535. Use plenty of clamps and strongbacks to hold the parts together.

Fig. 536. A "V" cut is made at the opening line after the case is sanded. Take light cuts to avoid tear-out.

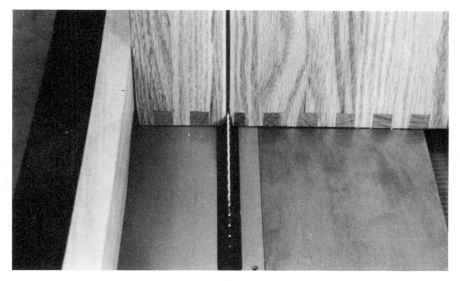

Fig. 537. Cut the box open with a fine-tooth blade. Do not cut through the stock. Separate the parts with a dovetail saw.

Fig. 538. Drive a brass machine screw through the corners to lock them. Drill a hole small enough so the screw cuts threads in the box.

Fig. 539. Cut the head of the screw off with a hacksaw.

Fig. 540. File the screw flush with the surface of the wood.

Projects for General Use

Making Picture Frames

Picture frames are fun to make. They incorporate many woodworking operations and challenges. Many picture frame operations allow you to use the shaper head. Flutes (Fig. 541), rabbets (Fig. 542) and coves (Fig. 543) are all common shaper operations employed on picture frames.

The rabbet for a frame using compound mitres can be made with a "V" cutter or a planer cutter (Fig. 544). The planer cutter is tilted to the 45° position for this cut. Remember to take light cuts.

Compound mitres can also add a challenge to picture frames. The stock can be tilted to the desired angle and cut like a simple mitre (Fig. 545). It may also be cut in the flat position, but this requires tilting both the blade and mitre gauge. Picture frames may incorporate special coves that must be cut with an inclined fence (Fig. 546). Review the procedures in Chapter 6 (page 151) before attempting this cut. Remember to remove most of the stock with a blade or dado head before making a cove cut.

Begin with simple picture frames using simple mitres. Stock with chamfered profiles (Fig. 547) is easy to fit when the corners do not match. Pare away at the chamfers until the corners appear to fit perfectly.

The mitres can be cut using the mitre gauge (Fig. 548). Make sure your set-up is accurate and the blade is sharp. A mitre jig can also be used to cut mitres. The stop block clamped to the fence ensures that all parts are of equal length (Fig. 549).

Be sure to consider glass size when making picture frames. Measure along the rabbet (Fig. 550). Project these lines to locate the cutting line (Fig. 551). It is more difficult to project the lines on frames with compound mitres (Fig. 552). Mark the rabbet and adjust the mark with the blade's path. Cut 1 end of all parts with compound mitres first (Fig. 553). A stop rod can be used to control the length of all the parts when the second mitre is cut.

If you wish to try advanced coves and compound mitre frames, try some of the profiles in Figs. 554 and 555. These profiles are full size; they are mirror images of each other. Photocopy them and glue them to both ends of your stock. They can guide the set-up of the saw.

One of the best ways to glue up picture frames is with a band clamp (Fig. 556). The clamp pulls uniformly on all 4 corners. When clamping frames with compound mitres, turn the frame upside down. As the band clamp is tightened, the parts lift like a pyramid (Fig. 557). This is the easiest way I know to assemble frames with compound mitres.

To reinforce mitre joints, and keep them from opening due to moisture changes, a key should be cut in the corners. The jig in Fig. 558 or the universal jig presented earlier in this chapter (pages 247–255) can be used for cutting the keyway (groove). A keyway is cut into all 4 corners. A key or feather is then cut and glued in place (Fig. 559). These keys are then trimmed flush with the frame (Fig. 560). Keys can be used on simple or compound mitres. Remember to keep the keyways shallow or they will come through the front of the frame.

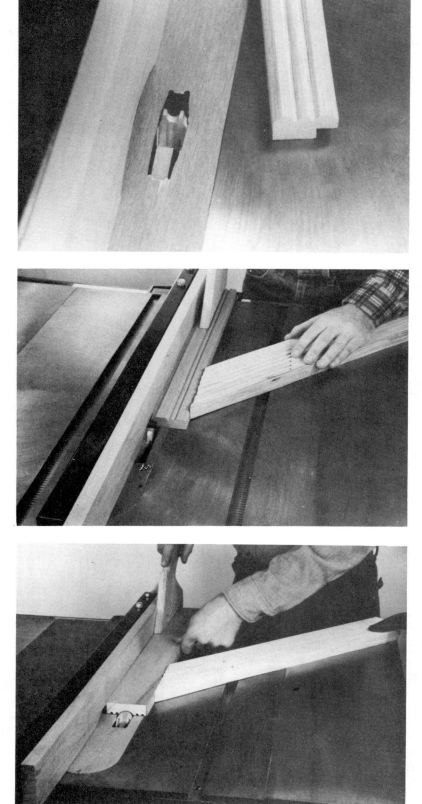

Fig. 541. The flute on this picture-frame part was cut with a shaper head.

Fig. 542. The rabbet for the glass on this frame part was cut with the shaper head. Two light cuts were required.

Fig. 543. The shaper head cuts an attractive cove on picture-frame parts.

Fig. 544. This planer cutter was tilted 45° to cut a rabbet. This part is for a frame with compound mitres.

Fig. 545. Compound mitres make picture frames more challenging.

Fig. 546. The cove on this picture frame is cut with an inclined fence. Most of the stock is first removed with a dado head.

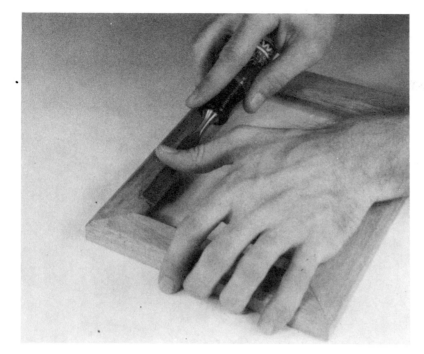

Fig. 547. Chamfered profiles are easy to fit when the corners do not match.

Fig. 548. Set up the mitre gauge carefully to obtain accurate mitres.

Fig. 549. The stop block clamped to the mitre jig ensures that all parts are the same length.

Fig. 550. Mark the glass size along the rabbet. Make the frame parts ⅛ inch (3 mm) larger than the glass. This allowance is for trimming the mitres.

Fig. 551. Project the marks on the rabbet onto the face of the frame to locate the cut.

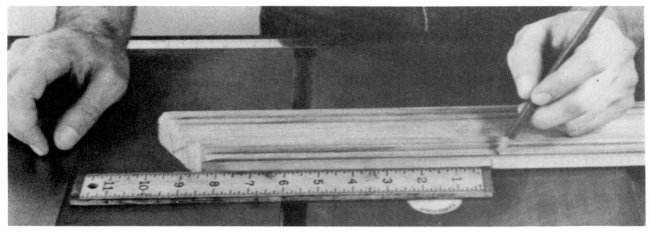

Fig. 552. It is difficult to project lines from compound mitres. Mark the rabbet and make the set-up carefully.

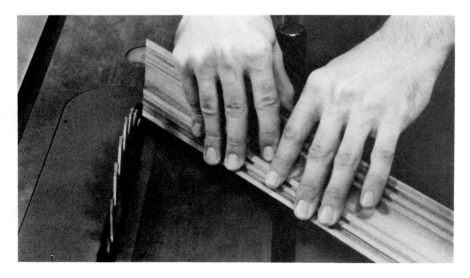

Fig. 553. For accuracy, cut one end of all compound mitres first. A stop rod can then be used to control length.

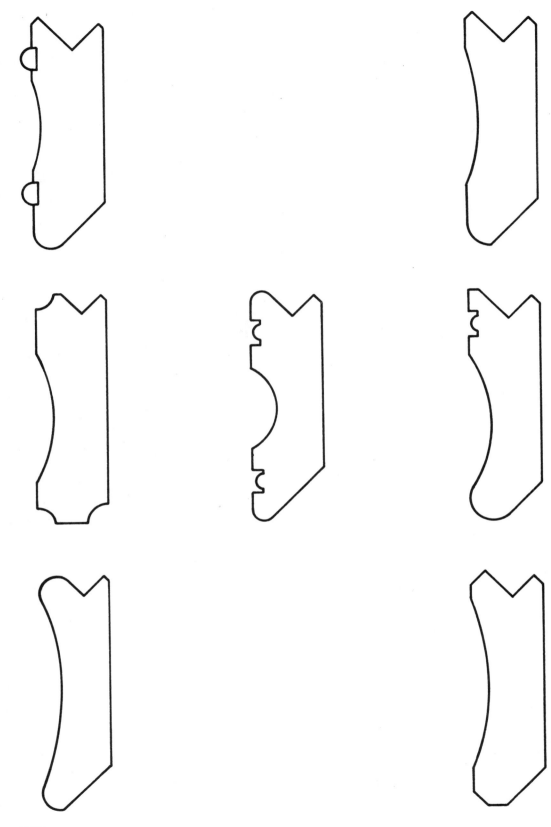

Fig. 554. These profiles will challenge your table saw skills. Photocopy them and glue them to your stock.

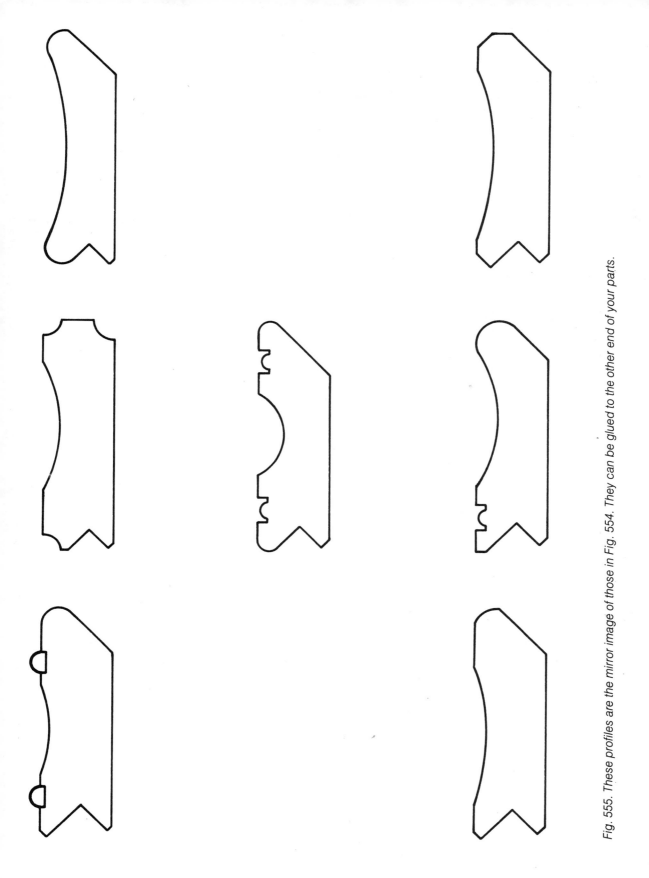

Fig. 555. These profiles are the mirror image of those in Fig. 554. They can be glued to the other end of your parts.

Fig. 556. A band clamp pulls all 4 corners uniformly. It is easy to adjust pieces held with a band clamp.

Fig. 557. Turn frames with compound mitres upside down for clamping. As the clamp is tightened, they lift like a pyramid.

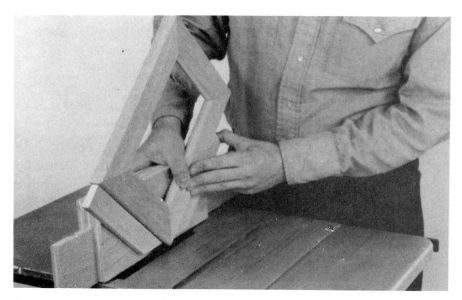

Fig. 558. This jig may be used to cut keyways in all 4 corners of the frame.

Fig. 559. Glue the keys in the keyways. Make the keys out of a different wood for contrast.

Fig. 560. The keys are sanded flush with the edges of the frame. The contrasting color gives a decorative effect.

For simple mitres, a spline can be cut. A universal jig (Fig. 561) is used to cut the groove. A spline is then used to reinforce the mitre. The spline locates parts and keeps them from slipping when they are glued together. Remember to keep all faces (or backs) in contact with the jig. Any error will be doubled if you do not. This means the mitres will not line up.

Mats and finish can affect the overall appearance of any frame. Plan ahead; remember the objects within the frame (Figs. 562 and 563) are more important than the frame.

Remember the following tips before beginning any picture frame project:

1. Review the mitre unit in Chapter 5 (pages 77–84).
2. Plan your shaping and cutting sequence and mark your stock before you begin. Keep 1 face and edge true for controlling the stock.

3. Allow at least 40 percent more stock than you need for set-up and mitre errors.
4. Use a sharp, hollow-ground combination blade to cut the mitres. Dull blades waste time and wood.
5. Be sure the blade is perpendicular to the table.
6. Use a jig and stop rod for accurate mitres. Lines drawn on the stock are not accurate enough.
7. Cut stock oversize; if the mitres need to be trimmed, the glass will still fit.
8. Work from the longest to shortest parts. Long errors can always be cut shorter.
9. Fit parts dry. Test the fit of the glass. Mark the position of the pieces at the corners. This allows you to put them back together the same way.
10. Sand all the parts well before assembly. It is difficult to sand the moulding on an assembled frame.
11. Use glue sparingly. It is difficult to remove glue from the corners of an assembled frame.

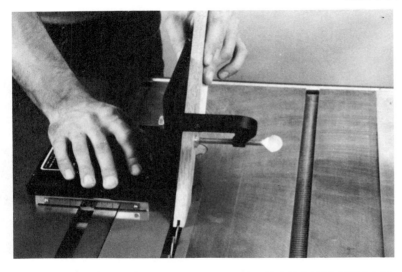

Fig. 561. Grooves for splines can be cut with this universal jig.

Fig. 562. This pecan frame was stained black and filled with white paste wood filler. The photo draws your eye.

Fig. 563. This frame and its message are hung prominently at Cliffe Cabinets.

Making Wall Clocks

Wall clocks are similar to picture frames. The clock frame holds a clock face and the picture frame holds the picture. Clocks are deeper and have less wood showing on the face. Usually the edge grain shows on the front of the clock, and the face grain shows on the front of a picture frame. Typical clock profiles are shown in Fig. 564. The clock face is either housed in a dado or it is held in a rabbet. Both methods hold the dial equally well.

There are many types of faces, motors and hands available. I made a burl-face clock with veneer (Fig. 565). Inexpensive paper face (Figs. 566 and 567) and porcelain-glazed metal face (Fig. 568) are also available. Select your materials from the many suppliers of clock parts. Faces can be manufactured or of your own design.

The motor size determines the position of the face in relation to the frame. Use the motor to determine placement of the dado or rabbet. Determine what type of decorative edge you wish to have surrounding the face, and rip your parts accordingly. Some faces look better if they are set back from the front of the frame. Others look better with less wood around them. Experiment with scraps or cut-offs for best results.

Begin with the faces. Paper faces must be backed with plywood . Make sure the glue you use is compatable with the face (Fig. 569). Wood glue does not hold thin metal faces to wood very well. Smooth out any bubbles (Fig. 570), and clamp the face to the plywood backing. Thin metal pieces may not require clamping, since other types of glue will be used.

Use the face to determine dado size. Cut the dado with a saw blade or dado head. Check the fit of the face in the dado (Fig. 571). It is easier to shape and dado pieces 12–18 inches (30.5–45.7 cm) long. Longer pieces tend to be warped or twisted. They do not shape as well as shorter pieces. Crosscut longer pieces into parts that are easier to handle. Avoid pieces under 12 inches (30.5 cm). They are likely to kick back or cause an accident.

The mitres can be cut several different ways. The stock can be placed on edge and fed with the mitre gauge (Fig. 572). The mitre gauge is turned 45° for this operation. This method will not work with very wide parts.

A mitre jig will also work for cutting the clock mitres. A shop-made jig or a commercial jig will work equally well. Set the jig up carefully. The blade may also be tilted for cutting the mitres. Set the mitre gauge at 90° and tilt the blade to 45° (Fig. 573). Adjust the blade and mitre gauge carefully. Adjustment errors will make the mitres difficult to fit. Use a stop block or rod to control part length. All parts of a square frame must be of equal length if the mitres are to fit well.

Review the section on mitres in Chapter 5 (pages 77–84) before beginning. There are many tips on blade selection, saw set-up and causes of poor-fitting mitres.

After the parts are cut, dry fit the clock (Fig. 574). You may wish to stain the inner parts before gluing the clock together. This will keep stain and finish off the clock face. Do not stain and finish the mitres. This will affect the strength of the mitre joint. The mitres can be reinforced with a spline or feather if desired. Clean off any excess glue after assembly, and select hands that look nice with the face (Fig. 575). Bolt the motor in place (Fig. 576) and attach the hands. Install a battery and test the movement. Handle the motors carefully. They are precision movements, and can be damaged easily.

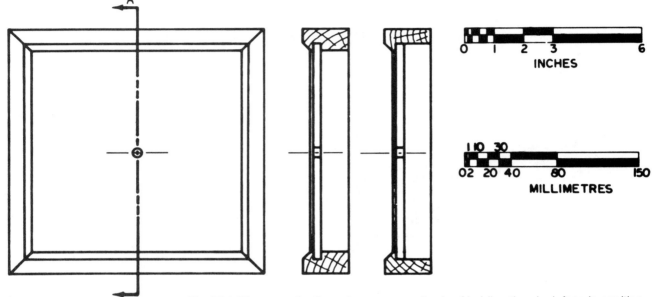

Fig. 564. These are the 2 most common methods of holding the clock face in position.

Fig. 565. This clock has a burl-veneer face. The veneer face provides an additional woodworking challenge.

Fig. 566. The inexpensive paper face on this clock must be glued and clamped carefully to avoid wrinkles and bubbles.

Fig. 568. This porcelain-glazed metal face is very easy to work with. It is thick enough to require no backing.

Fig. 567. This paper face has a plastic coating that makes it easier to work with.

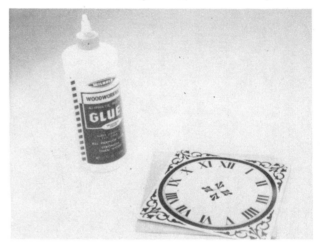

Fig. 569. Make sure the glue you use is compatible with the face. White or yellow glue works well with paper faces.

Fig. 570 (right). Be sure to smooth out any bubbles before clamping the face to a backer.

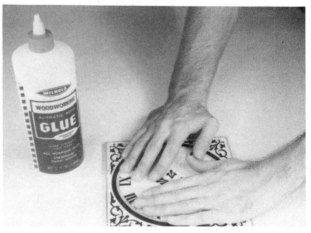

Fig. 571. The groove in this piece is cut to hold the clockface. Mitres will be cut later to make the frame.

Fig. 572. Mitres can be cut with the stock on edge. The blade is set at 90° and the mitre gauge is set at 45°.

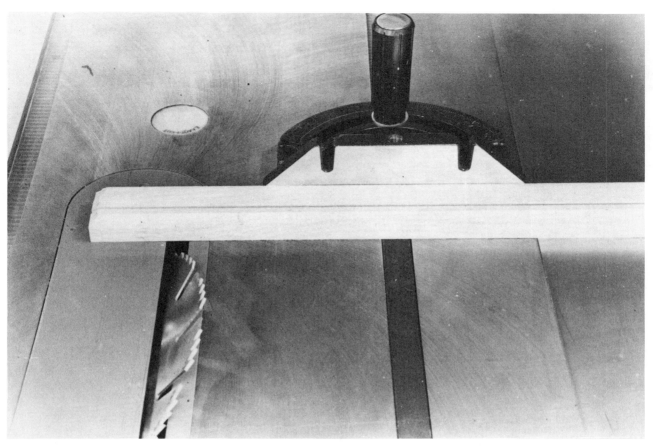

Fig. 573. The blade may be tilted to 45° to cut the mitre. Set the mitre gauge to 90° before the blade is tilted.

Fig. 574. Clamp up the clock dry to be sure the parts fit together well. Be sure to sand (and possibly finish) the inner surfaces before gluing.

Fig. 575. Assemble the motor and select hands that look nice with the face.

Fig. 576. Bolt the motor in place before attaching the hands. Handle the motors carefully. They can be damaged easily.

Making a Brush Holder

The brush holder (Fig. 577) is a nice addition in most bathrooms. It keeps brushes, combs and other clutter off the sink. This is a simple project. The biggest challenge is cutting the cove.

Study Fig. 578 and develop a bill of materials. Cut the back, and disc sand the ends to the correct radius (Fig. 579). Rout the edge to the desired shape. Sand the face and edges lightly.

Lay out the cove on the end of the tray (Fig. 580). Remove most of the stock with a saw blade (Fig. 581) or a dado head. Set up the auxiliary fence and cut the cove (Fig. 582). Be sure to hold the stock against the fence with featherboards or another straightedge. Review the cove-cutting section in Chapter 6 (pages 147–156) before beginning the cove cut. This can be a dangerous operation if procedures are not followed carefully and correctly.

Make a sanding block to sand the cove (Fig. 583), or use a hand scraper. I found the swan-neck scraper to be the best tool to smooth this type of cove.

Glue and nail the caps on the end of the tray. Be sure to predrill the nail holes, or the stock may split when nailed. The caps are oversize. After the wood filler covers the nail holes, sand the ends to size.

Center the tray on the back and drill 3–4 holes. Countersink the holes and screw the back to the tray (Fig. 584). Apply the stain and finish of your choice. A water-resistant finish should be used to protect the wood. The brush holder can now be mounted.

Fig. 577. This brush holder eliminates clutter around the sink. It is a simple project to build.

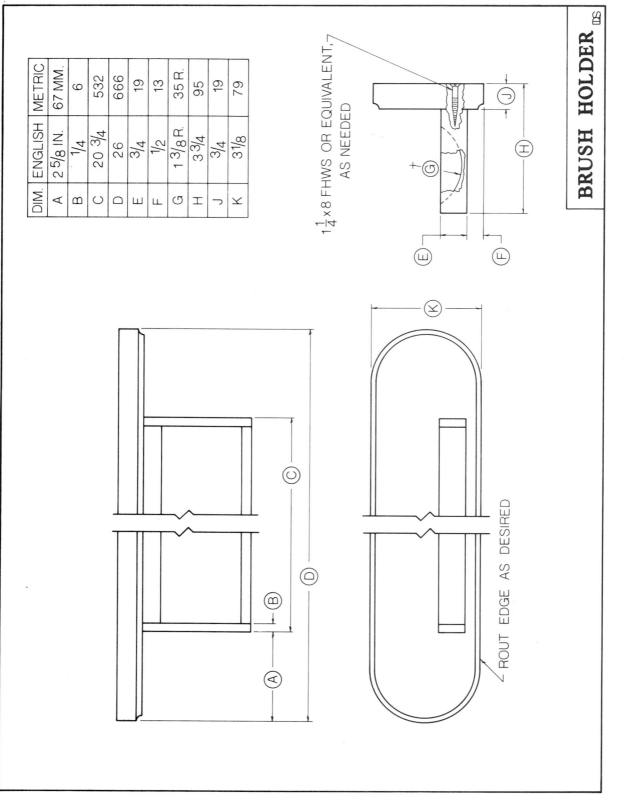

DIM.	ENGLISH	METRIC
A	2 5/8 IN.	67 MM.
B	1/4	6
C	20 3/4	532
D	26	666
E	3/4	19
F	1/2	13
G	1 3/8 R.	35 R.
H	3 3/4	95
J	3/4	19
K	3 1/8	79

1 1/4 × 8 FHWS OR EQUIVALENT, AS NEEDED

ROUT EDGE AS DESIRED

BRUSH HOLDER

Fig. 578. Study the plan for the brush holder before you begin.

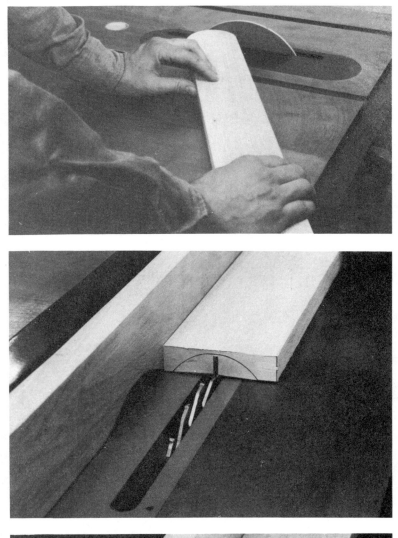

Fig. 579. The sanding disc can be used to smooth the ends of the back.

Fig. 580. The cove is laid out on the end of the tray. A piece of paper was glued to the end of this piece.

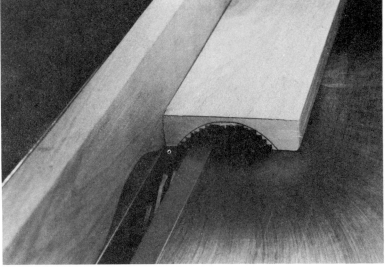

Fig. 581. Remove most of the stock inside the cove area with a saw blade or dado head.

291

Fig. 582. Set up an auxiliary fence to cut a cove. Note the feather-boards. They help control the work.

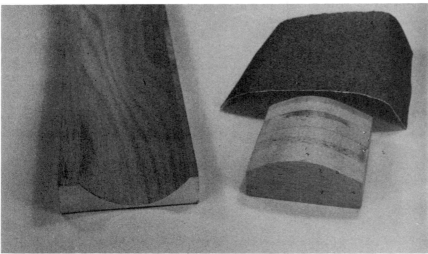

Fig. 583. A curved sanding block can be made to sand the cove. Begin sanding with a 60-grit abrasive.

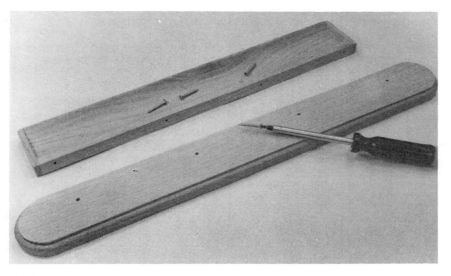

Fig. 584. Screw the back onto the tray with flathead screws. Be sure to countersink the heads.

Making a Bathroom Storage Cabinet

This bathroom storage cabinet (Fig. 585) provides many challenging table saw operations. There are grooves, dadoes, mortise-and-tenon joints, rabbets, raised panels and lap joints in the storage cabinet. The joints must be made exactly in order to have a cabinet of furniture-store quality. The cabinet sides can be made of plywood or solid wood. I used plywood because I had some short pieces on hand.

Study the drawings (Fig. 586) carefully before you begin. Make sure you understand how all the parts fit together. Review the related operations in the previous chapters. Be sure you can perform the operation safety and correctly; practice on some scraps if necessary.

Rip the stock for the faceplate. Cut the lap joints, and glue the parts together (Fig. 587). While the glue is drying, work on the sides. Cut the dado for the top and bottom of the cabinet. Rout 2 grooves for the metal shelf tracks between the dadoes. The sides should look like the one in Fig. 588.

Fit the sides to the top and bottom. Cut the nailers to size and assemble the cabinet. Use glue and nails to hold the parts. Make sure the cabinet is square. After the parts are assembled (Fig. 589), rout a rabbet in the sides and the nailers for the back. Square the corners with a chisel, and install the back. Use glue and nails (Fig. 590) to hold the back in position.

Remove the faceplate from the clamps and clean up the joints. Remove any excess glue and sand the joints smooth. Attach the faceplate to the cabinets (Fig. 591). Use glue and nails to anchor it. Clamp it in position when nailing. Be sure to drill pilot holes for the nails to avoid splitting the sides or faceplate.

Cut the door parts to size. Make up the mortises and tenons (Fig. 592). Cut the raised panels (Fig. 593), and sand them well. Once they are glued in the frame, they are difficult to sand. Test the fit of the door parts (Fig. 594) and make any needed adjustments. Glue and clamp the door together (Fig. 595). Make sure the door is square and the panel is centered. Use small nails to pin the panels in the center of the frame.

Fig. 585. This bathroom storage cabinet provides many table saw challenges. It is also a useful addition to your home.

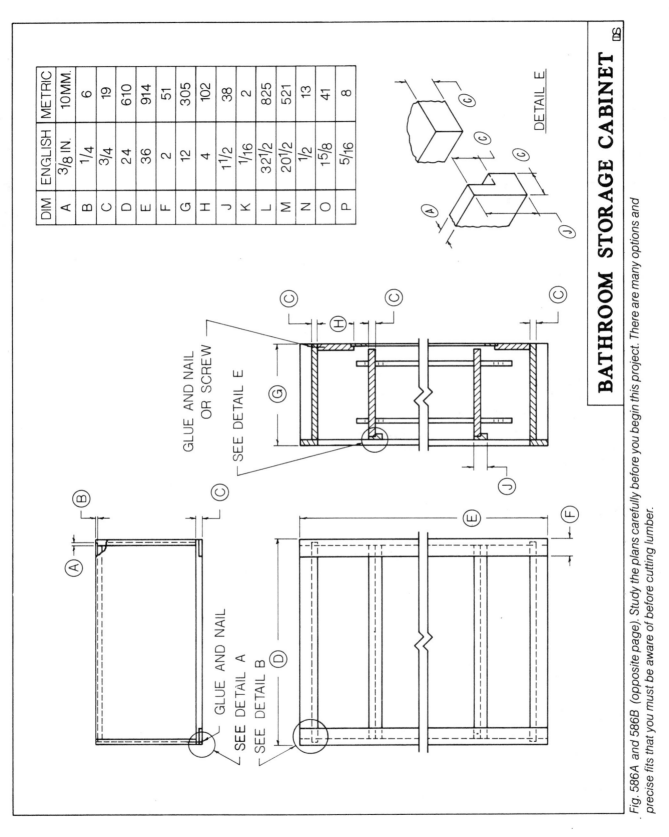

DIM	ENGLISH 3/8 IN.	METRIC 10MM.
A	3/8	6
B	1/4	19
C	3/4	19
D	24	610
E	36	914
F	2	51
G	12	305
H	4	102
J	1½	38
K	1/16	2
L	32½	825
M	20½	521
N	½	13
O	15/8	41
P	5/16	8

DETAIL E

GLUE AND NAIL
OR SCREW

SEE DETAIL E

GLUE AND NAIL

SEE DETAIL A

SEE DETAIL B

BATHROOM STORAGE CABINET

Fig. 586A and 586B (opposite page). Study the plans carefully before you begin this project. There are many options and precise fits that you must be aware of before cutting lumber.

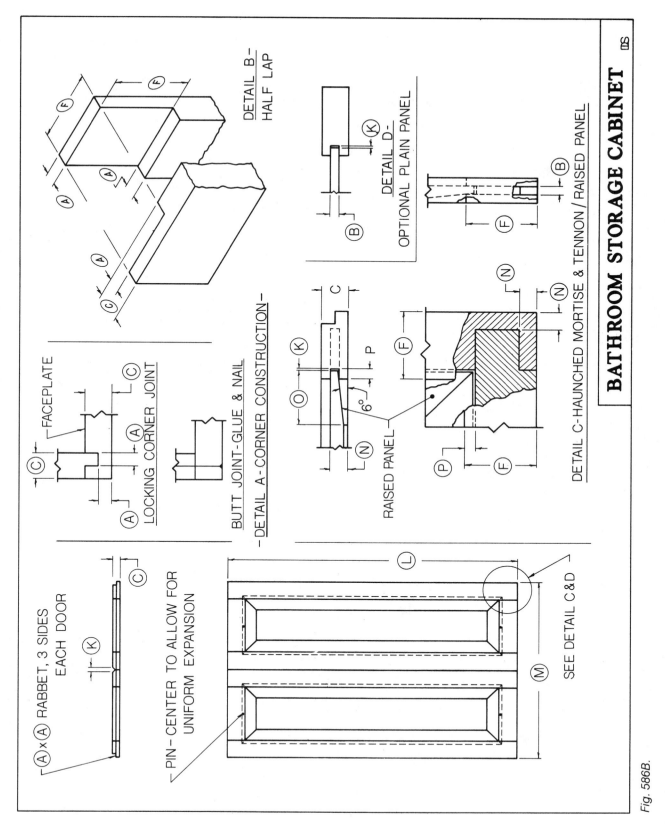

BATHROOM STORAGE CABINET

DETAIL B – HALF LAP

DETAIL D – OPTIONAL PLAIN PANEL

DETAIL C – HAUNCHED MORTISE & TENNON / RAISED PANEL

RAISED PANEL

FACEPLATE

LOCKING CORNER JOINT

BUTT JOINT – GLUE & NAIL

– DETAIL A – CORNER CONSTRUCTION –

(A) x (A) RABBET, 3 SIDES EACH DOOR

PIN – CENTER TO ALLOW FOR UNIFORM EXPANSION

SEE DETAIL C&D

Fig. 586B.

295

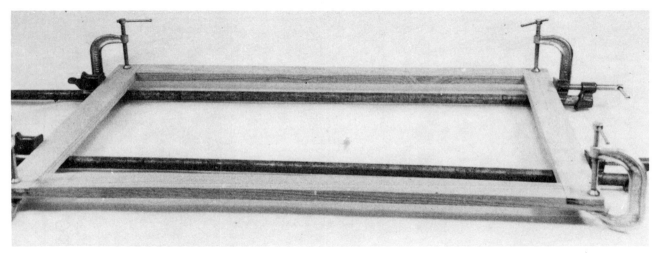

Fig. 587. Glue and clamp the faceplate together. Use the glue sparingly to avoid glue blemishes in the finish.

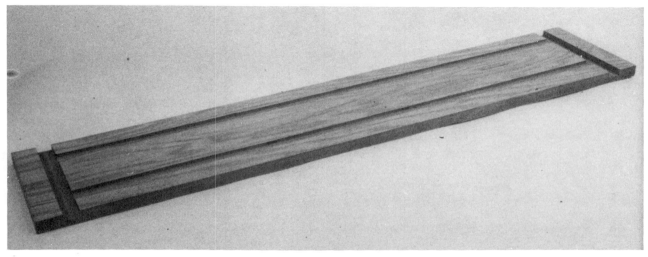

Fig. 588. After all cuts are made in the side, it should look like this.

Fig. 589. Assemble the parts, and rout the nailers and sides for the back. Square up the arc made by the router with a chisel.

Fig. 590. Use glue and nails to hold the back in position.

Fig. 591. After the faceplate is sanded, it may be attached to the cabinet.

Fig. 592. Cut the grooves, mortises and tenons on the door parts. The dado head is being used to cut the haunch on the door rail.

Fig. 593. Cut the raised panels carefully. The straightedge keeps the panel from dropping through the throat plate.

Fig. 594. Make a trial assembly of the door parts before gluing them together. Sand the panel completely. It will be difficult to sand in the assembled door.

Fig. 595. Make sure the door is square and the panel is centered when you glue up the door. Pin the center of the panel from the back side.

Rabbet the shelf fronts (Fig. 596), and glue them to the shelves (Fig. 597). Use the glue sparingly so there is no excess glue damage to the finish.

Cut the rabbet on the doors with a shaper head or dado head (Fig. 598). Remember, the rabbet is cut on only 1 edge of the door. The edge facing center is bevelled slightly, but not rabbeted. The bevel provides clearance when opening. If the door were not bevelled, the back corner would hit the other door as it was opened.

Determine the location of the hinge on the door (Fig. 599), and mark the position of the screws. Provide an indentation for the drill bit using an awl. Drill the holes carefully. Avoid drilling through the door. Install the hinge (Fig. 600). Avoid damage to the screws by using the correct screwdriver.

Position the door on the faceplate and mark the screw locations carefully (Fig. 601). Self-closing hinges tend to move around while they are being mounted. Hold the door securely when marking the hinge position and screwing the door in place.

Install the shelf tracks in the dadoes on the cabinet sides. Make sure a reference point is used for installation. This will keep the shelves from rocking. Fit the shelves in position; trim the length if they rub against the tracks or sides.

After all the parts have been fitted and marked, the hardware can be removed for finishing. Fill all holes, and sand the cabinet parts carefully. Be sure to sand with the grain. Apply the stain and finish of your choice and reassemble the cabinet. It may now be installed.

Fig. 596. The rabbet on the shelf front was made using a single blade and 2 cuts. A dado head or shaper head may also be used.

Fig. 597. The shelf front is glued and clamped to the plywood shelf. The front makes the shelf rigid and covers the plywood edge.

Fig. 598. The rabbet on the door was cut with the dado head. Rabbet only 1 edge of the door.

Fig. 599. The top (or bottom) of the hinge is marked. The position of the holes in the hinge is then marked. Note the hinge marks on the door.

Fig. 600. After pilot holes are drilled, the screws are driven through the holes in the hinge. Be careful not to damage the screwheads.

Fig. 601. The door is positioned on the faceplate, and the screw holes are marked. Hold the door securely while marking the screw holes.

Building a Nightstand

The nightstand (Fig. 602) is one of the most challenging projects in this section. There are many table saw operations included in this project. The cabinet may be built with or without a door. In addition to being used as a nightstand next to the bed, it may also be used as an end table next to your favorite easy chair.

Study the drawings (Fig. 603A–D) carefully before you begin; make sure you know how the parts are to be machined and assembled. Develop a bill of materials and a plan of procedure. Break the plan of procedure down into subassemblies such as: faceplate, top, cabinet assembly, door and drawer. This will allow you to work on different areas of the project when certain assemblies are in the clamps.

Rip the faceplate stock to size. Cut the parts to length and make the lap joints. Make a trial cut in some cut-offs so you are certain the lap joint is set up correctly. Glue and clamp the parts together (Fig. 604) after a trial fit.

Cut the parts of the cabinet, and assemble them to the faceplate (Fig. 605). Sand and trim the faceplate before assembly. Cut notches in the corner blocks so clamps may be used to hold them in place. After the glue cures, the base moulding may be installed.

Lay out the parts for the top (Fig. 606). Cut the spline joints and the mitres. Glue and clamp the parts together after a dry fit (Fig. 607). Sand the top and remove any excess glue (Fig. 608). Cut some keys into the mitres (Fig. 609). Keep them below center so they will not be cut away when the edge is shaped (Fig. 610). Use the shaper head (Fig. 611) or a router to shape the edge of the top. Use this same set-up to shape the top edge of the base moulding (Fig. 612).

Cut and sand the raised panel (Figs. 613 and 614). Make the other door parts and assemble the door (Fig. 615). Rabbet all 4 edges of the door with a shaper head (Fig. 616), dado head or router. Center the panel and pin it (Fig. 617) in position. Locate the hinges on the door, drill pilot holes and screw the hinges in place (Fig. 618).

Locate the door on the faceplate and mark the position of the holes (Fig. 619). Drill pilot holes and screw the hinges in position.

Cut the drawer parts and fit the drawer together without glue. Stain and finish the drawer front before you glue the drawer together. This gives the nightstand a professional look (Fig. 620).

Install the drawer guides and fit the drawer to the opening. Screw the top in place. Remove the hardware and sand all the parts. Apply the stain, and finish and reassemble the nightstand.

Fig. 602. This nightstand offers many challenges to the table saw. It may be made with or without a door, and also looks nice as an end table next to your favorite chair.

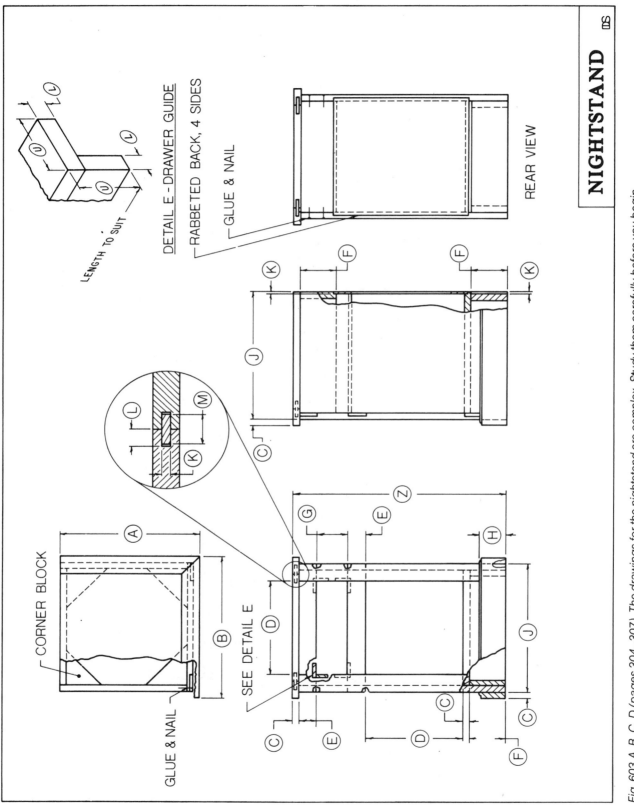

CORNER BLOCK

GLUE & NAIL

SEE DETAIL E

DETAIL E - DRAWER GUIDE

RABBETED BACK, 4 SIDES

GLUE & NAIL

LENGTH TO SUIT

REAR VIEW

NIGHTSTAND

Fig. 603 A, B, C, D (pages 304–307). The drawings for the nightstand are complex. Study them carefully before you begin.

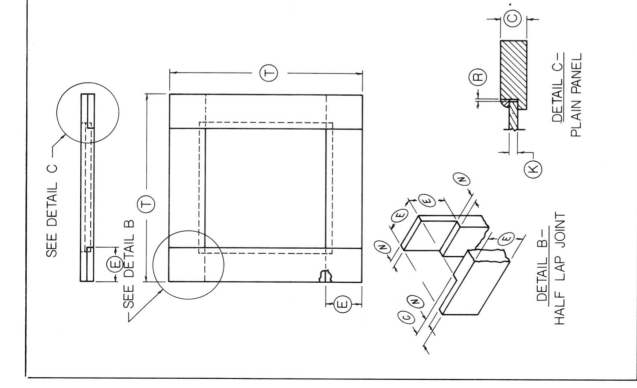

DIM.	ENGLISH	METRIC
A	15 3/4 IN.	400 MM.
B	16 1/2	419
C	3/4	19
D	11	279
E	2	51
F	4	102
G	3 1/2	89
H	3	76
J	15	381
K	1/4	6
L	1/2	13
M	7/8	22
N	3/8	10
O	11 1/2	292
P	1 1/4	32
Q	1 5/8	41
R	1/16	2
S	5/16	8
T	10 7/8	276
U	1 3/4	44
V	3/16	5
W	3 7/16	87
X	13 1/2	343
Y	10 3/8	262
Z	24	610

NIGHTSTAND

SEE DETAIL C

SEE DETAIL B

DETAIL C—
PLAIN PANEL

DETAIL B—
HALF LAP JOINT

Fig. 603B.

305

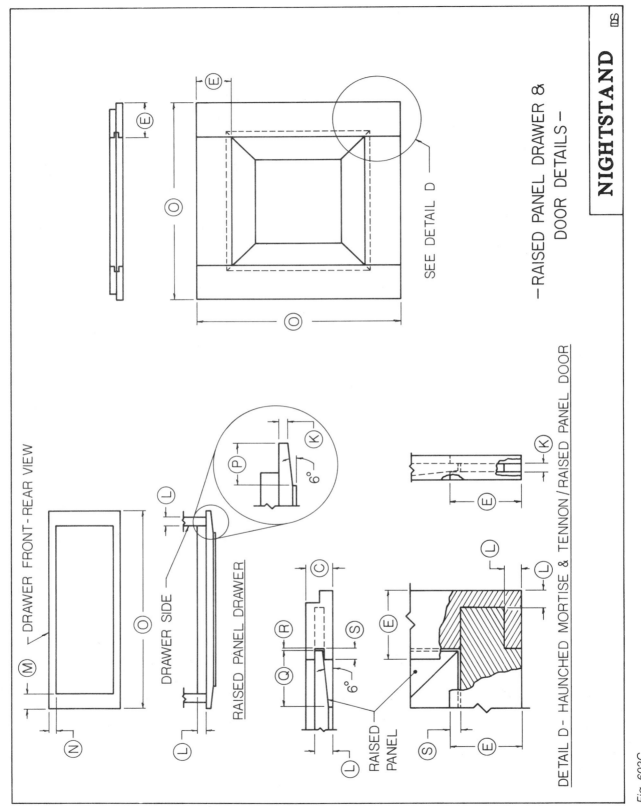

NIGHTSTAND

—RAISED PANEL DRAWER &
DOOR DETAILS—

SEE DETAIL D

DRAWER FRONT-REAR VIEW

DRAWER SIDE

RAISED PANEL DRAWER

RAISED PANEL

6°

DETAIL D - HAUNCHED MORTISE & TENNON/RAISED PANEL DOOR

Fig. 603C.

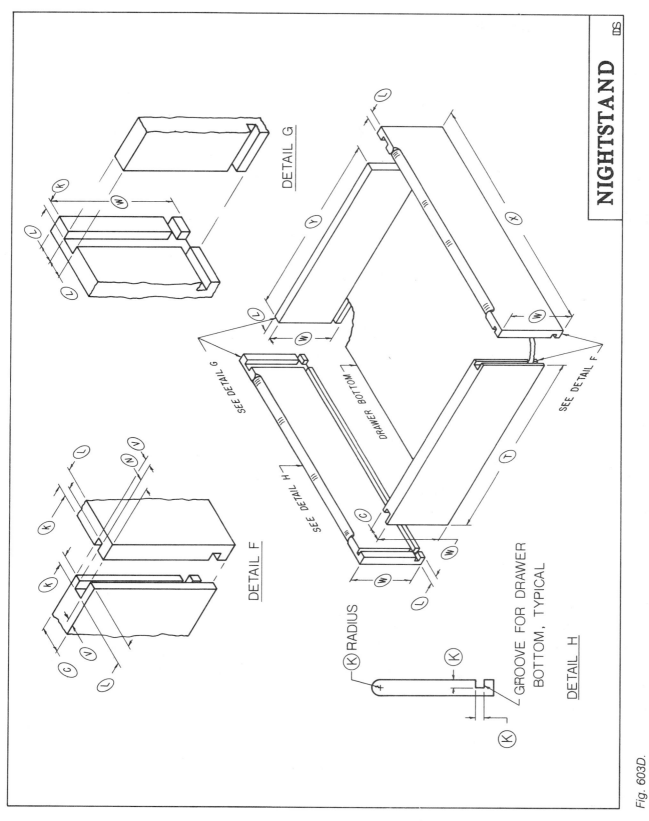

NIGHTSTAND

DETAIL G

SEE DETAIL G

SEE DETAIL H

DRAWER BOTTOM

SEE DETAIL F

DETAIL F

(K) RADIUS

GROOVE FOR DRAWER BOTTOM, TYPICAL

DETAIL H

Fig. 603D.

307

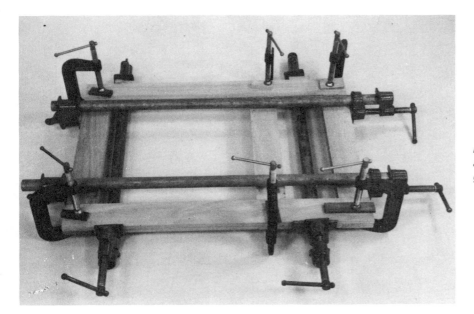

Fig. 604. After the lap joints are cut and fitted, the faceplate can be glued together.

Fig. 605. The faceplate is trimmed and glued to the cabinet parts. Nails may be used to reinforce the butt joint. Notch the corner blocks so they are easy to clamp.

Fig. 606. Lay out the parts for the top and mark them carefully. Chalk works well because it is easy to remove.

Fig. 607. Assemble the top after cutting the splines and mitres. Clamp the parts securely.

Fig. 608. Sand the top carefully after the glue cures.

Fig. 609. Cut keys into the mitres. The universal jig was used for this operation.

310

Fig. 610. The keys are below the centerline. They will not be cut away when the edge is shaped.

Fig. 611. The shaper head can be used to cut a decorative edge on the top. Take light cuts!

Fig. 612. The base moulding is shaped on the same set-up as the top. Work slowly and take light cuts.

Fig. 613. Cut the raised panel using the procedure outlined in Chapter 6 (pages 187 and 188).

Fig. 614. Sand the raised panel with a small sander. Sand it completely before assembling the door.

Fig. 615. Glue and clamp the door after fitting. Make sure the door is square and the panel is centered.

Fig. 616. The shaper head was used to cut the rabbet on the 4 door edges.

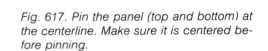

Fig. 617. Pin the panel (top and bottom) at the centerline. Make sure it is centered before pinning.

Fig. 618. Locate the hinges, drill the pilot holes and screw the hinges in position.

Fig. 619. Locate the door carefully. Mark the screw holes with an awl and drill pilot holes. Attach the door and test the fit.

Fig. 620. The drawer front was stained and finished before the drawer was glued together. This gives the nightstand a professional look.

Building a Food Preparation Table

The food preparation table in Fig. 621 was designed for a client who wanted a cutting area and preparation surface for his kitchen. The drawers store knives and other kitchen tools. The drawer fronts (Fig. 622) are bird's-eye maple. A locking corner joint was used to join the drawer front to the sides.

This table was made of maple. It features knockdown construction. The rails go through the legs and are held securely with wedges (Fig. 623). The top is located on 2 dowels, and rests on top of the legs.

The top can be glued up and planed to thickness or it can be purchased as a completed bench top. The com-

pleted bench top is more expensive, but less labor and machinery are needed. The drawer guides are screwed to the tabletop. The drawer sides are dadoed to travel on the guides.

Study the drawings (Figs. 624–628) carefully before you begin. Closed-grain woods are best for this table. Start the building sequence with the legs and rails, then make the top and construct the drawers. Select your wood with care. Avoid checks, knots and cracks. All parts of the leg and rail unit should be free of defects. Set aside any stock with interesting grain patterns. This stock can be used for drawer fronts.

Lay out the tenons on the rails and cut them with the dado head. Read the section on mortise-and-tenon joints in Chapter 6 (pages 132–138) before you begin. Make the tenons slightly oversize. This allows you to smooth the exposed surfaces with a chisel.

Lay out and cut the mortises on the edges of the legs. Fit the tenons, and glue up the leg assembly. After the glue dries, the mortises can be cut for the rails. Keep the unit square while fitting the rails. After the joint is made, the holes for the wedge must be drilled and fitted. Use details A, B and C (Figs. 624 and 625) for laying out mortises and wedges. Note that the hole is larger than the wedge. This allows the wedge to pull the unit together snugly.

Cut and carve the wedge carefully. When it is installed (Fig. 623), it can enhance the overall appearance of the table. Make an extra wedge or 2, in case they are lost when the table is disassembled.

Glue up the tabletop and plane it to thickness. A water-resistant glue would be best for the tabletop. Glue the dowels into the top of 2 opposing legs (Fig. 624). Position the top on the legs. Mark the location of the blind holes into which the dowels will fit. Bore these holes and test the fit of the top on the legs. If the top is warped, some shimming or planing may be needed.

Study the drawer details and assembly drawing (Figs. 626 and 627) before cutting the drawers. Note the alternate drawer front, and decide which drawer you wish to make. Cut the joints accurately. Study the drawer section in Chapter 6 (pages 192–206) before you begin. Assemble the drawer without glue to test the fit of the parts. Make any needed adjustments, and glue the drawers together.

Cut the drawer guides (Fig. 628) to fit the dadoes on the drawer sides. Locate the guides on the underside of the tabletop. Use Phillips® head screws to secure the guides (Fig. 629). The Phillips® screwdriver will go into the hole without interference. Adjust the drawers for smooth operation and apply the finish. I used a nontoxic oil finish on my table. I also made some knife racks to fit in the drawers. These racks were designed to fit my client's knife assortment.

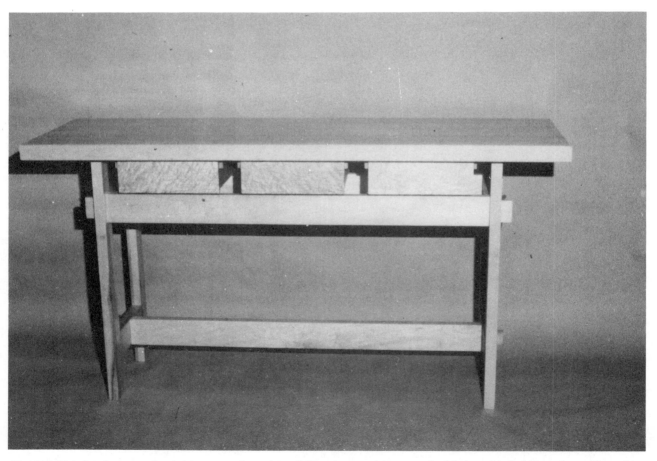

Fig. 621. This food preparation table can make a nice addition to a pantry or country kitchen. It is held together with wedges, and may be dismantled for transportation.

Fig. 622. The locking corner adds to the quality of this table. Note the bird's-eye maple drawer fronts.

Fig. 623. Wedges hold these through mortise-and-tenon joints securely. Contrasting wood color adds accent to the table.

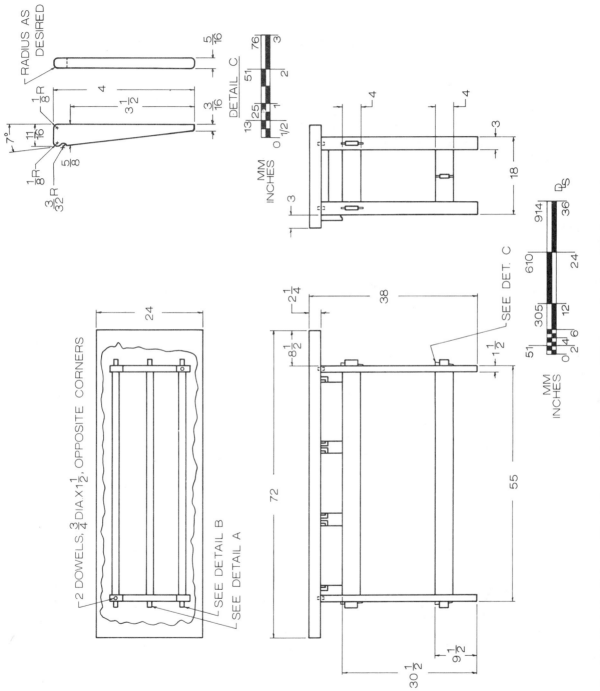

Fig. 624. Study the 3 views of the table presented here. They will help you develop a bill of materials.

318

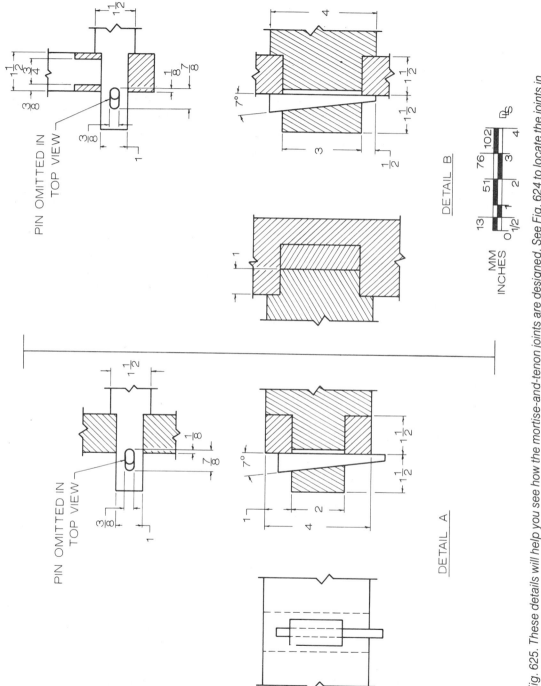

PIN OMITTED IN
TOP VIEW

DETAIL B

PIN OMITTED IN
TOP VIEW

DETAIL A

MM
INCHES

Fig. 625. These details will help you see how the mortise-and-tenon joints are designed. See Fig. 624 to locate the joints in the correct position.

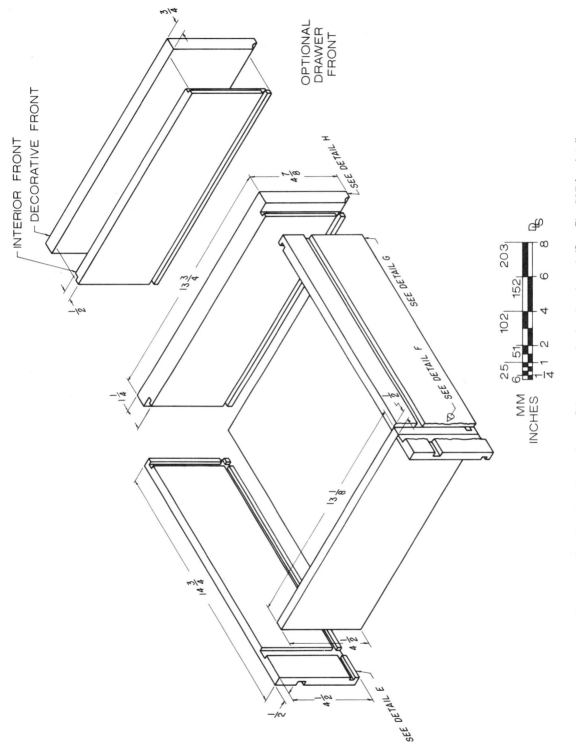

INTERIOR FRONT
DECORATIVE FRONT

OPTIONAL DRAWER FRONT

$\frac{3}{4}$

$\frac{1}{2}$

$13\frac{3}{4}$

$1\frac{1}{4}$

$4\frac{7}{8}$

SEE DETAIL H

SEE DETAIL F

SEE DETAIL G

$\frac{1}{2}$

SEE DETAIL D

$13\frac{1}{8}$

$14\frac{3}{4}$

$\frac{1}{2}$

$4\frac{1}{2}$

$4\frac{1}{2}$

$\frac{1}{2}$

SEE DETAIL E

MM   25 51 102 152 203
6   Ø
INCHES $\frac{1}{4}$ 1 2 4 6 8

Fig. 626. This drawer detail gives you 2 options for drawer fronts. Others may also be developed. (See Fig. 627 for details E–H.)

320

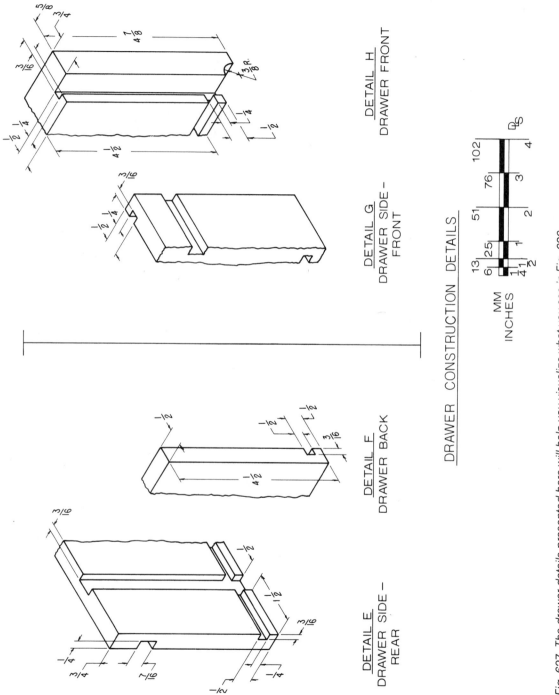

DETAIL H
DRAWER FRONT

DETAIL G
DRAWER SIDE –
FRONT

DETAIL F
DRAWER BACK

DETAIL E
DRAWER SIDE –
REAR

DRAWER CONSTRUCTION DETAILS

Fig. 627. The drawer details presented here will help you visualize what you see in Fig. 626.

321

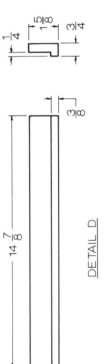

DETAIL D

$14\frac{7}{8}$

$\frac{3}{8}$

$\frac{1}{4}$

$1\frac{5}{8}$

$\frac{3}{4}$

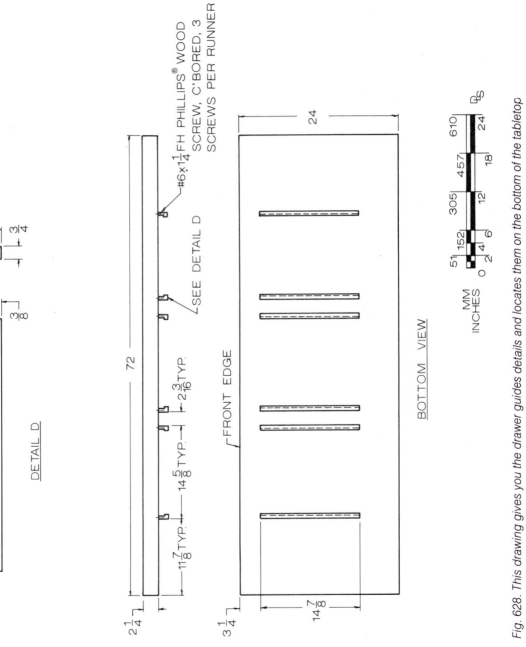

#6x1$\frac{1}{4}$ FH PHILLIPS® WOOD
SCREW, C'BORED, 3
SCREWS PER RUNNER

SEE DETAIL D

FRONT EDGE

$2\frac{3}{16}$ TYP.

$14\frac{5}{8}$ TYP.

$11\frac{7}{8}$ TYP.

72

$2\frac{1}{4}$

24

$14\frac{7}{8}$

$3\frac{1}{4}$

BOTTOM VIEW

MM
INCHES

51 152 305 457 610
0 2 4 6 12 18 24

Fig. 628. This drawing gives you the drawer guides details and locates them on the bottom of the tabletop

322

Fig. 629. Use a Phillips® screwdriver to mount the guides. It fits easily into the counterbored holes.

Building a Gun Cabinet

These gun cabinets (Figs. 630 and 631) have been quite popular. Despite the fact that many collectors store their guns in vaults, I have sold 6 of these cabinets in the past year. The cabinet with 2 doors in the base (Fig. 630) was my first design. It fits in the average house with 8-foot (2.4-m) ceilings. The cabinet with the drawer base (Fig. 631) was designed for lower ceilings such as those found in basement, recreation and hobby rooms.

Both gun cabinets are a challenge to the woodworker. There are lap, mitre, mortise-and-tenon and rabbet joints in both gun cabinets. The drawer base offers the challenge of drawer construction with raised panel fronts. The door base offers the challenge of raised panels and haunched mortise-and-tenon joints. This base could be made as a separate unit (Fig. 632). It could be used as a storage cabinet for books, records or stereo components.

This project is large, and errors will be expensive. Study the plans and related sections in the book before you begin. Make your cuts accurately, and keep your assemblies square. Little errors tend to compound themselves as construction continues.

Before cutting any parts, study the 3 drawings of the gun cabinet (Figs. 633–635) and decide which base you wish to make. Make the faceplate for the base and upper cabinet at the same time. While the glue is curing, all of the doors can be made. Use your straightest, truest stock for the doors. Study the door details (Figs. 636–638) before you begin. Cut all the joints carefully. Glue and clamp the doors. Keep the clamps in a true plane so the doors do not twist.

After the glue dries, cut the rabbets for the glass with a router. Square up the corners and make some quarter-round moulding. Shape the edge of a wide board, and cut the moulding away from the larger piece. Three of the outside edges of each door must also be rabbeted (Fig. 637). This may be done on the table saw or with a router.

The base doors have a haunched mortise and tenon and hold a panel (Fig. 638). Cut the raised panels or plywood panels and sand them thoroughly. They are very difficult to sand when they are in the door frame. Glue and clamp these doors after a trial fit.

Note: The panels are not glued to the groove. They float freely in the groove. This allows the panel to expand and contract with changes in the humidity. Usually the panel is centered and pinned in position (Fig. 617).

Cut the base and upper cabinet parts. Make all necessary joinery cuts, and dry fit the parts together. Test the unit for squareness and fit. Make sure the faceplate is slightly larger than the cabinet. This allows the faceplate to be trimmed for an exact fit. Sand the inside of all parts before assembly.

Glue and clamp the base and upper cabinet parts together. After the glue cures, they can be routed to accommodate the back. Sand and install the back.

The top of the base and upper cabinet can now be constructed. Both parts are plywood, with solid stock splined to them. The corners are mitred and keyed. The key is closer to the bottom on the base top and closer to the top on the upper top. This keeps the key intact when the edges are shaped.

Position and mount the tops. They should be fastened with wood screws. No screws should be visible inside the upper cabinet.

Cut the base moulding and fit it to the case. Use a fine-tooth blade to cut the mitres. Screw the base moulding to the cabinet from the back.

If you are making the drawer base, the drawers should be constructed now. Study the drawer details and assembly drawings (Figs. 639 and 640). Select the appropriate side guides, and make the correct allowances in drawer size. Cut the drawer joints and test the fit of the parts. Assemble the drawer dry, and check for fit and squareness. Glue up the drawers if the fit is correct.

Make the fronts for the drawers and screw them to the false fronts. Mount the drawer guides to the drawer sides. Slim the sides of the cabinet, and mount the drawer guides to the cabinet. Test the fit of the drawers to the cabinet, and make any needed adjustments.

Study the gun barrel and gun butt cutouts (Fig. 641), and make a template. Fit the gun butt part to the bottom of the cabinet and make the cutouts. Do the same for the gun barrel part. Make sure these cutouts are correct for the guns being stored. Double-barrelled guns may require larger cutouts. Sand these parts carefully. Do not install them until the finish has been applied.

Fit the hinges to the doors. Use 3 hinges on the upper doors. This keeps them truer and minimizes the chance of warp. Mount the doors on the cabinets, and do any necessary hand fitting. Bevel the mating edges of the doors with a block plane. This will keep the back edge of the door from rubbing as the door is opened.

Do not make the doors fit too tightly. Remember, 2 coats of finish on both doors will make the fit even closer. It is not much fun to plane door edges after the finish has been applied. Fit the door pulls and/or drawer pulls, and remove all hardware for final sanding and finishing.

Make the top for each unit and shape the edges. The mitres should be keyed. Add the trim moulding under the top of the upper unit, and fit the 2 units together. Use bolts and "T" nuts for this.

Fill all holes, raise all dents and check all surfaces for glue blemishes. Sand all parts carefully before applying the stain and finish. Rub out the finish and install the glass in the upper doors. Work carefully when installing the glass. Predrill the holes in the moulding, and drive the nails carefully. Keep the glass clean, and protect the finish by working on carpet scraps.

Install the gun butt cutout, and mount the gun barrel cutout to the back. Adjust the barrel cutout height to accommodate the longest and shortest barrel in the gun collection.

It may also be desirable to install locking devices on the doors if small children play near the cabinet. Locks will not keep burglars out, however; they just break the glass and take the guns.

Fig. 630. These cabinets are 2 of the 6 that I have sold in the past year. The one on the left is oak, and the one on the right is walnut.

Fig. 631. This drawer base makes the cabinet shorter. This style is popular in base-
ments or recreation rooms with low ceilings.

Fig. 632. The door base could be made as a separate unit. It could be modified for book, album or stereo component storage.

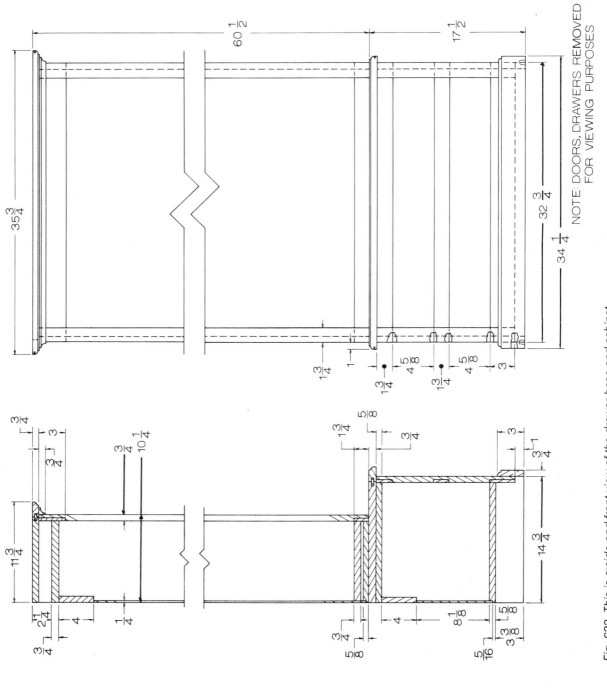

NOTE: DOORS, DRAWERS REMOVED FOR VIEWING PURPOSES

Fig. 633. This is a side and front view of the drawer base and cabinet.

326

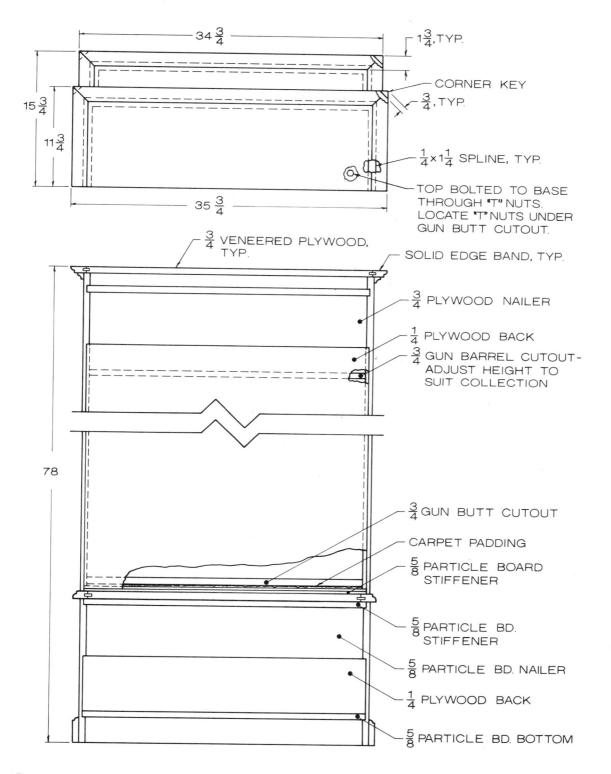

Fig. 634. This is a rear and top view of the drawer base and cabinet.

$34\frac{3}{4}$

$1\frac{3}{4}$, TYP.

CORNER KEY

$15\frac{3}{4}$

$\frac{3}{4}$, TYP.

$11\frac{3}{4}$

$\frac{1}{4} \times 1\frac{1}{4}$ SPLINE, TYP.

TOP BOLTED TO BASE THROUGH "T" NUTS. LOCATE "T" NUTS UNDER GUN BUTT CUTOUT.

$35\frac{3}{4}$

$\frac{3}{4}$ VENEERED PLYWOOD, TYP.

SOLID EDGE BAND, TYP.

$\frac{3}{4}$ PLYWOOD NAILER

$\frac{1}{4}$ PLYWOOD BACK

$\frac{3}{4}$ GUN BARREL CUTOUT- ADJUST HEIGHT TO SUIT COLLECTION

78

$\frac{3}{4}$ GUN BUTT CUTOUT

CARPET PADDING

$\frac{5}{8}$ PARTICLE BOARD STIFFENER

$\frac{5}{8}$ PARTICLE BD. STIFFENER

$\frac{5}{8}$ PARTICLE BD. NAILER

$\frac{1}{4}$ PLYWOOD BACK

$\frac{5}{8}$ PARTICLE BD. BOTTOM

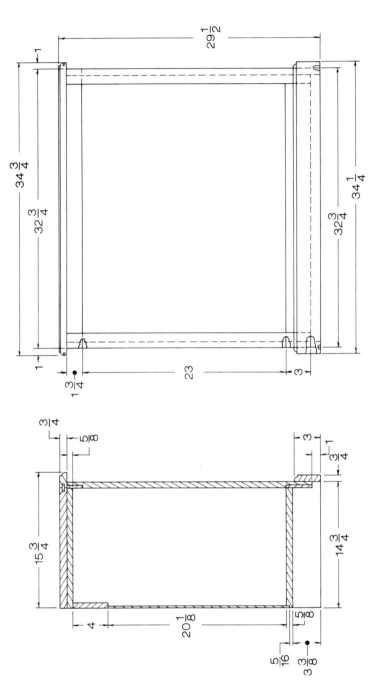

NOTE: DOORS REMOVED FOR
VIEWING PURPOSES

Fig. 635. This is a front and side view of the door base. The doors were removed for clarity.

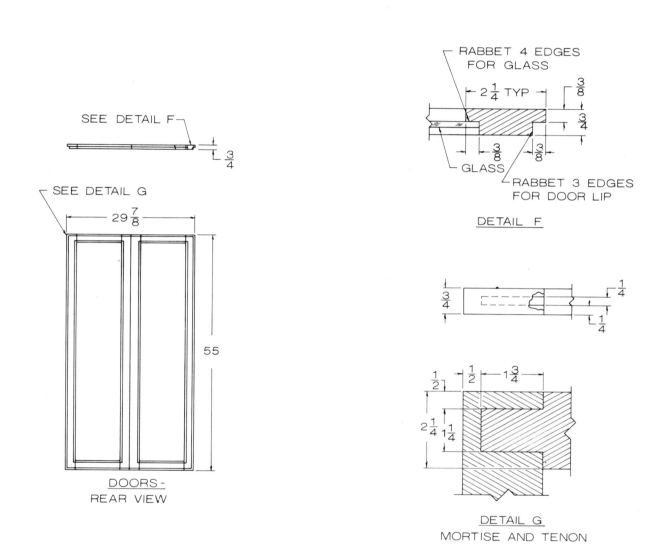

SEE DETAIL F

$\frac{3}{4}$

SEE DETAIL G

$29\frac{7}{8}$

55

DOORS -
REAR VIEW

RABBET 4 EDGES
FOR GLASS

$2\frac{1}{4}$ TYP

$\frac{3}{8}$

$\frac{3}{4}$

$\frac{3}{8}$

$\frac{3}{8}$

GLASS

RABBET 3 EDGES
FOR DOOR LIP

DETAIL F

$\frac{3}{4}$

$\frac{1}{4}$

$\frac{1}{4}$

$\frac{1}{2}$

$\frac{1}{2}$

$1\frac{3}{4}$

$2\frac{1}{4}$ $1\frac{1}{4}$

DETAIL G
MORTISE AND TENON

Fig. 636. This is a detail drawing of the upper glass doors.

329

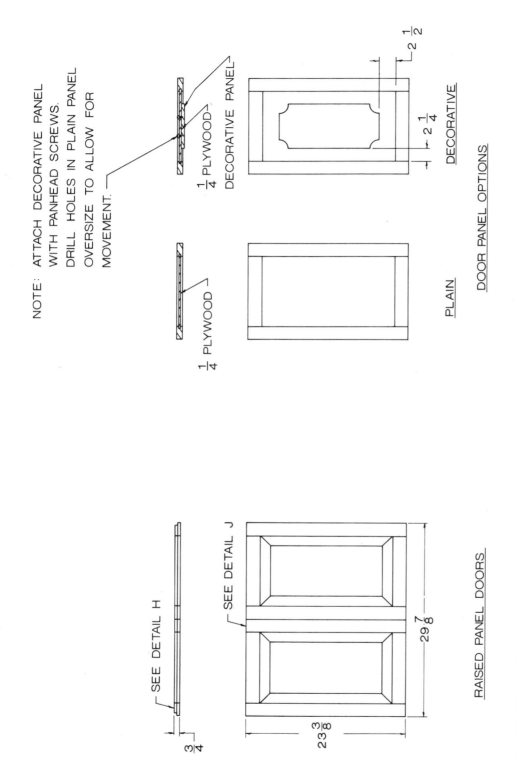

NOTE: ATTACH DECORATIVE PANEL WITH PANHEAD SCREWS. DRILL HOLES IN PLAIN PANEL OVERSIZE TO ALLOW FOR MOVEMENT.

$\frac{1}{4}$ PLYWOOD

DECORATIVE PANEL

$\frac{1}{4}$ PLYWOOD

$2\frac{1}{2}$

$2\frac{1}{4}$

DECORATIVE

PLAIN

DOOR PANEL OPTIONS

SEE DETAIL H

SEE DETAIL J

$\frac{3}{4}$

$29\frac{7}{8}$

$23\frac{3}{8}$

RAISED PANEL DOORS

Fig. 637. This detail drawing is of the lower panel doors. Note the door options.

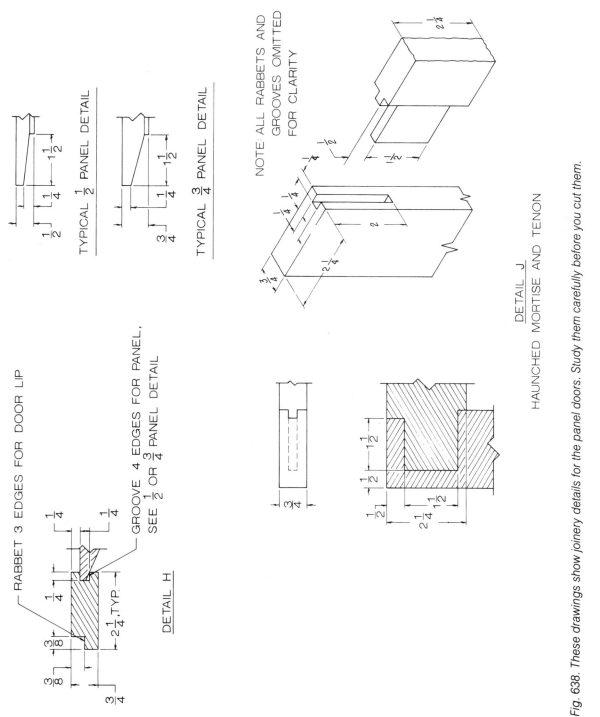

TYPICAL $\frac{1}{2}$ PANEL DETAIL

TYPICAL $\frac{3}{4}$ PANEL DETAIL

RABBET 3 EDGES FOR DOOR LIP

GROOVE 4 EDGES FOR PANEL, SEE $\frac{1}{2}$ OR $\frac{3}{4}$ PANEL DETAIL

DETAIL H

NOTE: ALL RABBETS AND GROOVES OMITTED FOR CLARITY

DETAIL J
HAUNCHED MORTISE AND TENON

Fig. 638. These drawings show joinery details for the panel doors. Study them carefully before you cut them.

331

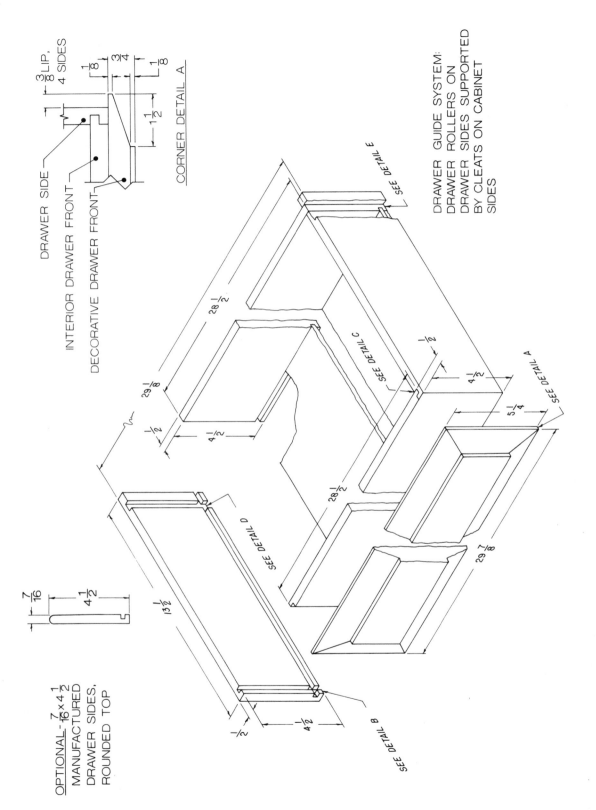

Fig. 639. Here is an assembly drawing of the drawers used in the drawer base. Note the 2-piece drawer front.

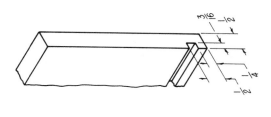
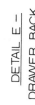

DETAIL E —
DRAWER BACK

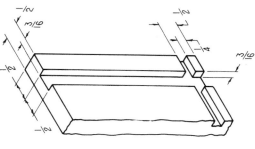
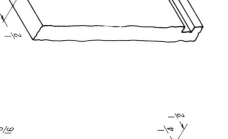

DETAIL D —
DRAWER SIDE-REAR

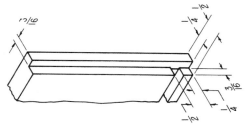

DETAIL C —
INTERIOR DRAWER FRONT

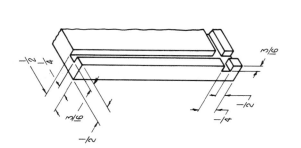

DETAIL B—
DRAWER SIDE-FRONT

Fig. 640. Study these drawer joinery details before making the drawer.

333

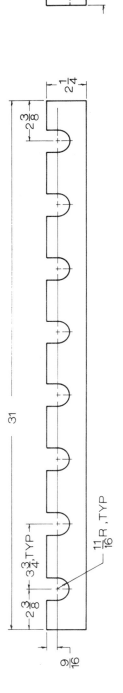

GUN BARREL CUTOUT

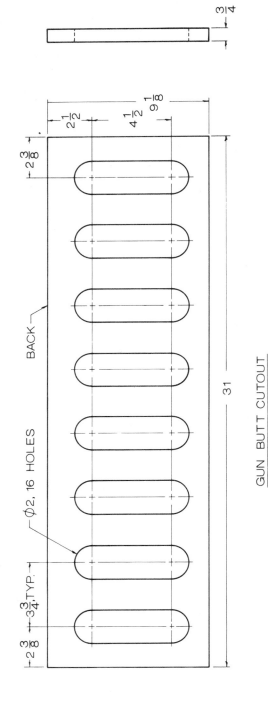

GUN BUTT CUTOUT

Fig. 641. Make full-size templates from these drawings and lay out the gun-barrel and gun-butt cutouts.

Building a Hall Chest

The hall chest (Fig. 642) offers many of the same challenges as the nightstand and gun cabinet. Study the plans and dimensions (Fig. 643) carefully before you begin. Note the door detail and drawer detail (Figs. 644 and 645). The door can be made many different ways. The decorative drawer front should match the door style. If you use an overlay style door, you should also use an overlay style drawer.

The doors can also be made out of plywood and banded with decorative moulding similar to that in Figs. 387 and 388. Decide on which type of door you wish to make before you begin.

Begin by making the faceplate. You can use mortise-and-tenon or lap joints. Practice your set-up on scrap stock to be sure it is correct. The sides and bottom of the case can now be cut. Note that the carcass assembly uses butt joints (Fig. 643). You can substitute a dado joint if you wish.

The top is edge-banded plywood. The solid edge band is splined to the plywood. The mitres can be keyed for reinforcement. Keep the keys below center so that they will not be cut away when the edge is shaped. Be sure to shape the base moulding at the same time. Install the base moulding and fasten the top to the cabinet.

Now make the drawers and doors. If your shop is crowded, it may be easier to make the doors and drawers before you assemble the cabinet. Once the cabinet is built, it takes up a lot of bench or floor space. Metal drawer guides with rollers may be substituted for the wooden guides if desired. Remember, this will alter the drawer dimensions. Purchase the slides before you make the drawers. This will assure a correct fit.

Install all hardware and adjust the doors and drawers. Mount the decorative drawer front to the drawer. Remove the hardware and prepare to finish. Stain and finish as desired.

Fig. 642. The hall chest makes a nice storage cabinet for gloves and sweaters. It can be adapted to many other uses.

DIM.	ENGLISH	METRIC
A	16 3/4 IN.	425 MM.
B	16	406
C	3/4	19
D	2	51
E	15 3/8	391
F	4 1/2	114
G	16 1/4	413
H	36	914
J	34 1/2	876
K	31/2	89
L	4 5/8	117
M	1/4	6
N	7/8	22
O	1/2	13
P	1 3/4	44
Q	30	762
R	9	229
S	3/8	10
T	1 1/4	32
U	1/16	2
V	13 3/4	349
W	13 5/8	346

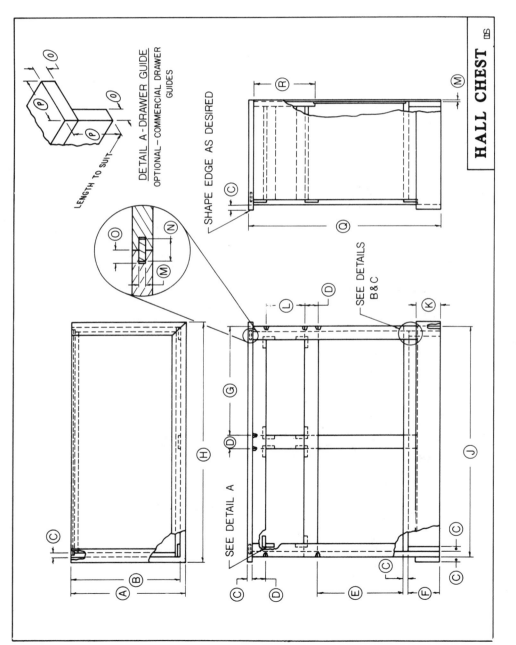

DETAIL A - DRAWER GUIDE
OPTIONAL - COMMERCIAL DRAWER GUIDES

LENGTH TO SUIT

SHAPE EDGE AS DESIRED

SEE DETAIL A

SEE DETAILS B & C

HALL CHEST

Fig. 643. Study these 3 views of the hall chest carefully before beginning. You may wish to change the butt joints in the base to dado joints. Make additional drawings if you change joinery.

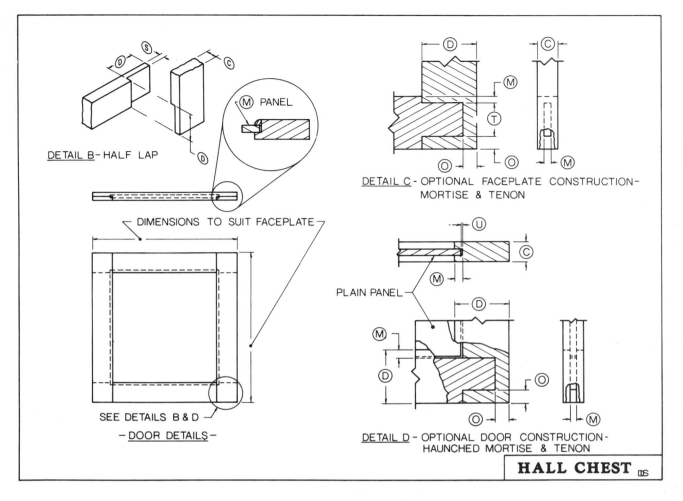

DETAIL B - HALL LAP

M PANEL

DIMENSIONS TO SUIT FACEPLATE

SEE DETAILS B & D

- DOOR DETAILS -

DETAIL C - OPTIONAL FACEPLATE CONSTRUCTION-
MORTISE & TENON

PLAIN PANEL

DETAIL D - OPTIONAL DOOR CONSTRUCTION-
HAUNCHED MORTISE & TENON

HALL CHEST

Fig. 644. Study your options for door and faceplate construction. Lap joints are easier to make, but mortise-and-tenon joints are more challenging. Overall door dimensions are not given. You must first decide if they will be flush, rabbet or overlay doors.

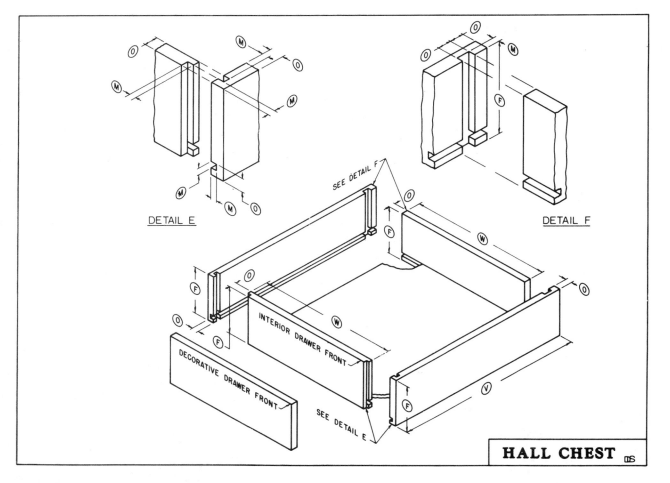

DETAIL E

DETAIL F

SEE DETAIL F

SEE DETAIL E

INTERIOR DRAWER FRONT

DECORATIVE DRAWER FRONT

HALL CHEST DS

Fig. 645. Check the drawer dimensions before you begin. Any error in the faceplate will change these dimensions. Metal drawer guides will also change the dimensions.

Building a Cocktail Table

This cocktail table is easy to build and looks nice with most types of furniture. Some cocktail tables are made with a solid top (Fig. 646). Others have a frame top with a plastic laminate insert (Fig. 647). These stand up better to spills and sweating glasses. A plunge router was used to rout the splines in the mitred corners. They reinforce the corners and enhance the overall appearance. You may wish to make a larger coffee table using the same construction details. This can be done by lengthening the rails and top.

Study the drawing and details (Figs. 648–650) before you begin. Make sure you know which parts get rabbeted, and which face of the stock has a lap joint cut on it. Mark your stock carefully.

Begin making the table by gluing up the solid stock top. If you are using a frame top, rabbet the frame parts first. Cut the legs to size and rabbet 4 of the parts.

Shape the radius on the top of the legs. Shape the edges of the solid stock top or frame parts while the saw is set up for shaping. Cut the mitres in the frame top and fit them dry. If they fit correctly, glue and clamp them together using a band clamp.

Glue the 2 parts of the leg together and clamp them with parallel clamps or "C" clamps. If you use "C" clamps, protect the surface with a clamp pad. Use a thin scrap for the clamp pad.

Cut the lap joints on the outer face of the rails. Cut the groove for the "Z" brackets on the inside face of the rails. Study the details in Fig. 649 to determine the location of these cuts.

A universal jig or tenoning jig would make the lap joints easier to cut. Make the shoulder cut with the mitre gauge and the cheek cut with the tenoning jig. Sand all parts before assembly.

Assemble the legs and the rails. Use glue and screws or nails. If you use nails, predrill the nail holes to avoid splitting the wood. Make sure the table sits evenly before nailing or screwing the parts in position.

Cut the panel for the tabletop and glue the plastic laminate to it. Use contact cement for this purpose. Trim the laminate to size after it is glued in position.

Mount the top to the table with the "Z" brackets. The brackets allow the wood to expand and contract without breaking the glue joints in the table. Wooden brackets can be substituted if the "Z" brackets are not available. This may alter the position of the groove on the rails.

Remove the top and sand all parts. Stain and finish can now be applied.

Fig. 646. This cocktail table has a solid stock top. It was made of 6 narrow pieces glued together.

Fig. 647. This cocktail table has a frame top. The center is a plastic laminate panel. These stand up better than solid stock.

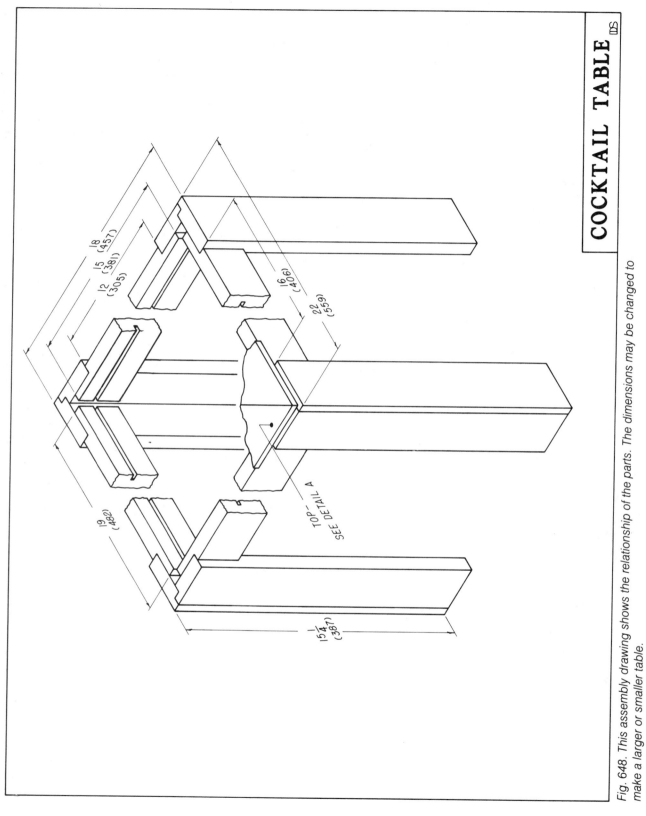

COCKTAIL TABLE

18
(457)

15
(381)

12
(305)

16
(406)

22
(559)

19
(482)

15 1/4
(387)

TOP—
SEE DETAIL A

Fig. 648. This assembly drawing shows the relationship of the parts. The dimensions may be changed to make a larger or smaller table.

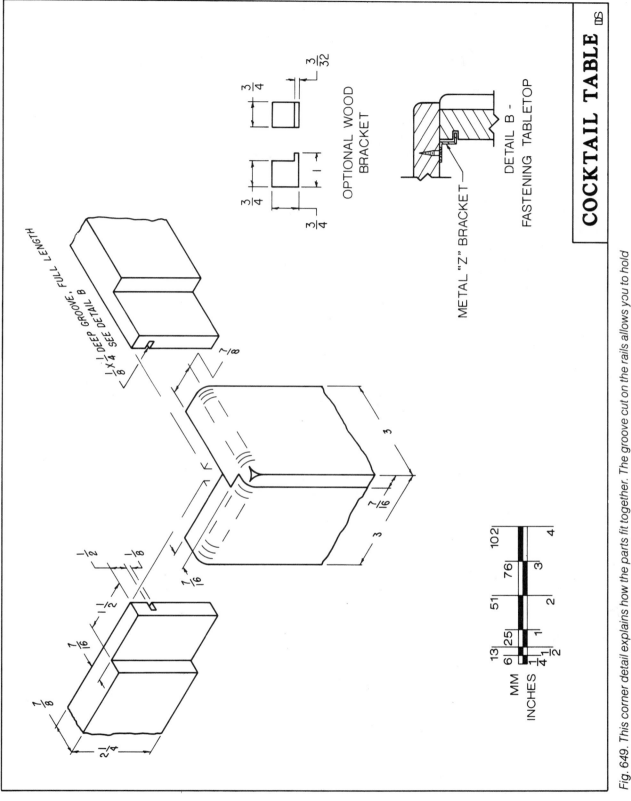

$\frac{1}{8} \times \frac{1}{4}$ DEEP GROOVE, FULL LENGTH
SEE DETAIL B

$\frac{7}{8}$

$\frac{1}{2}$

$\frac{1}{8}$

$\frac{1}{2}$

$1\frac{1}{2}$

$\frac{7}{16}$

$\frac{7}{16}$

$\frac{7}{16}$

3

3

$\frac{7}{8}$

$2\frac{1}{4}$

$\frac{3}{4}$

$\frac{3}{32}$

$\frac{3}{4}$

1

$\frac{3}{4}$

OPTIONAL WOOD BRACKET

METAL "Z" BRACKET

DETAIL B -
FASTENING TABLETOP

MM	6	13	25	51	76	102
INCHES	$\frac{1}{4}$ $\frac{1}{2}$	1	2	3	4

COCKTAIL TABLE

Fig. 649. This corner detail explains how the parts fit together. The groove cut on the rails allows you to hold the top down and cope with expansion and contraction.

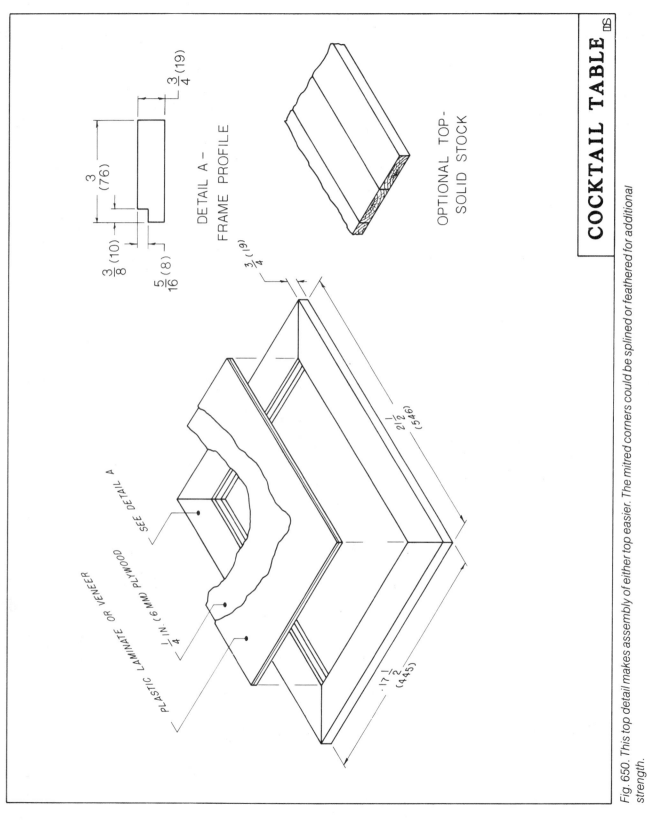

$\frac{3}{8}$ (10)

$\frac{5}{16}$ (8)

$\frac{3}{4}$ (19)

3
(76)

DETAIL A –
FRAME PROFILE

$\frac{3}{4}$ (19)

OPTIONAL TOP-
SOLID STOCK

PLASTIC LAMINATE OR VENEER

$\frac{1}{4}$ IN. (6 MM) PLYWOOD

SEE DETAIL A

$21\frac{1}{2}$
(546)

$17\frac{1}{2}$
(445)

COCKTAIL TABLE

Fig. 650. This top detail makes assembly of either top easier. The mitred corners could be splined or feathered for additional strength.

Building a Storage Trunk

This storage trunk (Fig. 651) looks similar to the old steamer trunks. It is ideal for storing tools, clothing or record albums. It can be lined with cedar, or special compartments can be added to hold your tools.

If you make compartments or trays for your tools, you will have a chance to cut some finger joints or other challenging joinery. Study the plans (Figs. 652 and 653) before beginning. Plan your sequence for cutting the sheet stock. You may need help supporting the sheet stock if you do not have a take-off table behind your saw.

The storage trunk is simple to build. All joints are butt joints reinforced with nails. You could use rabbet joints instead if you wish to modify the plan. The trim is resawn from ¾-inch (19-mm) stock. It is about ¼ inch (6 mm) thick. Make sure the trim is wide enough to accommodate the hinges and catches you plan to use. In addition to resawing, the top trim is also mitred. This will provide some challenge in the assembly.

Cut and assemble the sheet stock. Use glue and nails to assemble the box. Remember, the box is sawn open after it is finished. Keep nails away from the path of the saw blade. A nail could dull your saw blade or break off a carbide tip.

Resaw enough stock to trim the box. You may want to use wood of a contrasting color for the trim. If you are making a tool box, select a hard wood. This will protect the box from damage on the job and in transit.

Glue and nail the trim in position. Keep nails out of the saw's path. Be sure to sand the plywood box before adding the trim. It will be difficult to sand after the trim is installed.

Set the fence and saw the box open. Use a fine-cutting blade to minimize tear-out. Saw the ends first, then saw the front and back. Handle the trunk carefully so the kerf around the trunk is even. You may also make a kerf all the way around the trunk on the saw, and saw it open with a handsaw.

Mount the hinges, handles and catches to the trunk. For strength, I used "T" nuts and machine screws. Wood screws might pull out if the trunk were heavily loaded. Metal feet or corners can also be added to the top and bottom of the box to reduce wear and protect the corners.

Fig. 651. This storage trunk looks like the old steamer trunk. It is easy to build and has a number of uses.

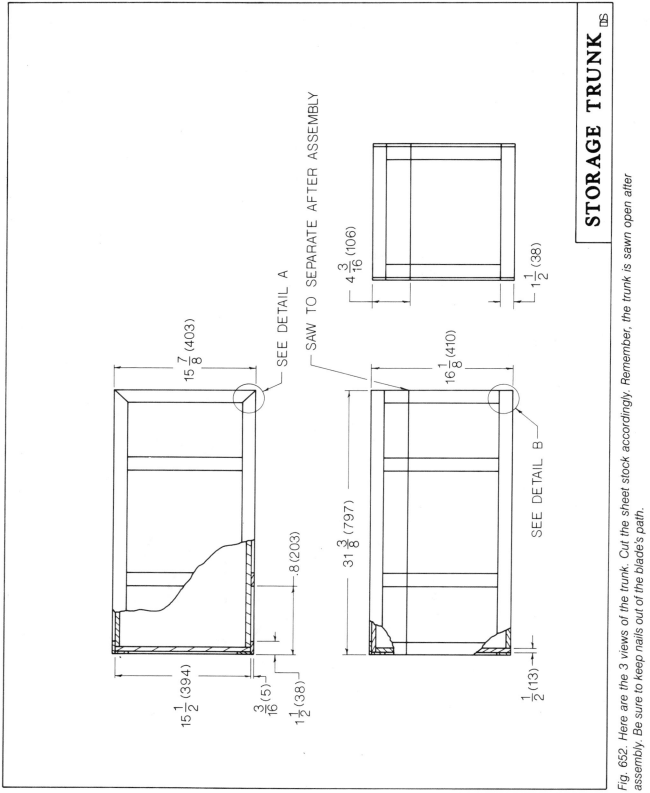

SEE DETAIL A

SAW TO SEPARATE AFTER ASSEMBLY

15 7/8 (403)

4 3/16 (106)

1 1/2 (38)

31 3/8 (797)

16 1/8 (410)

SEE DETAIL B

15 1/2 (394)

3/16 (5)

1 1/2 (38)

.8 (203)

1/2 (13)

STORAGE TRUNK Ⅲ

Fig. 652. Here are the 3 views of the trunk. Cut the sheet stock accordingly. Remember, the trunk is sawn open after assembly. Be sure to keep nails out of the blade's path.

344

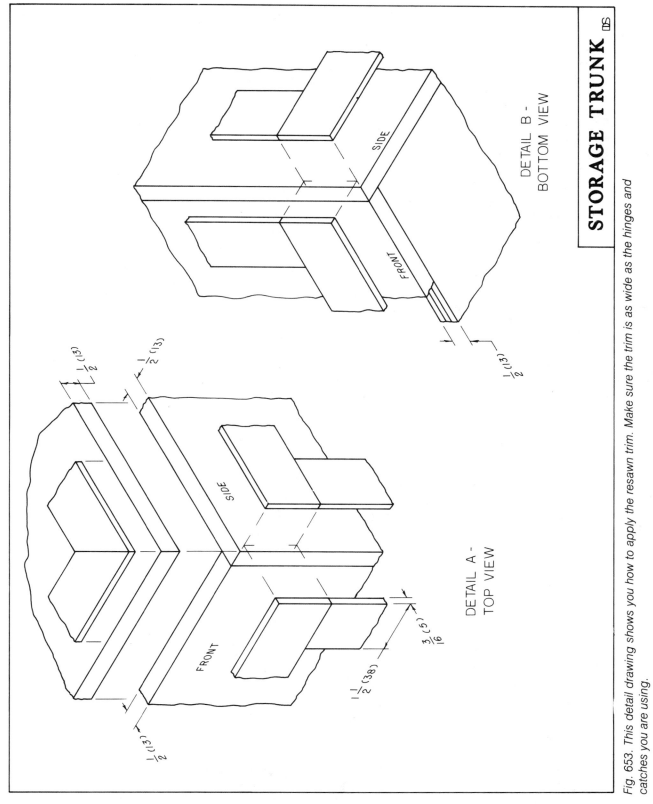

DETAIL B -
BOTTOM VIEW

DETAIL A -
TOP VIEW

SIDE

FRONT

SIDE

FRONT

$\frac{1}{2}$ (13)

$\frac{1}{2}$ (13)

$\frac{1}{2}$ (13)

$\frac{1}{2}$ (13)

$\frac{3}{16}$ (5)

$1\frac{1}{2}$ (38)

STORAGE TRUNK

Fig. 653. *This detail drawing shows you how to apply the resawn trim. Make sure the trim is as wide as the hinges and catches you are using.*

345

Building the Raised Panel Chest

The raised panel chest is one of my favorite projects. I have built approximately 20 of them and supervised the construction of 100 more. The banak chest (Fig. 654) is all solid stock. The walnut chest (Fig. 655) has a veneer top. A burl veneer (Fig. 656) was used, and it added to the overall beauty of the piece. This piece is in a prominent lawyer's private collection.

Hinges and lid supports (Fig. 657) are the only hardware. You could add a locking mechanism, but the cleaner the chest, the better it looks.

The plan (Fig. 660) shows a plywood top with a solid-stock frame. This frame is a challenge because all 4 corners must be tight. Make sure your plywood top is perfectly square. This will make it easier to cut the frame.

The section view (Fig. 659) shows raised panels in the chest. There are 10 panels. This requires a great deal of gluing, cutting and sanding. You can substitute ¼-inch (6-mm) plywood panels for the raised panels. These also look very nice. If you are making raised panels, make 3 large panels. The extra panel can be used as a replacement for all 3 sizes if needed.

The front view (Fig. 658) shows stub mortise-and-tenon joints in the corners. These joints should be replaced with a haunched mortise and tenon for strength and durability. The extra face-grain gluing makes a joint that is less likely to fail.

The leg detail (Fig. 661) shows a leg that is quite a challenge. The top is rounded over with a shaping cutter, and the front is cove-cut. The 2 parts are mitred and cut on the band saw for extra line. A plywood triangle is attached to the rabbet for support. This also allows the legs to be attached to the bottom of the chest.

Look over all of the plans before you begin. Review the related operations in Chapters 6 and 7 before you cut the parts. This review will reduce the chance of error.

Begin by cutting all the rails and stiles. Allow additional length for the joints. Cut the groove on the inside of all the rails and stiles. Make the tenons to fit the groove. Cut the haunch on the tenons, and drill out the mortises. Clean up the mortises with a sharp chisel. Dry fit the frames and measure the openings to determine panel size. The panels should be ⅛ inch (3 mm) shorter and narrower than the groove to groove measurement.

Cut the panels and sand them. Fit them to the rails and stiles. Sand all the parts and assemble them. Do not glue the panels in place. They should be free to move. Pin them in position (Fig. 617) so they do not move off center.

Cut the rabbet on the ends of the sides. Cut a matching groove on the ends of the front and back. Glue the chest parts together and clamp them with bar clamps. Protect the surfaces of the box with clamp pads. Make sure the assembly is square before the glue begins to cure.

Cut the parts for the bottom, and rabbet the inside of each part. Cut the edge banding for the top, and cut a groove on the inside edge. This groove will accommodate the spline. Shape the edges of the edge banding and bottom frame parts. Mitre the bottom frame parts and glue them together. Use a band clamp to hold them in alignment until the glue cures.

Fit the edge banding to the top and glue up the assembly. A band clamp will pull the mitres together. If necessary, a few bar clamps may also be used to pull the edge banding closer to the plywood.

Cut the bottom and rabbet it. Glue it into the frame. After the glue cures, you may wish to put a feather in the mitres. Use a universal jig to guide the stock while cutting the kerf. Feathers may also be cut in the lid.

Fig. 654. The banak chest is all solid stock. Banak made sanding of the panels very easy because it is soft.

Cut the stock for the legs (Fig. 661). You may have to glue up 2 thicknesses of stock for the legs. Lay out the arc and the cove on the legs. Cut the coves first, then cut the rabbets. Shape the arc at the top, and blend the curves together with a hand plane or abrasives.

Cut the mitres and fit the pieces together. Lay out and cut the curves in leg parts. This is done with a band saw or sabre saw. Sand the curves smooth. Cut the plywood triangles and glue up the legs. Keep the parts aligned and held firmly. Nail the plywood triangle in position if desired. Sand the legs and mount them to the box.

Fit the hinges to the box and install the lid supports. Adjust the lid supports. They should keep the lid from slamming. This protects the hands and fingers of the user.

Remove all hardware, and sand the parts 1 last time. Apply stain and finish as desired. *Hint:* You may wish to stain the raised panels before they are installed in the frame. This ensures that the whole panel is stained. If the panel ever shrinks, no unstained wood will show.

Fig. 655. This walnut chest has a veneer top. Clear solid stock for the top was hard to find.

Fig. 656. A burl veneer was selected for the top of this walnut chest. This added to the overall beauty.

Fig. 657. Hinges and lid supports are the only hardware used on the chest. This gives it a clean look. A locking mechanism could be added if desired.

347

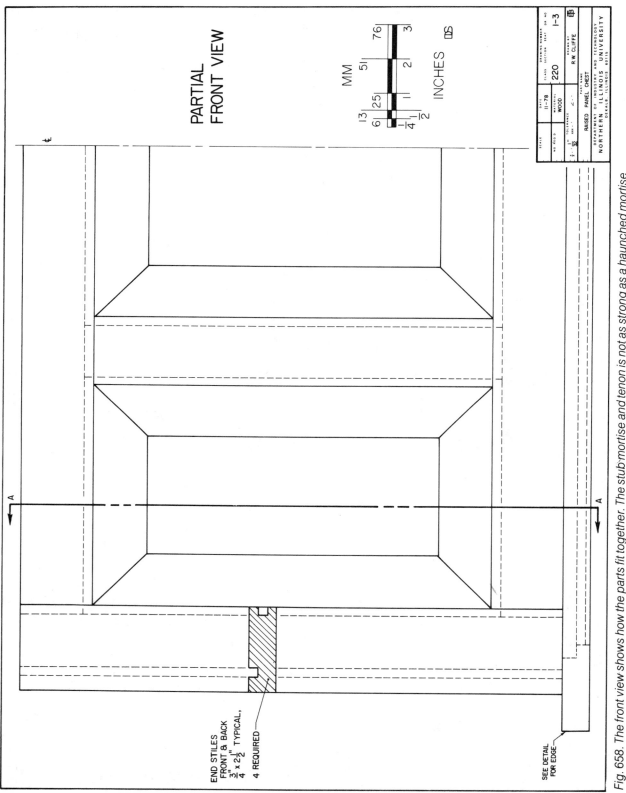

PARTIAL
FRONT VIEW

MM

INCHES

END STILES
FRONT & BACK
$\frac{3}{4}$" x $2\frac{1}{2}$" TYPICAL,
4 REQUIRED

SEE DETAIL
FOR EDGE

Fig. 658. The front view shows how the parts fit together. The stub mortise and tenon is not as strong as a haunched mortise and tenon. You may wish to modify this joint.

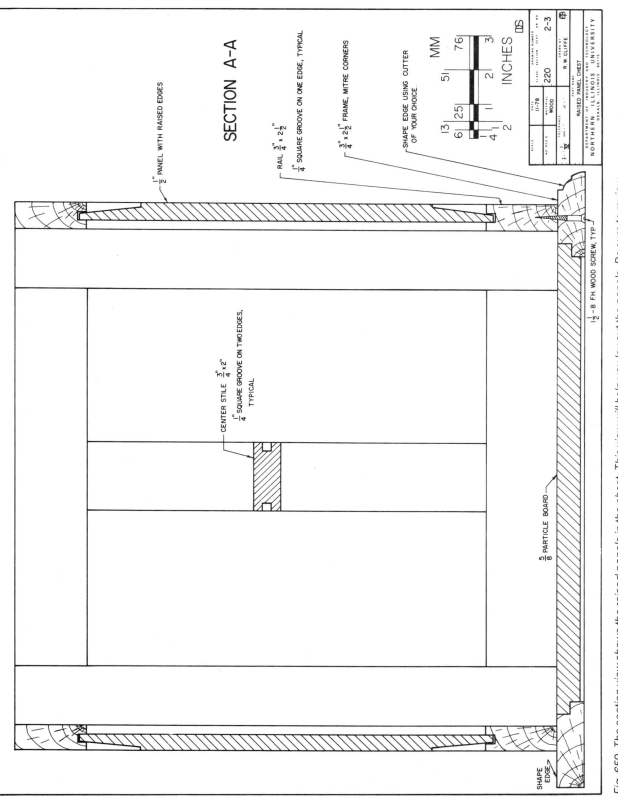

SECTION A-A

$\frac{1}{2}$" PANEL WITH RAISED EDGES

RAIL $\frac{3}{4}$" × $2\frac{1}{2}$"

$\frac{1}{4}$" SQUARE GROOVE ON ONE EDGE, TYPICAL

$\frac{3}{4}$" × $2\frac{1}{2}$" FRAME, MITRE CORNERS

SHAPE EDGE USING CUTTER OF YOUR CHOICE.

CENTER STILE $\frac{3}{4}$" × 2"
$\frac{1}{4}$" SQUARE GROOVE ON TWO EDGES, TYPICAL

$\frac{5}{8}$ PARTICLE BOARD

SHAPE EDGE

$1\frac{1}{2}$ - 8 FH WOOD SCREW, TYP.

MM
13   6   25   51   76
INCHES
6   $\frac{1}{4}$ 1   2   3

DS

SCALE   DATE 11-76   CLASS SECTION 220   TEXT OR NO 2-3

NO REQ'D   MATERIAL WOOD   DRAWN BY R W CLIFFE

TOLERANCE

PART NAME
RAISED PANEL CHEST
DEPARTMENT OF INDUSTRY AND TECHNOLOGY
NORTHERN ILLINOIS UNIVERSITY
DEKALB, ILLINOIS 60115

Fig. 659. The section view shows the raised panels in the chest. This view will help you lay out the panels. Be sure to review the unit in Chapter 6 on raised panels (pages 187 and 188).

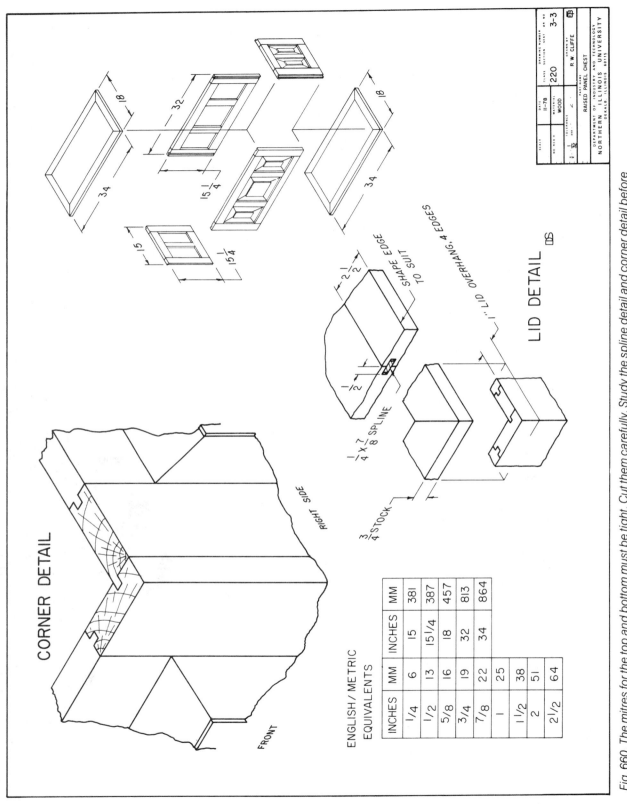

CORNER DETAIL

RIGHT SIDE

FRONT

LID DETAIL

SHAPE EDGE TO SUIT

2 1/2

1/2

1/4 X 7/8 SPLINE

3/4 STOCK

1" LID OVERHANG, 4 EDGES

18

34

32

15 1/4

15

15 1/4

18

34

ENGLISH / METRIC EQUIVALENTS

INCHES	MM	INCHES	MM
1/4	6	15	381
1/2	13	15 1/4	387
5/8	16	18	457
3/4	19	32	813
7/8	22	34	864
1	25		
1 1/2	38		
2	51		
2 1/2	64		

RAISED PANEL CHEST

WOOD

DATE 11-78

CLASS SECTION 220

DRAWING NUMBER 3-3

DRAWN BY R W CLIFFE

DEPARTMENT OF INDUSTRY AND TECHNOLOGY
NORTHERN ILLINOIS UNIVERSITY
DEKALB ILLINOIS 60115

Fig. 660. The mitres for the top and bottom must be tight. Cut them carefully. Study the spline detail and corner detail before you cut any wood.

350

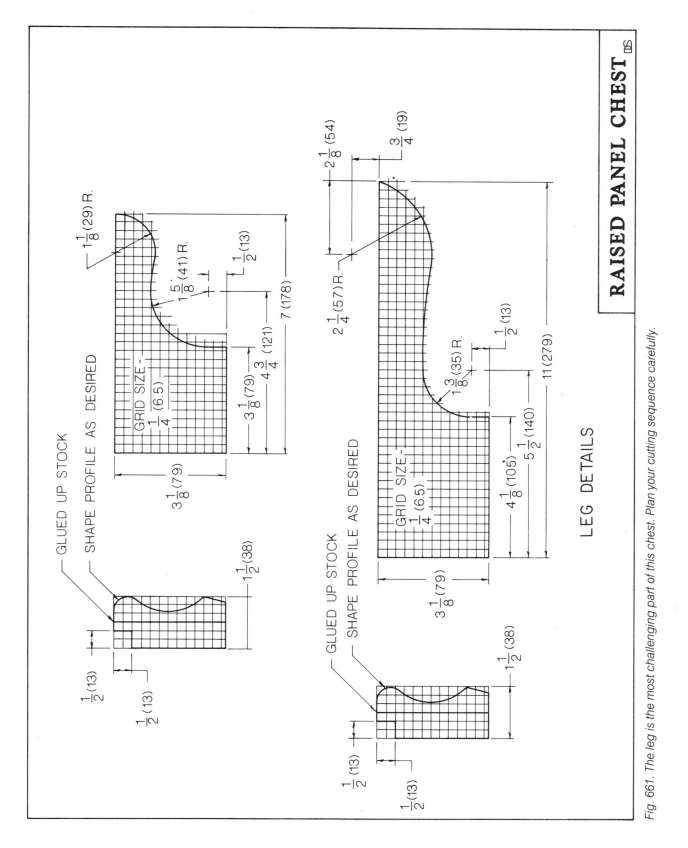

RAISED PANEL CHEST

GLUED UP STOCK

SHAPE PROFILE AS DESIRED

$1\frac{1}{8}$(29) R.

$1\frac{5}{8}$(41) R.

$\frac{1}{2}$(13)

GRID SIZE -
$\frac{1}{4}$(6.5)

$3\frac{1}{8}$(79)

$4\frac{3}{4}$(121)

7 (178)

$3\frac{1}{8}$(79)

$\frac{1}{2}$(13)

$\frac{1}{2}$(13)

$1\frac{1}{2}$(38)

$2\frac{1}{8}$(54)

$\frac{3}{4}$(19)

$2\frac{1}{4}$(57) R.

$1\frac{3}{8}$(35) R.

$\frac{1}{2}$(13)

11 (279)

$4\frac{1}{8}$(105)

$5\frac{1}{2}$(140)

GLUED UP STOCK

SHAPE PROFILE AS DESIRED

GRID SIZE -
$\frac{1}{4}$(6.5)

$3\frac{1}{8}$(79)

$\frac{1}{2}$(13)

$\frac{1}{2}$(13)

$1\frac{1}{2}$(38)

LEG DETAILS

Fig. 661. The leg is the most challenging part of this chest. Plan your cutting sequence carefully.

INDEX